THE LETTERS

OF

WILLIAM HAZLITT

The Publication of this work has been aided by a grant
from the Andrew W. Mellon Foundation

THE GOTHAM LIBRARY
OF THE NEW YORK UNIVERSITY PRESS

The Gotham Library is a series of original works
and critical studies, published in paperback primarily for student use. The Gotham hardcover
edition is primarily for use by libraries and the
general reader. Devoted to significant works and
major authors and to literary topics of enduring
importance, Gotham Library texts offer the best in
literature and criticism.

Comparative and Foreign Language Literature:
Robert J. Clements, Editor
Comparative and English Language Literature:
James W. Tuttleton, Editor

THE LETTERS
OF
WILLIAM HAZLITT

EDITED BY

Herschel Moreland Sikes

ASSISTED BY

Willard Hallam Bonner

AND

Gerald Lahey

New York · New York University Press · 1978

Library of Congress Cataloging in Publication Data

Hazlitt, William, 1778-1830.
The letters of William Hazlitt.

(The Gotham library of the New York University Press)
Includes bibliographical references.
1. Hazlitt, William, 1778-1830—Correspondence.
2. Authors, English—19th century—Correspondence.
I. Sikes, Herschel Moreland. II. Bonner, Willard
Hallam, 1899- III. Lahey, Gerald B.
PR4773.A44 1978   824'.7   78-54079
ISBN 0-8147-4986-0
ISBN 0-8147-4987-9 pbk.

Manufactured in the United States of America

Preface

It is most regrettable that Professor Herschel M. Sikes did not live to see the publication of the Hazlitt correspondence which he had brought near to completion. It would have been a culminating event in his lifelong interest in Hazlitt, beginning with his doctoral dissertation on Hazlitt at New York University. It would have likewise fittingly complemented a distinguished teaching career begun at Hunter College of the City University of New York and continued at Arizona State University. Professor Sikes has assembled the most comprehensive collection of letters, judiciously annotated, that has yet been made.

Inevitably, additions have been necessary in the light of some dozen or more newly discovered letters. Moreover, one hopes that such alterations and revisions of the existing but unfinished text as seemed desirable and necessary would have met with the approval of Professor Sikes, who was the principal initiator of a publication so unequivocally needed by students of the Romantic period.

Professor Sikes included in his manuscript the following special acknowledgment of assistance: "Because of the special problems involved in the 'Liber Amoris' letters (those addressed to Sarah Walker, P.G. Patmore, and James Sheridan Knowles), they have been prepared and annotated by Willard Hallam Bonner, Professor Emeritus of the English Department of the State University of New York at Buffalo, editor of *The Journals of Sarah and William Hazlitt: 1822-1831* (1959). Professor Bonner had completed a study of that correspondence as this volume was being planned. I wish to express my appreciation to Professor Bonner for dividing his own work and making possible now the first complete publication of the manuscripts in which they occur." Professor Bonner's bibliographical description and analysis of this portion of the correspondence will be found in Appendix B.

Acknowledgment of indebtedness is gratefully made to the following: The Abinger Collection, Duke University; the Bodleian Library, Oxford; Bristol University Library, The British Library Board, The Lockwood Memorial Library of the State University of New York at Buffalo, the Wordsworth Collection, Cornell University; the Houghton Library, Harvard University; the Henry E. Huntington Library and Art Gallery; the City of Liverpool Library; the Pierpont Morgan Library; the Newberry Library; the Henry W. and Albert A. Berg Collection, the New York Public Library, Astor, Lenox and Tilden Foundations; the Historical Society of Pennsylvania; the Carl and Lily Pforzheimer Foundation, Inc.; the Princeton University Library; the John Rylands Library; the Charlotte Ashley Felton Memorial Library, Stanford University; the National Library of Scotland; the Scottish Record Office; the Victoria and Albert Museum; Dr. Williams's Library, Gordon Square, London; Yale University Library.

Professor Sikes has particularly recorded his personal gratitude for the generosity of the following for making available privately owned manuscripts: Lord Abinger, Sir Geoffrey Keynes, Mr. and Mrs. Donald Hyde, Professor Willard Bissell Pope. For their assistance he has been grateful to Professor Robert Halsband, Dr. John Frost, Professor Douglas Grant; to Professor J. Max Patrick, a special indebtedness for advice and encouragement.

The supplemental editors wish especially to thank for encouragement and assistance: Professor Elizabeth Schneider and Dean Robert R. Raymo of the New York University Graduate School, College of Arts and Science.

Contents

HAZLITT AS A YOUNG MAN

Introduction

I.

Admirers and critics of Hazlitt's *Essays* have heard from the beginning their frequently very personal voice. The fact has led a few to wonder whether even his private correspondence could add much. But the letters (mainly falling into three categories: those to editors and publishers, those to family and friends, and a special group centered upon Hazlitt's *inamorata* Sarah Walker) do indeed add innumerable delightful and vividly intimate glimpses of Hazlitt not to be found elsewhere. Especially notable (to take but one example) is the so-called "Liber Amoris" group of letters. By comparison with the mild, lunar light of self-revelation that shines through the *Essays,* they present an incandescent blaze of confessional fervor which, even in a period of exuberant self-portraiture, surpasses all in passionate frankness. The publication in 1823 of his *Liber Amoris,* his partially autobiographical record of a disastrous infatuation, brought down upon Hazlitt the thundering disapproval of the gods of prudery and the dismay of friends. Even as late as 1894, the decade of the liberated Nineties, Richard Le Gallienne, professing to publish for the first time the original Ms material which served in part as the source for the love story, dared not "tell all." Despite the fact that his publication was a "Privately Printed" and discreetly "limited edition" of five hundred copies "for subscribers," Le Gallienne "edited," suppressed, and bowdlerized. Consequently the present publication of these letters in their fullness and uninterrupted continuity provides a unique and original specimen of the workings of the Romantic imagination.

To refer first, for example, to attitudes somewhat different from those revealed in the *Essays*. Those who think of Hazlitt as the *enfant terrible* of aggressive dissent, as the pre-eminently angry man of his day, unrelenting in his sharp-edged hostility to monarchy and arbitrary rule, and all of its supporters, will find some of the letters a little surprising.

Notable is Hazlitt's deferential, even docile, behavior towards such figures as Francis Jeffrey, editor of *The Edinburgh Review,* and Macvey Napier, staff member of the *Review,* editor of the various *Supplements* to the *Encyclopaedia Britannica,* and ultimately editorial successor to Jeffrey. In writing to Jeffrey about work submitted to him, Hazlitt is almost solicitous of supervision: the work is ". . . entirely in your hands, if you will be at the trouble to prune its excrescences." Hazlitt apologizes for his own headstrong impetuosity: "I know that I am somewhat 'splenetive and rash' and submit the whole to your decision." We recall that this is written by a journalist-critic of about forty years of age. As relations between editor and contributor developed, Hazlitt began to appear as the serious student grateful for Jeffrey's tutorial guidance: "I . . . am proud of having required so few corrections . . . I am much obliged to your indulgence to me . . . and hope to stand less in need of it in the future." A year later, and Hazlitt is still the submissive apprentice, almost contrite in acknowledging deficiencies: "With respect to what you say of my writing, I have no objection to make than that it is too favourable. I confess to all the faults." In the matter of his critical judgment, Hazlitt defers to Jeffrey's alterations: "I am very sensible of my want of discretion. . . ."

Although equally respectful to Macvey Napier, Hazlitt is slightly more defensive of his own manner than he was with Jeffrey. Interestingly we learn that his sharp and provocative style of statement was as deliberately adopted for effect as that of such writers as Shaw or Chesterton, and for comparable reasons. Of material submitted, he writes to Napier, "... I dare say your objections to several of the observations are well-founded. I confess I am apt to be paradoxical in stating an extreme opinion when I think the prevailing one not quite correct. I believe however this way of writing answers with most readers better than the logical. I tried for some years to express the truth and nothing but the truth, till I found it would not do." He hastens to add that although his paradoxical manner is credible, it requires interpretation on the part of the public. The difference between his "logical" and his "paradoxical" mode can be seen clearly by comparing Hazlitt's essay "On the Qualifications Necessary to Success in Life" (No. 18 of *The Plain Speaker*) with his epistolary essay written especially for his young son—"On the Conduct of Life, or Advice to a School-boy" (letter no. 99 in this volume). Even in respect of his master obsession with political issues, Hazlitt offers to submit to Napier's corrections: "As to political innuendos [*sic*], and one or two things relating to proposed articles, you can omit or retain at your pleasure."

Again, for all of his stubborn independence and sturdy individualism, Hazlitt does not hesitate to ask Jeffrey for such "puffing" of his "Characters of Shakespear" (and his *Round Table*) as the influential editor of the *Edinburgh Review* can legitimately give. Hazlitt urges "... the necessity of circumstances. My friends praise what I write, but I do not find that the public read it. .... A single word from you would ... make what I write a marketable commodity ... do Dear Sir, extend a friendly hand to help me out. ...." In the last of further requests, Hazlitt advises: "... your notice would at once lift me from the character of a disappointed author to that of a successful one."

Jeffrey did give Hazlitt personal, professional, and journalistic support, and advances and loans as well. Jeffrey writes to him of his willingness to pay him in advance for prospective articles: "I take the liberty of enclosing £100, a great part of which I shall owe you in a few weeks, and the rest you shall pay me back in reviews when you can do so without putting yourself to any uneasiness." That Jeffrey's offers were not grudgingly made is clear: "If you really want another £100 tell me so plainly, and it shall be at your service." The letters not only show Jeffrey in a much more kindly light than he is generally represented in but that considerable sums of money flowed into—and out of—Hazlitt's hands. (Why was he seemingly always in need?) We learn with pleasure that Hazlitt found Jeffrey's personal company an equally gratifying experience: "I have seen the great little man, and he is very gracious to me—*Et sa femme aussi!* . . . He is a person of infinite vivacity."

Besides his associations with his journalistic colleagues, we are given lively glimpses of Hazlitt's relations to his parents, his studies and school-fellows, his friends, and his son. We also can note in the early letters a certain nervous irritability, a temperament too easily turned up to a tight pitch. Especially charming are his early letters containing glimpses of the young, self-conscious Dissenter, praising the sermons of "Chapel" or "Meeting," dutifully disdaining the allegedly uninspiring ramblings of the Church pulpit. There is a delightful letter to his father, a little sally of pietistic edification utilizing the favorite homiletic situation of both Evangelical and Dissenting minister: the deathbed. At his terminal hour, we are bid to gaze upon the peace and tranquillity of the Good Man with duty fulfilled; then upon the remorseful agonies of the Bad Man whose life has been devoted to the World and to Pleasure. A long letter to Leigh Hunt discloses the long-range, more serious effects of minority, Dissenting mentality—of being born in exile. Hazlitt expresses a deep sense of isolation, his feelings of being proscribed and neglected by his friends and the world, and his stubborn resentment of it. In a happier mood, we read his response to a practical joke, turning on a burlesque announcement of Hazlitt's death. Hazlitt's answer gives us considerable information about his daily routine, his personal and domestic habits: his morning rising, eating, drinking; his mode and manner of living. We have a single courtship letter to Sarah Stoddart, the wife of his first unfortunate marriage. Hazlitt's attentions to his prospective bride seem a little elephantine. She learns that he has been having dreams of his first love, and that when his thoughts turn to her (Sarah Stoddart), they rise little higher than a vision of "sitting down with you to dinner over a boiled scrag-end of mutton and hot potatoes."

Hazlitt is often accused of being destitute of any faculty of self-criticism. His somewhat pensive essay-letter to his son, "a poignant letter" as Professor Wardle rightly calls it (*Hazlitt:* p. 311), disposes of such a charge. The father speaks in a valedictory voice: "As my health is so indifferent, and I may not be with you long, I wish to leave you some advice ... for your conduct of life." We are surprised to encounter a different, a self-transformed Hazlitt, a truly "New Pygmalion." He is something between a prudential Polonius and a worldly Lord Chesterfield, a cool detached spectator standing on the shore of life calmly calculating its ebb and flow, counselling the prospective voyager to keep to the quiet coastal waters. In a world not likely to be improved, Hazlitt advises that "the best way is to slide through it as contentedly and innocently as we may." In an especially self-critical mood, Hazlitt relates that his Dissenting, minority background placed him in a cultural outpost of England, encouraged a narrow-minded, right-tight mentality, aggressively contemptuous of all that lay outside of its own provincial range. Whatever its virtues, he sternly warns his son against it. Hazlitt looks back to Augustan urbanity, recommending a manner that is "courteous, mild, and forbearing." He praises the admired Augustan virtues celebrated in the *Rape of the Lock,* those of "good nature and good sense." For all that, the Romantic Hazlitt appears momentarily at the end of the letter. He applauds especially the lives of painters, contemplates their enviable longevity, and emphasizes their sustained interest and vital absorption in their work which overflows into life. "There is a kind of immortality about this sort of ideal and visionary existence. . . ."

On the whole, the remarkable letter Hazlitt wrote his son is perhaps more melancholy and monitory than inspiring. It is melancholy in its astringent view of the frugal satisfactions to be found in the lives of authors and scholars. It is melancholy towards the end: ". . . when the feast is finished and the lamps expire," then falls the darkening shadow of Sarah Walker. It is monitory in warning the son against the cramping effects of minority psychology. But the positive side of the warning is Hazlitt's insistence on a design for living inclusive of a large-hearted tolerance and a large-minded understanding of the varieties of human opinion, of the diverse ways and manners of men, virtues not conspicuously displayed in the author's Essays.

We also recall that Hazlitt has been chided for a dismal lack of humour about his militant rage against the politics of his day. However, in a letter of 1827 to C.C. Clarke, still more valedictory

[13]

in tone, Hazlitt can be seen gaily and light-heartedly self-critical. Inspired by a recent close brush with death, "the shadowy world" as he terms it, he analyzes his own failings in gentle self-mockery, confessing those "sins" which have brought him down: "Delicacy, moderation, complaisance, the *suaviter in modo,* whisper it about, my dear Clarke, these are my faults and have been my ruin." They are obviously among the virtues recommended in the aforementioned letter to his son. In that same letter in which Hazlitt had celebrated the "visionary existence" of the artist, he had further exalted it as that unique life-style ". . . that dallies with Fate and baffles the grim Monster, Death." But destiny, not casting Hazlitt in the mould of the painter, permitted the fell sergeant to be unduly swift in his arrest; worse—more exorbitant in his fees. Hazlitt's last recorded words (they are to Jeffrey) dictated on his deathbed read: "I am dying; can you lend me £10, and so consummate your many kindnesses to me?" Perhaps the expiring Hazlitt was permitted the happy recollection of an early letter from Jeffrey, offering money if needed and saying consolingly, "We cannot let a man of genius suffer." To this last request, Jeffrey responded promptly and generously.

Considerably more complex are those unique letters recording Hazlitt's infatuation with Sarah Walker, his youthful *Infelice* (as he called her) whose puzzling image dominates the letters to P.G. Patmore and J.S. Knowles, his confidential friends. Sarah was the daughter of Hazlitt's landlord, the latter a tailor by occupation. She was about twenty years old (less than half Hazlitt's age), a young lady of perplexing character and elusive charm. Hazlitt is hardly a typical Shropshire Lad despite the long association of the family and his own intermittent connection with Wem of Shropshire. Yet these letters, like their author's life, are a poignant illustration of Housman's pervasive theme: "The troubles of our proud and angry dust/ Are from eternity and shall not fail." Born in Dissent and Romanticism, Hazlitt lived with a double intensity within his own imagination. Besides his defeated aspirations to become either a "metaphysician" or a great painter, perhaps Hazlitt's most piercing disappointment prior to his meeting with Sarah Walker was the defeat of his idol Napoleon at Waterloo. The Emperor was to Hazlitt "the child and champion of the Revolution" which had overturned the ancient dynasties of Europe, whose arbitrary rule was so abhorrent to Hazlitt. He has recorded the feeling that a favouring Providence had sent him Sarah Walker (the "heroine" of that sequence of letters in this volume) as a consolation for Waterloo. A central image appearing in the letters is that of a small bust of Napoleon, which, through its extended association with Sarah, comes to symbolize both Hazlitt's political and amorous idealizations and their soul-shattering defeat. The little image gets smashed in the run of events. As in the novels of Hardy or Hemingway, love which seemed sent as a gracious compensation to relieve the stern privations and denials of life turned out to be made of the same intractable stuff.

Hence the peculiar anguish of these letters. In the Romantic vision-poem, *Kubla Khan,* we read: "A damsel with a dulcimer/ In a vision once I saw: . . ." Like all visions, it has dissolved, leaving the visionary beholder contemplating only a frenzied self-abandonment characterized by "flashing eyes" and "floating hair." Hazlitt writes of Sarah Walker: "She came . . . a vision . . . to make me amends for all . . . now . . . she has vanished like a dream, an enchantment; it torments me and it makes me mad."

A rationally detached, yet friendly and sympathetic observer has described Hazlitt in this wildly distraught interval of his life. Benjamin R. Haydon writing to Mary Russell Mitford says: "He has fallen in love with a lodging-house hussy, who will be his death." He explains that Hazlitt's "torture," which is "beyond expression," is owing to the fact that "His imagination clothed her with that virtue" which made Hazlitt "downright in love with an ideal perfection, which has no existence but in his own head." Contemplating the spectacle, Haydon exclaims: "What a being it is! His conversation is now a mixture of disappointed revenge, passionate remembrance, fiending hopes, and melting lamentation" (Stoddard, pp. 210-211).

In the *Liber Amoris,* Hazlitt says of Sarah that she descended: ". . . from the heavens . . . a vision of love and joy . . . and now . . . she has vanished from me." He broods over the loss: It is "like a dream, an effect of enchantment." The victim of *La Belle Dame,* Keat's symbol of the falsely idealizing imagination, says: "And there she lulled me asleep/ And there I dream'd," only to awaken "On the cold hill's side." Hazlitt, when the dream dissolves, laments: "I am left to perish." He compulsively returns to the

[15]

experience: "I have tasted the sweets of . . . illusion and now feel the bitterness." Hence we encounter a persistent ambivalence of mind in the strenuous and tempestuous prose of these letters as they unfold the consuming and unconsumated *l'affaire Sarah Walker.* The burden of the letters, that of the disastrous enthrallment of a baffled middle-aged journalist and literary critic by the youthful daughter of his landlord is, despite its grotesque *mésalliance,* by virtue of its turbulent intensity more nearly tragic than comic.

More particularly, it is an archetype of the Romantic malady or predicament of double mental vision: a paralysis of discrimination between the opposing data of the idealizing imagination and of the critical judgment. The Romantic writers symbolized the workings of the delusive imagination by potions of exotic sweetness derived from esoteric sources: "She fed me roots of relish sweet,/ And honey wild, and manna dew, . . ." Such is Keats' account in *La Belle Dame sans Merci* of the sorceress who typifies the perverted working of the imagination. To the speaker in *Kubla Khan,* likewise, the same kind of potion is given: "For he on honey-dew has fed,/ And drunk the milk of Paradise." But the rub is that the transforming power of the imagination is only half effective; it creates, not sustained delusion but confusion. Hence in his *Ode to a Nightingale,* Keats chides the imagination as the dream loses credibility: "Adieu! the fancy cannot cheat so well,/ As she is famed to do, deceiving elf!" Having split the sensibility of perception, it leaves the victim in suspenseful perplexity: "Was it a vision or a waking dream?/ Fled is that music: —do I wake or sleep?" The malady so subtly described by Keats, so vividly by Coleridge is the dilemma of the discordant ambivalence of the divided mind so characteristic of the Romantic temperament, so gaily exploited in the ironic counterpoint of Byron's *Don Juan.*

The *Liber Amoris,* it should be noted in passing, wears what Hazlitt said of his fateful Sarah, "an equivocal face." Compared to the letters (those to Sarah Walker, P.G. Patmore, and J.S. Knowles) it seems to some critics a nearly symbiotic extension. To others, biographer-critics, such as P.P. Howe and Professor Ralph M. Wardle, the *Liber Amoris* appears more the product of the shaping hand of the artist. Howe, as early as 1916 in the *Fortnightly Review* (January-June, v. 102, NS 99), noted that all of the events of the book had happened to Hazlitt, that the letters were the "raw material" of it, and that Hazlitt determined to imitate Montaigne and "say as author what he felt as man." Hazlitt had produced a work of "imaginative art . . . founded on fact." Professor Wardle, considering especially the letters from Hazlitt to Patmore, observes that they ". . . differ markedly from the versions which Hazlitt printed in *Liber Amoris* . . ." *(Hazlitt,* p. 306 n.). Actually, the letters and the *Liber Amoris* taken together are a literary centaur, substantially related yet separate species; in design and form they are distinct and different. The equine portion, symbolizing the letters, includes a little more of the violent and the sensual; the human part, the *Liber Amoris* stresses a little more the high sentimental.

Both the letters and the *Liber Amoris* give us a picture of a mind split down the middle. It is not the psychopathic condition of the clinical "split personality," in which there is an alternate and exclusive dominance of a single half at a given time. Still less is it the perennial human situation of the mind confronted with unusually difficult or painful choices—the "divided mind" theme of so much conventional critical analysis of Victorian mental conflict. Hazlitt refers to his predicament as that of a divided mind but makes it clear that by the phrase he means what he also calls his "half-disordered mind." The spell cast by *La Belle Dame* induces a serious disorientation of the whole personality. There is a helpless awareness of the self groping with a distorted and obstructed sense of reality. It is the mental predicament in which the visionary or idealizing imagination says one thing; the critical judgment says the opposite. Both are concurrently operative. The Romantic personality was especially aware of this kind of split, of its own "cheating" fancy. But unable effectually to halt the cheating process of the imagination, it is correspondingly aware of its own inner warfare of division. Hazlitt's letters vividly illustrate the prolonged strain of such a split, a fact of which he reveals himself agonizingly and helplessly aware. He sees his Sarah as a shy "Vestal" virgin, also as "a young witch," enthralling other men within her "serpent arms . . . her eyes glancing and her cheeks on fire. . . ."

Pervasively the letters (and the *Liber Amoris*) express Hazlitt's suspension between heaven and hell as he scrutinizes Sarah

[17]

Walker's "equivocal face." The face presents itself to him as a smoothly polished marble surface reflecting in ideal form his own imaginative compulsions. Yet it is simultaneously perceived as something alien and deceiving. In both the letters and the *Liber Amoris,* antithetical images and allusions multiply like the endlessly repeating images of opposing mirrors. In nearly delirious suspense, in simultaneous belief and disbelief, Hazlitt questions the character of Sarah. Are you, he asks, a phantom of delight or a demon destroyer, an ethereal St. Cecilia or another Circe; a shy, demure maiden or a sinuous, seductive serpent-form; an ecstatic vision or a lodging-house decoy, angel or witch, strumpet or saint, Madonna or harlot? These are quite literally the very antitheses which flood through his letters.

Despondingly aware of his own hyphenated sensibility, of the futile effort to distinguish concerning the mind's movements "what they half-create,/ And what perceive," *(Tintern Abbey),* Hazlitt apologizes in the letters for his own irresolvable mental predicament: "You will perhaps excuse this as a picture of a divided mind." He repeats with significant variation in the *Liber Amoris:* "You see by this letter the way I am in, and I hope you will excuse it as the picture of a half-disordered mind." But the realization of the predicament renders it only more keenly perplexing. Hazlitt reached the point in March of 1822 when the nerve-lacerating stress became such that he felt he would "bear anything but this horrid suspense." He dwells upon his alternating symptoms, ". . . my depressions and my altitudes, my wanderings and pertinacity. . . ." He meditates: "If I knew she was a mere abandoned creature, I should try to forget her: but till I do know this, nothing can tear me from her. . . ." The conviction grows upon him that proof of her promiscuity will ". . . satisfy my soul I have lost only a lovely frail one." The thought obsesses him: "Yet if I only knew she was a whore, *flagrante delicto,* it would wean me from her, and burst my chain."

By May he is determined to free himself from the thrall of this ". . . strange, almost . . . inscrutable girl." Hazlitt, like Hamlet, worn by vacillation is resolved that ". . . the play's the thing" whereby he will break the unresolved tension between rage and rapture, between whether to adore or to abhor. Thought hardens into decision, and in hot haste he commands his friend Patmore:

"TRY HER through some one (anyone) E. for example, . . ." At the end of May, he is again urging Patmore to execute the virginity-test: "Could you ascertain this for me, by any means or through any person (E. for example) who might try her as a lodger?" In June he is still imploring Patmore, stressing immediacy: "I entreat you to get some one to work to ascertain for me, without loss of time, whether she is a common sporter, or not?" His final plea for help is in July, when he exclaims: "The bond grows tighter . . ." and again impatiently demands to know concerning the chastity-ambush: "Where is E—? Why tarry the wheels of his chariot? When, how shall I be released from these horrors?" His last imperious words: ". . . get anybody to see what flesh she is made of, and send her to hell if possible."

Of the eventual trial of Sarah, Hazlitt has left us a record of the actual attempt, wherein Sarah preserves her virginity as effectually, if not as triumphantly, as Pamela. The attempt took place finally in the spring of 1823 about the time, perhaps, when Hazlitt was making ready for the press his *Liber Amoris.* His terse, staccato journal or diary of the ambush covers a period of twelve days, from the fourth to the sixteenth of March. One of Hazlitt's more recent scholarly biographers, Professor Herschel Baker, has referred to this trial and the document recording it as "astonishing and dismaying" *(William Hazlitt:* p. 425). At any rate it records an investigation as bizarre as the magical "chastity-test" scene in *The Changeling.* But considering Hazlitt in the light of the psychological impasse being discussed, we can understand his vain hope for release from baffling thralldom by a kind of improvised shock treatment, a desperate, kill-or-cure counter-potion whereby he may re-integrate his "half-disordered" mind. Benjamin Haydon reveals to us, in his letter to Miss Mitford, Hazlitt's urgent need to be done with the affair: "He will sink into idiotcy if he does not get rid of it" (Stoddard: pp. 210-211). The journal recounts the experiences of Hazlitt's commissioned agent, who took lodgings with the Walkers to "try" the girl.

The diary was first published in mutilated form in *Lamb and Hazlitt* by Dodd, Mead and Company in New York (1899) and again in London (1900) by Elkin Mathews, both edited by the grandson, William Carew Hazlitt. All mention of bodily intimacies or improprieties of speech were altered or omitted. So closely did the editor relate the episode to the book that he entitled it: "LIBER AMORIS. PART II." It would have been more appropriately presented as *"The Patmore Letters: Epilogue."* The episode of the chastity-test belongs to the letters, not to the *Liber Amoris,* a more sentimental and less aggressive account of the affair. It is one of those scenes that illustrate the distinctly different character of the book. Hence, contrary to W. Carew Hazlitt's assumption, the document does intimately and vitally belong to the spirit of the letters. It further illustrates (still without resolving) Hazlitt's confused turmoil of mind and gives the grotesque sequel to Hazlitt's demands upon his friend as recorded in the letters. The trial of Sarah left Hazlitt much as he was originally, still groping in a mist of ambivalence, recording in the trial-diary the same discordant vision: ". . . in Hell, my only consolation . . . in Heaven . . . my only reward." Yet at the same time and place, he notes: "the little ideot," creature of a "marble" heart, seductively wearing a smiling "mask." Because of the closely complementary character of this document, it has been placed in *Appendix A* after the letters.

Recurring to more sympathetic moments appearing at intervals near the close of the letters, we find Hazlitt dwelling finally in something like the darker regions of Dante's *Inferno:* "I am pent up in burning, impotent desires which can find no vent or object." Sarah had become a fateful Eros: "She has shot me through . . . the barbed arrow is in my heart. I can neither endure it nor draw it out, for with it flows my life's-blood." He knew at last that he was destined to watch Sarah's image inexorably recede from his view. He dwelt upon it in dream and reverie: ". . . when I entirely lose sight of thee, no flower will ever bloom on earth to glad my heart again." Still the image dwindled and vanished from his outer vision: "She was my life—it is gone from me, and I am grown spectral." Sarah left him a gray ghost languishing in a haunted landscape of the mind, in "that deep romantic chasm" of *Kubla Khan,* wailing for his demon-love.

II.

Portions of William Hazlitt's letters were first printed interspersed in the rather untidy and disorderly compilations of biographical material published by his son, William Jr. and much more copiously and with scarcely better arrangement, by the grandson, William Carew Hazlitt. The first publication is the *Literary Remains/ of the late/ William Hazlitt./ with a/ notice of his life by/ his son* . . . In Two Volumes./ London,/ Saunders and Otley, Conduit Street./1836. William the Younger included about a dozen of his father's letters. Three that are extant reveal inaccuracies of transcription as well as mutilations of the text. Although the others do not survive in holograph, they appear elsewhere in fuller and presumably more accurate form. The *Literary Remains* is still the chief source for seven of Hazlitt's letters.

The publications of William Carew Hazlitt, the grandson, are fourfold: *Memoirs/ of/ William Hazlitt./ with portions of his correspondence./ by/ W. Carew Hazlitt* . . . in Two Volumes./ London:/ Richard Bentley,/ Publisher in ordinary to Her Majesty./ 1867, containing sixteen letters. Next in time is *Four Generations of a Literary Family/ The Hazlitts in England, Ireland, and America/ Their Friends and Their Fortunes/ 1725-1896.* In two volumes, London and New York/ George Redway/1897. The materials included under this more pretentious title furnished over a dozen additional letters. Next came *Lamb and Hazlitt/ Further Letters and Records/ Hitherto Unpublished/* edited by William Carew Hazlitt, New York, 1899; and London, Elkin Mathews, Vigo Street,/ MDCCCC. It contained some half dozen letters. Last in appearance, bearing a title faintly dynastic in tone, was *The Hazlitts: An Account of Their Origin and Descent,* Edinburgh: Ballantyne, Hanson and Co., 1911. Sixteen letters were reprinted. Original Mss in the possession of the grandson have disappeared, having been sold in small batches without records of purchasers. For example, some half dozen letters written by Hazlitt on his first visit to France (October 1802 to January 1803) have disappeared. Such letters would enlighten us on the formative period of his life, his first serious study of painting, and details of his life and work in Paris while studying at the Louvre.

Two editors of newly published Hazlitt letters may be grouped together: P.G. Patmore and Richard Le Gallienne. Patmore in *My Friends and Acquaintance:* . . . London, 1854, included in Volume III a section entitled "Extracts of Letters from W. Hazlitt to P.G. Patmore. . . ." He included portions of five letters.

In an 1893 edition of the *Liber Amoris,* Richard Le Gallienne published two letters in an Appendix, one in part. In 1894, Le Gallienne brought out a handsomely printed edition of the *Liber Amoris,* "Privately Printed," and limited to five hundred copies. In this edition, he included a section entitled "Correspondence Now First Literally Transcribed from the Original MSS." The section included eleven letters from Hazlitt to P.G. Patmore but embodying numerous errors and omissions.

So widely dispersed are Hazlitt's extant letters that even P.P. Howe in preparing the *Complete Works* of Hazlitt did not find it possible to include them. Manuscript locations range from the National Library of Scotland in Edinburgh, which owns more than a score, to the Huntington Library of San Marino, California, which owns one. Others are located at the Yale University Library, which owns nearly a score to Francis Jeffrey alone, and the State University of New York at Buffalo, where the letters to P.G. Patmore and numerous others are in the Goodyear Collection of the Lockwood Memorial Library. Except for the more than two dozen letters published by W. Carew Hazlitt, which presumably do not survive in manuscript form, two to P.G. Patmore, and a few addressed to editors and printed in magazines, the originals have been recovered and can be seen fully and accurately reproduced for the first time in a single collection. Often bowdlerized and expurgated, the letters as presented by William Carew Hazlitt are unreliable. Collation of extant manuscripts with those printed in the grandson's memoirs reveals misdatings, misspellings of names, omission of words, passages, and marginalia, and some re-phrasing.

If unfortunate in his life, Hazlitt has been especially favored in his spiritual "life-beyond-life." He has had a succession of devoted, scholarly, and unusually judicious biographers. P.P. Howe stands at the beginning of the company of modern scholarly biographers and editors of Hazlitt and his writings: Editor of the *Centenary Edition of the Complete Works of / William Hazlitt, / After the Edition of / A.R. Waller and Arnold Glover,* 21 vols., 1930-1934, J.M. Dent and Sons, Ltd. London and Toronto, as well as the author of the *Life of William Hazlitt,* London, 1922, Martin Secker; revised edition in 1928. A new edition of the *Life,* Hamish Hamilton, London, appeared in 1947. With reference to new letters, Howe stated in his "Preface" to the first American edition (New York,

George H. Doran Company, 1922): "Hazlitt, it may be remarked, was not by temperament a letter-writer, and to the forty-odd examples of his correspondence which have been hitherto known (excluding the somewhat specialized *Liber Amoris* group), I have succeeded in adding eighteen." Among these latter were the "Unpublished Letters" of Hazlitt from originals in the British Museum. Howe published them in two successive issues of *The Athenaeum,* those of 8 and 15 August, 1919, pages 711-712 and 742-744 respectively. The first group contained seven letters of 1816-1817 to Macvey Napier; the second, six letters of 1829-1830, also to Napier.

Howe published additional "New Hazlitt Letters" in *The London Mercury* in March of 1923 (pages 494-498). They included three letters to different correspondents and three fragmentary notes to Archibald Constable. Howe wrote: "No more is claimed for these letters than that they provide a slight addition to the eighteen more substantial ones given for the first time in the writer's recently published 'Life.' Letters of Hazlitt are of comparative rarity, the number now public totalling some seventy against upwards of eight hundred bearing the signature of Charles Lamb." In *The London Mercury* for May of 1924 (page 73), Howe again published: "Hazlitt Letters: An Addition." This is interesting for its biographical significance. Howe's final contribution consisted of "Three Hazlitt Letters," brief and miscellaneous, appearing in *The Times Literary Supplement* for 21 March 1936 (page 244). In the *Centenary Edition,* Howe reproduces of this correspondence only about a dozen letters in his "Notes."

Among succeeding biographers who have added notably to our knowledge of new letters is Professor Herschel Baker. In his *William Hazlitt* (1962), he has presented numerous letters hitherto unpublished, especially utilizing the collection of Hazlitt letters to Francis Jeffrey of the Yale University Library.

The last of the principal biographers of Hazlitt to further significantly our knowledge of unpublished Hazlitt letters is Professor Ralph M. Wardle, whose *Hazlitt* appeared in 1971. Professor Wardle has drawn largely not only upon all previously available correspondence but has made generous use of the original letters addressed to P.G. Patmore and others, many of which, although published by Richard Le Gallienne in 1894, were neither fully nor accurately reproduced. Professor Wardle's biography also contains detailed reference to the most recent accession of previously unpublished Hazlitt letters, the "Nine New Hazlitt Letters and Some Others," published by Professor Stanley Jones in the *Etudes Anglaises, XIX, Année, No. 3,* Juillet-Sept., *1966,* together with Professor Jones' article "Hazlitt and *John Bull," Review of English Studies,* N.S. v. 17, no. 66, May, 1966. The latter article reprints a Hazlitt letter from the *John Bull* weekly newspaper of 22 June 1823, which in slightly altered and shortened form appears in the *Liber Amoris.*

Gerald Lahey, Professor Emeritus
Faculty of English Literature
College of Arts and Science
New York University.

The Letters
of William Hazlitt

A reference list of their first publication, either in part or in full. Unless the notation "in part" appears, it is to be assumed that publication was in full. (Also see the List of Abbreviations and Bibliographical Note following.)

No. 1	To the Rev. William Hazlitt	*Memoirs:* I: 7.
No. 2	To Grace Loftus Hazlitt	Wardle, p. 311.
No. 3	To John Hazlitt	*Remains:* I: viii-x.
No. 4	To Grace Loftus Hazlitt	*Four Generations:* I: 67-69.
No. 5	To the Rev. William Hazlitt	*Remains:* I: xix-xxiii.
No. 6	To the Rev. William Hazlitt	*Remains:* I: x-xv.
No. 7	To the Editor of the Shrewsbury *Chronicle*	*Remains:* I: xxiv-xxvii.
No. 8	To the Rev. William Hazlitt	*Remains:* I: xxix-xxxi, in part.
No. 9	To the Rev. William Hazlitt	*Remains:* I: xxxi-xxxii, in part.
No. 10	To the Rev. William Hazlitt	*Lamb and Hazlitt,* pp. 33-36.

No. 11	To the Rev. William Hazlitt	*Remains:* I: xxxiii-xxxiv, in part.
No. 12	To the Rev. William Hazlitt	*Lamb and Hazlitt,* pp. 44-47.
No. 13	To the Rev. William Hazlitt	*Four Generations:* I: 79.
No. 14	To the Rev. William Hazlitt	K.N. Cameron: *Shelley and His Circle:* I: 219-220. Harvard University Press, 1961.
No. 15	To the Rev. William Hazlitt	*Remains:* I: xxxviii-xl.
No. 16	To the Rev. William Hazlitt	*Remains:* I: xl-xliii.
No. 17	To the Rev. William Hazlitt	*Remains:* I: xliii-xliv.
No. 18	To the Rev. William Hazlitt	*Remains:* I: xlv-xlvi.
No. 19	To the Rev. William Hazlitt	*Remains:* I: xlvi-xlix.
No. 20	To the Rev. William Hazlitt	*Remains:* I: xlix-l.
No. 21	To William Godwin	Baker, p. 140.
No. 22	To Joseph Johnson	*Four Generations:* I: 96.
No. 23	To William Godwin	(Hitherto unpublished).
No. 24	To the Rev. William Hazlitt	*Four Generations:* I: 97-99.
No. 25	To Joseph Johnson	*Four Generations:* I: 100.
No. 26	To William Godwin	Baker, p. 166.
No. 27	To Joseph Hume	*Lamb and Hazlitt,* pp. 67-76.
No. 28	To Sarah Stoddart	*Memoirs:* I: 153-155.
No. 29	To the Right Honorable William Windham	Howe, 107.
No. 30	To William Godwin	Baker, 171.
No. 31	To William Godwin	C. Kegan Paul, *William Godwin: Friends and Contemporaries,* 2 vols. London, 1876: II: 175, in part.
No. 32	To the Rev. William Hazlitt	*Publications of the Modern Language Association,* v.77, 1962, pp. 341-342. (E.J. Moyne)
No. 33	To Henry Crabb Robinson	Howe, 111-113.

No. 34	To Henry Crabb Robinson	Howe, 113-114.
No. 35	To Sarah Stoddart Hazlitt	*Lamb and Hazlitt,* pp. 99-102.
No. 36	To William Cobbett	Cobbett's *Political Register,* 24 Nov. 1810.
No. 37	To Thomas Hardy	*Lamb and Hazlitt,* p. 106.
No. 38	To Thomas Robinson	Howe, 122.
No. 39	To Henry Crabb Robinson	Howe, 124-125.
No. 40	To James Perry	Baker, 193, in part.
No. 41	To the Curator, Lucien Bonaparte Collection	*The Hazlitts,* p. 475.
No. 42	To Francis Jeffrey	Baker, 208-209.
No. 43	To Francis Jeffrey	Baker, 209, in part.
No. 44	To Francis Jeffrey	Baker, 209, in part.
No. 45	To Francis Jeffrey	Baker, 209, in part.
No. 46	To Charles Ollier	*Four Generations:* I: 115-116.
No. 47	To Francis Jeffrey	Baker, 209, in part.
No. 48	To Francis Jeffrey	(Hitherto unpublished)
No. 49	To the Editor of *The Examiner*	*The Examiner,* 29 Oct. 1815.
No. 50	To Francis Jeffrey	Baker, 210.
No. 51	To Archibald Constable	*Etudes Anglaises,* 19, July-Sept., 1966, pp. 264-266. (Jones)
No. 52	To Macvey Napier	*The Athenaeum,* Friday, August 8, 1919, p. 711 (Howe)
No. 53	To Macvey Napier	*The Athenaeum,* August 8, 1919, pp. 711-712 (Howe).
No. 54	To Leigh Hunt	*The London Mercury,* March, 1923, p. 494 (Howe).
No. 55	To Archibald Constable	*Etudes Anglaises,* 19, July-Sept., 1966, p. 269 (Jones).
No. 56	To Macvey Napier	*The Athenaeum,* August

		8, 1918, p. 712 (Howe).
No. 57	To Archibald Constable	*Etudes Anglaises, 19,* July-Sept., 1966, p. 270 (Jones).
No. 58	To Macvey Napier	*The Athenaeum,* August 8, 1918, p. 712 (Howe).
No. 59	To Macvey Napier	*The Athenaeum,* August 8, 1919, p. 712 (Howe).
No. 60	To Macvey Napier	*The Athenaeum,* August 8, 1919, p. 712 (Howe).
No. 61	To Archibald Constable	*Etudes Anglaises,* 19, July-Sept., 1966, p. 272 (Jones).
No. 62	To Archibald Constable	*Etudes Anglaises,* 19, July-Sept., 1966, p. 273 (Jones).
No. 63	To Francis Jeffrey	Baker, 358, n., in part.
No. 64	To the Editor	*The Examiner,* January, 1817.
No. 65	To Francis Jeffrey	*The London Mercury,* v. 12, 1925, p. 411 (Howe).
No. 66	To Macvey Napier	*The Athenaeum,* August 8, 1919, pp. 712-713 (Howe).
No. 67	To Francis Jeffrey	Baker, p. 214.
No. 68	To Archibald Constable	*Etudes Anglaises,* 19, 1966, July-Sept., p. 274 (Jones).
No. 69	To Francis Jeffrey	Wardle, p. 198, in part.
No. 70	To Francis Jeffrey	Wardle, p. 203, in part.
No. 71	To B. W. Procter	(Hitherto unpublished).

No. 72	To Archibald Constable	*The London Mercury,* March 1923, p. 496 (Howe).
No. 73	To Archibald Constable	*The London Mercury,* March 1923, p. 496 (Howe).
No. 74	To Archibald Constable	*The London Mercury,* March 1923, p. 496 (Howe).
No. 75	To P.G. Patmore	*Personal Recollections of Lamb, Hazlitt, and Others,* edited by Richard Henry Stoddard, N.Y. 1876, p. 65
No. 76	To Francis Jeffrey	Wardle, 224, in part.
No. 77	To Archibald Constable	Wardle, 227 n. in part.
No. 78	To Macvey Napier	*Selections from the Correspondence of the Late Macvey Napier, Esq.,* edited by Macvey Napier, Jr., London, 1879, pp. 22-23.
No. 79	To Archibald Constable	*Times Literary Supplement,* 21 March, 1936, p. 244 (Howe).
No. 80	To Archibald Constable	*Etudes Anglaises,* 19, July-Sept., 1966, p. 276 (Jones).
No. 81	To Mr. James Balfour, W.S.	*Etudes Anglaises,* 19, July-Sept., 1966, p. 277 (Jones).
No. 82	To the Editor	*Edinburgh Magazine,* Jan. 1819.
No. 83	To P.G. Patmore	*Works:* 6: 385.
No. 84	To Whitmore and Fenn	*Works:* 9: 251.
No. 85	To Benjamin Robert Haydon	Baker, 242.

No. 108	To Taylor and Hessey	Howe, 311, in part.
No. 109	To P.G. Patmore	Patmore, *My Friends and Acquaintance*, 1854, III: 177, 178, 179, in part.
No. 110	To P.G. Patmore	Le Gallienne, *Liber Amoris*, 1893, Appendix III: lxxxi-xc, in part.
No. 111	To Taylor and Hessey	Howe, 316, in part.
No. 112	To P.G. Patmore	Patmore, *My Friends and Acquaintance*, 1854, III: 176-177, in part.
No. 113	To William Hazlitt	(Hitherto unpublished).
No. 114	To P.G. Patmore	Le Gallienne, *Liber Amoris*, 1894, "Correspondence," 216-219.
No. 115	To P.G. Patmore	Patmore, *My Friends and Acquaintance*, 1854, III: 182-185.
No. 116	To P.G. Patmore	Le Gallienne, *Liber Amoris*, 1893, Appendix III: xci-xcii.
No. 117	To P.G. Patmore	Patmore, *My Friends and Acquaintance*, 1854, III: 179-182, in part.
No. 118	To Sarah Walker	*Liber Amoris*, 1823, Part II: 102-103.
No. 119	To P.G. Patmore	*Memoirs:* III: 55-56.
No. 120	To P.G. Patmore	Le Gallienne, *Liber Amoris*, 1894, "Correspondence," 232-236, in part.
No. 121	To P.G. Patmore	Le Gallienne, *Liber Amoris*, 1894, "Correspondence," 236-237, in part.

No. 122	To P.G. Patmore	Patmore, *My Friends and Acquaintance,* 1854, III: 187, in part.
No. 123	To Francis Jeffrey	Baker, 417, in part.
No. 124	To James Sheridan Knowles	*Liber Amoris,* 1823, Part III: 127-149.
No. 125	To James Sheridan Knowles	*Liber Amoris,* 1823, Part III: 150-181.
No. 126	To James Sheridan Knowles	*Liber Amoris,* 1823, Part III: 182-192.
No. 127	To Francis Jeffrey	Baker, 418.
No. 128	To Francis Jeffrey	Wardle, 354, in part.
No. 129	To Jane Reynolds	*Times Literary Supplement,* 21 March, 1936, p. 244.
No. 130	To Thomas Noon Talfourd	Howe, 322.
No. 131	To Taylor and Hessey	*The London Mercury,* March 1923, p. 498. (Howe).
No. 132	To Thomas Cadell	*Four Generations:* I: 142.
No. 133	To Thomas Hood	Howe, 326, 327.
No. 134	To the Editor	*The London Magazine,* Nov. 1823.
No. 135	To Taylor and Hessey	*The London Mercury,* May 1924, p. 73. (Howe).
No. 136	To Francis Jeffrey	Keynes, *Bibliography of William Hazlitt,* 1931, p. 83.
No. 137	To Walter S. Landor	(Hitherto unpublished).
No. 138	To Walter S. Landor	*Four Generations:* I: 183-184.
No. 139	To William Hazlitt, Jr.	*Four Generations:* I: 185-186.
No. 140	To John Black	*The Hazlitts,* p. 479.
No. 141	To Henry Colburn	*Four Generations:* I: 193.
No. 142	To Henry Colburn	(Hitherto unpublished).

No. 143	To P.G. Patmore	*Works:* 13: 354.
No. 144	To Isabella Jane Towers	(Hitherto unpublished).
No. 145	To Charles Cowden Clarke	*Memoirs:* II: 217-218.
No. 146	To Charles Cowden Clarke	*The Times Literary Supplement,* 21 March, 1936, p. 244.
No. 147	To David Constable	Howe, 360-361.
No. 148	To Henry Hunt	*Four Generations:* I: 188-189.
No. 149	To Charles Cowden Clarke	*Four Generations:* I: 191.
No. 150	To Charles Cowden Clarke	*Four Generations:* I: 189-190.
No. 151	To Charles Cowden Clarke	*Lamb and Hazlitt,* p. 144.
No. 152	To the Postmaster, Salisbury	*Four Generations:* I: 195.
No. 153	To Leigh Hunt	
No. 154	To the Editor of *The Atlas*	*The Atlas,* 19 April 1829.
No. 155	To Macvey Napier	*The Athenaeum,* Friday, August 15, 1919, pp. 742-743. (Howe).
No. 156	To Macvey Napier	*The Athenaeum,* August 15, 1919, p. 743 (Howe).
No. 157	To Macvey Napier	*The Athenaeum,* August 15, 1919, p. 743 (Howe).
No. 158	To Basil Montague	(Hitherto unpublished).
No. 159	To Macvey Napier	*The Athenaeum,* August 15, 1919, p. 743 (Howe).
No. 160	To Macvey Napier	*The Athenaeum,* August 15, 1919, p. 743 (Howe).
No. 161	To Macvey Napier	*The Athenaeum,* August 15, 1919, p. 743 (Howe).

List of Abbreviations

Abinger

MS Collection, Lord Abinger,
Duke University

Autobiography

Autobiography by Leigh Hunt, ed. R.
Ingpen, 1903

Baker

William Hazlitt, by Herschel Baker,
Cambridge, Mass.; Harvard
University Press, 1962

Berg

Henry W. and Albert A. Berg
Collection, The New York Public
Library, Astor, Lenox and Tilden
Foundations

Bibliography

Bibliography of William Hazlitt, by
Geoffrey Keynes, 1931

Birrell

William Hazlitt, by Augustine
Birrell, 1902

[35]

Boston	Massachusetts Historical Society
Collected Letters	*Collected Letters of Samuel Taylor Coleridge,* edited by Earl Leslie Griggs. 4 vols. Oxford, Clarendon Press, 1956-1959.
Cornell	Wordsworth Collection, Cornell University
Diary	*Henry Crabb Robinson on Books and Their Writers,* edited by Edith J. Morley. 3 vols. London, 1938
Edinburgh	National Library of Scotland
Four Generations	*Four Generations of a Literary Family,* by W. Carew Hazlitt. 2 vols. London, 1897.
Haydon Diary	*The Diary of Benjamin Robert Haydon,* edited by Willard Bissell Pope, 5 vols. Cambridge, Mass.; Harvard University Press, 1960-1963.
Hazlitts	*The Hazlitts: An Account of Their Origin and Descent,* by W. Carew Hazlitt, Edinburgh, Ballantyne, Hanson and Co., 1911
Hornby	Hornby Library, Liverpool
Houghton	The Houghton Library, Harvard University
Huntington	The Henry E. Huntington Library and Art Gallery
Howe	*Life of William Hazlitt,* by P.P.

	Howe, new edition, London; Hamish Hamilton, 1947
Keynes	MS. Collection, Sir Geoffrey Keynes
Lamb and Hazlitt	*Lamb and Hazlitt: Further Letters and Records, Hitherto Unpublished,* edited by William Carew Hazlitt, London, Elkin Mathews, 1900.
Le Gallienne (1893)	*Liber Amoris or the New Pygmalion* by William Hazlitt with an Introduction by Richard Le Gallienne London: Elkin Mathews & John Lane . . . Bodley Head . . . 1893.
Le Gallienne (1894)	*Liber Amoris, or the New Pygmalion by William Hazlitt,* with Additional Matter now Printed for the First Time from the Original Manuscripts, with an introduction by Richard Le Gallienne: Privately Printed, 1894.
Letters	*Letters of Charles Lamb, to Which are Added those of His Sister Mary Lamb,* edited by E.V. Lucas. 3 vols. London; J.M. Dent and Sons, Ltd.; Methuen and Co. Ltd., 1935
Lockwood	Lockwood Memorial Library, State University of New York at Buffalo
Memoirs	*Memoirs of William Hazlitt, with Portions of his Correspondence,* by W.

[37]

	Carew Hazlitt; London, Richard Bentley, 1867.
Patmore	*My Friends and Acquaintance . . . with Selections from Their Letters,* by Peter George Patmore, London, Saunders and Otley, 3 vols. 1854
Remains	*Literary Remains of the late William Hazlitt, with a Notice* of His Life, by His Son . . . in Two Volumes; London, Saunders and Otley, 1836.
Stoddard	*Life, Letters, and Table Talk of Benjamin Robert Haydon.* Edited by R.H. Stoddard, New York, 1876.
Wardle	*Hazlitt,* by Ralph W. Wardle, University of Nebraska Press, Lincoln, 1971.
Dr. Williams	Dr. Williams's Library, Gordon Square, London.
Works	*The Complete Works of William Hazlitt,* edited by P.P. Howe after the edition of A.R. Waller and Arnold Glover; J.M. Dent and Sons, Ltd. London and Toronto, 21 vols., 1930-1934.
Yale	Yale University Library.

Bibliographical Note

One peculiarity of Professor Sikes' text should be mentioned. In his script, Hazlitt never used *and* but always the ampersand "&." Professor Sikes' text originally embodied this usage; but throughout the typescript wherever it appears, Professor Sikes crossed it out to change it to *and*. One may only conjecture his reason. Perhaps it was done because all of the printed correspondence in the publications of the Hazlitts, son and grandson, likewise substituted the *and* for the original Ms ampersand. As it was necessary to rely upon these texts frequently as the only copies of lost originals, it would have produced a "mixed" final text to have had letters, some uniformly with and some uniformly without the ampersand. Professor Sikes apparently wished to avoid this irregularity. For the sake of consistency, newly discovered letters which have been added have been similarly edited to conform to the original practice.

Asterisks have been placed after many letter dates (the latter within square brackets) if they are conjectural. The asterisks refer to works of biographers and editors whose judgment about the conjectured dates supports that of the present text.

THE LETTERS
OF
WILLIAM HAZLITT

No. 1

To the Reverend William Hazlitt[1]

MS. Lockwood.
Address: The Rev. Mr. Hazlitt/London/To the care of Mr. David Lewis.

12 of Nov[1786]*

My Dear papa

I shall never forget that we came to america. If we had not came to america we should not have been away from one and another, though now it can not be helped, I think for my part that it would have been a great deal better if the white people had not found it out. Let the [Indians have][2] it to themselves for it was made for them, I have got a little of my grammar sometimes I get three pages and sometimes but one I do not sifer any at all. mamma peggy and Jacky are very well and I am to

I still remain your most
affectionate son
William, Hazlitt

---

* Cf. Howe, p. 4.

[1] Hazlitt's father was born in the village of Shronell, county Tipperary, in 1737 and died at Crediton, Devonshire, on 16 July 1820. At the age of eighteen, "a poor Irish lad," he left his father's farm to prepare himself for the Presbyterian ministry. After graduating at Glasgow University with an M. A. in 1760, he joined the Unitarians and became minister of Wisbeach, Cambridgeshire. There, in 1766, at the age of twenty-nine, the Reverend William Hazlitt married Grace Loftus (1746-1837), the daughter of an ironmonger. Shortly after they moved to Marshfield near Bath where their first child, John (1767-1837), was born. In 1770 Mr. Hazlitt received a call from the Earl Street Meeting House in Maidstone, Kent. Margaret, called Peggy, was born there in 1770 (died unmarried in 1844), and William on 10 April 1778. After ten years at Maidstone, during which the Reverend Hazlitt had enjoyed an intellectual circle that included Joseph Priestley and Richard Price, ardent Unitarian reformers, and had met Benjamin Franklin, the family moved back to Ireland to a congregation at Bandon, County Cork. A sympathiser with the cause of American independence, Mr. Hazlitt risked charges of treason to befriend the American prisoners held nearby at Kinsale. "My father," wrote Peggy in her Diary, "who never disguised his sentiments, gave great

No. 2

To Grace Loftus Hazlitt [1]

MS. Lockwood.

London December 20 [1787] *

My dear Mother,[2]

I shall come up [3] in a day or two. Father has been very unkind to me. And I shall try if you will not be so. I am just going out I don't know where to bide out a good while.

Good bye I shall se
you in two or three days
I am
[Unsigned]

---

offence by his freedom in writing and speaking at a time when the unbridled licence of the army (who took liberties in Ireland that they dared not do at home) made it dangerous to offend the haughty officers, who seemed to think wearing a sword entitled them to domineer over their fellow-subjects." With the encouragement of a Unitarian group in America, the Reverend Hazlitt sailed with his family from Cork on 3 April 1783 and arrived in New York on 26 May. They resided for three years in Philadelphia, Dorchester, and Weymouth, Mass., while Mr. Hazlitt preached in various meeting houses. In Dorchester, now part of Boston, he helped to found the first Unitarian Church. But disappointed in his prospects of a permanent settlement in America, Mr. Hazlitt returned alone to England and obtained a place at Wem, Shropshire. William's first letter was written at Dorchester about a month after his father had embarked. The family joined him in London nine months later, in August 1787. Cf. E.J. Moyne: *A Journal of Margaret Hazlitt*, Lawrence, Kansas: University of Kansas Press, 1967.

2 *Others* written above.

---

* In all probability, this undated letter is of a later period, written by William Hazlitt, the Younger, Hazlitt's son. Cf. Professor Wardle's comment on it in his *Hazlitt*, p. 311. The present dating is Professor Sikes'. Likewise note No. 1.

1 This is the first of the very few letters from William Hazlitt to his mother that have survived. He was on a visit to London with his father and brother John, who had shown his artistic talent by painting the portraits of American citizens in and around Boston. Now, at twenty, John was left in London to study under Sir Joshua Reynolds and "to live by his gift as a painter of miniatures." Cf. Howe, p. 5.

2 Hazlitt originally began with "My dear P"—presumably "Papa"—but crossed out *P*.

3 *down* crossed out.

No. 3

To John Hazlitt

MS. Lockwood.
Address: John Hazlitt/No. 288, High Holborn/London.

Wem, Saturday morning [March 1788]*

Dear brother

I received your letter this morning, to my great satisfaction. We were all glad to hear you were well and that you have so much business to do. We cannot be happy without being employed. I want you to tell me whether you go to the academy or not and what pictures you intend for the exhibition.[1] Tell the exhibitioners to finish their exhibition soon that you may soon come and see us. You must send your picture to us directly. You want to know what I do. I am a busy body and do many silly things. I drew eyes and noses till about a fort night ago. I have drawn a little boy since, a mans face and a little boys front face taken from a bust. Next Monday I shall begin to read Ovid Metamorphosis and Eutropius. I shall like to know all the Latin and Greek I can. I want to learn how to measure the stars. I shall not I suppose paint the worse for knowing every thing else. I began to cypher a fort night after Christmas and shall go into the rule of three next week. I can teach a boy of sixteen already who was cyphering eight months before me. Is he not a great dunce. I shall be through the whole cyphering book this summer, and then I am to learn Euclid. We go to school at nine every morning. Three boys begin with reading the Bible. Then I and two others shew our exercises. We then read the Speaker.[2] Then we all set about our lessons and those who are first ready say first. At eleven we write and cypher. In the afternoon we

---

* Cf. Howe, p. 5; Wardle, p. 27.
[1] John Hazlitt exhibited four miniatures and a *Portrait of a Lady* at the Royal Academy in 1788.
[2] William Enfield's *Speaker, or Miscellaneous Pieces Selected from the Best English Writers* (1774) was used in many grammar schools such as the one William was now attending at Wem.

stand for places at spelling and I am almost always first. We also read and do a great deal of business besides. I can say no more about the boys here. Some are so sulky they wont play. Others are quarrelsome because they cannot learn and are fit only for fighting like stupid dogs and cats. I can jump four yards at a running jump and two at a standing jump. I intend to try you at this when you come down. We are not all well for poor Peggy has a great cold. You spelled Mr. Vaughans name wrong, for you spelled it Vaughn.[3] Write soon again. I wish I could see all those paintings that you see and that Peggy had a good prize. I don't want your old cloaths. I shall go to dancing this month. This is all I can say. I

am your affectionate brother,

Wm Hazlitt.

---

[3] Samuel Vaughan and "his two sons, English gentlemen of large property," had settled in Philadelphia where they met and befriended the Hazlitts. In her diary, Margaret Hazlitt recalls that the Vaughans "wished my father to take a school at German Town . . . and offered to advance him any money necessary to begin with" (*Four Generations* I, 24.)

No. 4*

To Grace Loftus Hazlitt

Four Generations, I, 67-69.

Friday, 9th of July 1790.

Dear Mother,

It is with pleasure I now sit down to write to you, and it is with pleasure that I do anything, which I know, will please you. I hope you have by this time received my letter, which I put in the Post Office on Tuesday evening. I intended to have written to you, in my last, but, as you see, I had not room for it, and therefore I shall fill up this sheet as your correspondent. On Tuesday night, after I had been at Mrs. Hudson's to tea, I took my Papa's letter to the Post Office. As it was half an hour past eight, when I left Mrs. Hudson's and I had a mile and half to go in half an hour I went there rather quickly, and got home a good while before the rest. As soon as I came home Mrs. Tracey told me that a gentleman, who appeared to be about 2 or 3 and 20 years old, had been here enquiring after me; he said that he saw my brother on Sunday last, and that I must enquire for him at the Mail Coach Office, without telling where it was, or what his name was, so that it was almost impossible for anybody to find out who it was. I accordingly went, about ten o'clock in the morning, to the Mail Coach Office to enquire for him; I told the man how it was, who said that it was almost impossible to find out who it was, but however he said that if I would stop about an hour he would make enquiry. I amused myself about an hour, with looking at the pictures in the shops and then I went again, but I came home without knowing who it was, any more than I did when I went. On Wednesday I and George Dickin went to Mr. Fisher's to dine. He is a very rich man, but—

* This letter and the two following, No. 5 and No. 6, present problems in dating. Hence Howe (pp. 7-10) observes a different chronological order. But cf. Wardle, pp. 30 ff. Also Moyne; *The Journal of Margaret Hazlitt,* Lawrence, Kansas: University of Kansas Press, 1967, p. 128.

The man who is a well-wisher to slavery, is always a slave himself. The King, who wishes to enslave all mankind, is a slave to ambition; The man who wishes to enslave all mankind, for his King, is himself a slave to his King. He like others of his brethren, I suppose, wished that Mr. Beaufoy[1] was out, or with the Devil, he did not care which. You see that he wished to have him out, merely because *"he would do to others as he would be done to."* The man who is a well-wisher to liberty, wishes to have men good, and himself to be one of them, and knows that men are not good unless they are so willingly, and does [not] attempt to force them to it, but tries to put them in such a situation as will induce them to be good. Slavery is not a state for men to improve in, therefore he does not wish them to be in that condition. In a state of liberty men improve. He therefore wishes them to be in such a state. —I have just received my Papa's letter, and the other things which I am much obliged to him for. I am concerned to hear you have so little money, but I hope that your portion is not in this world, you have trouble for a few days, but have joy for many. The RICH take their fill in a few years, are cut short in the midst of their career, and fall into ruin; Never to rise again. But the good shall have joy for evermore. —Be sure to tell me if I may sell my old Buckles.

Tuesday, 13th of July.

I yesterday received my Papa's kind letter. I am sorry you did not receive my letter in due season as I put it in on Tuesday according to my directions. I was very glad to hear of Mr. Tayleur's[2] present. I yesterday began a letter to my sister, and finished one to my brother. [3]

Tell my Papa, to tell John Kynaston that I understand the 2nd problem, and that the other is very right. Do not forget to remember me to him. I have translated 11 Fables and written 11 verbs. Remember me to Mrs. and Miss Cottons, and to every inquirer. Tell Kynaston I am very sorry Mrs. Tracey has not gotten him a place. The person who called on me last Tuesday was Isaac

---

[1] Henry Beaufoy (d. 1795), Quaker, Whig M. P., supporter of religious liberty, and one of the founders of the Unitarian New College, Hackney, which Hazlitt entered in 1793.

[2] A merchant member of the Unitarian group at Shrewsbury.

[3] These letters have not survived.

Kingston. [4] He called here on Friday after I had written the first part of this letter, he stayed about an hour, and drank tea here the day following. He said he attempted to get Papa to Cork, but found it was useless to attempt it. He was asked by a lady to vote against Hind, but he said he would vote against no one. He said that those who were against him staid away from the Election and that he carried the Election without opposition.

He said that he was sorry that Papa had not a better place, and wished that he would set up a school, that is a boarding school; and that there was no man in the world to whom he would sooner send his children. He has 3 boys, the eldest of which is 5 years old, within a few months.

I shall go to Mr. Clegg's to drink tea on Thursday, and shall go to the play on Friday. I shall write to Joseph Swanwick this week. I dined at Mrs. Corbett's on Saturday, and at Mrs. Chilton's on Sunday, which was not very agreeable. I have told you all the news, I know, almost and have not much more paper.—They were pressing on Saturday evening.[5] The world is not quite perfect yet; nor will it ever be so whilst such practices are reckoned lawful. Mrs. Tracey says I had better let my arm alone, until I come home; but I wish I could tell how to procure grains and then I would foment it in them. Adieu—Give my love to Papa. Mr. Kingston will call as he returns if he can.

I am, Your affectionate Son,
W. Hazlitt.

P.S.—I like my Balls very well, and have also received the money.

---

[4] Both Kingston and Joseph Hind were Unitarian ministers of the Manchester Group.

[5] The Press Gang to force men into military service had not yet been abolished.

No. 5

To the Reverend William Hazlitt[1]

Remains, I, xix-xxiii.

[July, 1790]

Dear Papa,

I this morning received your affectionate letter, and, at the same time, one from my brother and sister, who were very well, when they wrote. On Wednesday I received a Lexicon, which I was very glad of. I have, since that time, gotten to the 12th verse of the 14th chapter, which is 39 verses from the place I was in before. Mr. Clegg[2] came last Wednesday, and employed the time he staid in showing the Miss Traceys how to find the latitude and longitude of any place; which I can now do upon the globes with ease. Whilst he was here, I was as attentive as I could be. He came again on Saturday. And I came in a few minutes after he came. I drank tea at his house, the Thursday before, when he asked me to prepare the map of Asia, which Miss Traceys were at that time getting. I answered that I had already gotten it. I said it to him on Saturday, with Miss Traceys, without missing a single word. He, when he had finished with us, bid me have the map of Africa ready by the next time he should come, which I have done. He also asked me to read a dialogue with him, which I did. I should think he intends to teach me geography while I stay. On Thursday he took me and George,[3] with his two brothers, to the glass-house, and then we went to the new fort. On Friday I went to the play with Mr. Corbett,[4] at whose house I dined and drank tea. The play was

---

[1] This, the foregoing, and the next letter were written in Liverpool during a visit to a Unitarian family named Tracey. The father was a merchant whose wife had taken an interest in William and encouraged his first intensive efforts at reading.

[2] A tutor, probably related to James or Benjamin Clegg, prominent teachers in Unitarian academies.

[3] George Dickin of Wem, a neighbor's son, who was also visiting the Traceys.

[4] Another tutor.

"Love in many Masks,"[5] and the farce, "No Song, no Supper."[6] It was very entertaining, and was performed by some of the best players in London, as for instance, Kemble,[7] Suett,[8] Dignum,[9] the famous singer, Mrs. Williams, Miss Hagley, Miss Romanzini,[10] and others. Suett, who acted in the character of "Ned Blunt," was enough to make any one laugh, though he stood still; and Kemble acted admirably as an officer. Mr. Dignum sang beautifully, and Miss Hagley acted the country-girl with much exactness. Mr. Corbett says he will take us to another play before we go. So much for last week. I have been writing an hour now. Yesterday I went to Meeting by myself in the morning, where we had a very good discourse on the 10th of the 2nd chapter of Thess. 2nd—"With all deceivableness of unrighteousness." From this he drew several conclusions of the false pretences which are made by sin to her followers to happiness; how people are drawn away, by imperceptible degrees, from one degree of sin to another, and so on to greater. I sent a note to Mr. Yates[11] "this morning, requesting him to send me a dictionary and Horace. Was it right to express myself in this manner? "Mr. Hazlitt sends his compliments to Mr. Yates, and would be much obliged to him if he would send him a dictionary

[5] Henry Fielding's *Love in Several Masques* (1728).

[6] By Prince Hoare (1755-1834). *"No Song No Supper* was the first play I had ever seen. . . " *Conversations of James Northcote, Works,* XI, 270).

[7] John Philip Kemble (1757-1823), the greatest actor of his day. Hazlitt admired Kemble's "sensible, lonely Hamlet" and followed his illustrious career until 1817 when, in "Mr. Kemble's Retirement," he wrote: "Our associations of admiration and delight with theatrical performers are among our earliest recollections—among our last regrets" (*A View of the English Stage, Works,* V, 374).

[8] The comedian Richard Suett (1755-1805) was greatly admired for his acting the roles of Shakespeare's fools.

[9] Charles Dignum (1765-1827), tenor and actor, became famous as "Crop" in *No Song No Supper* at the Royalty Theatre, London in 1787.

[10] Thirty-six years later Hazlitt wrote: "I met Dignum (the singer) in the street the other day: he was humming a tune; and his eye, though quenched, was smiling. I could scarcely forbear going up to speak to him. Why so? I had seen him in the year 1792 [1790] (the first time I ever was at a play), with Suett and Miss Romanzini and some others, in *No Song No Supper;* and ever since, that bright vision of my childhood has played round my fancy with unabated, vivid delight. Yet the whole was fictitious, your cynic philosopher will say. I wish there were but a few realities that lasted so long, and were followed with so little disappointment" (*The Plain Speaker, Works,* XII, 193).

[11] John Yates (1756-1826), popular Unitarian preacher of Kaye Street, Liverpool. Cf. "Pulpit Oratory—Dr. Chalmers and Mr. Irving," *Works,* XX, 113.

and Horace." P. S. Papa desired me to remember him to you.

On Sunday, after I had come from Meeting, I went, but not willingly, to Mrs. Sydebotham's to dinner; in the afternoon we went to church, for the first time I ever was in one, and I do not care if I should never go into one again. The clergyman, after he had gabbled over half a dozen prayers, began his sermon, the text of which was as follows:-Zachariah, 3rd chapter, 2nd verse, latter part—"Is not this a brand plucked out of the fire?" If a person had come in five minutes after he began, he would have thought that he had taken his text out of Joshua. In short, his sermon had neither head nor tail. I was sorry that so much time should be thrown away upon nonsense. I often wished I was hearing Mr. Yates; But I shall see I do not go to church again in a hurry. I have been very busy to day; I got up at seven and wrote a note for Mr. Yates; and called on Mr. Nicholls[12] with it, who was at breakfast. I then went to the post-office, and there I stayed a good while waiting for my letter, but as they told me the letters were gone to Richmond, I came home to my breakfast. After breakfast I went with George, to buy some paper, down to Mr. Bird; when I came home I sat down to my French, but as Mrs. Tracey wanted some riband, I went to Mr. Bird's for some; but, as you may suppose, I was not a long time going there. I had almost forgotten to tell you that I wrote to Joseph Swanwick[13] last week. I have every thing ready for Mr. Dolounghpryée,[14] who comes this evening. I have also made myself perfect in the map of Africa. As I have now given you all the news I can, I shall lay by for the present, and to-morrow, for my observations and reflections. Tell Kynaston[15] I have done the first sum, and understand it quite well. I cannot play any tune on the harpsichord but "God save the King." Farewell for the present.

I shall have satis pecuniae, dum tu habeas opportunitatem, mittendi aliquam partem mihi.[16]

---

[12] A tutor at the Manchester Academy.

[13] A boyhood friend at Wem.

[14] According to W. Carew Hazlitt this odd spelling represents John De Lemprière (1765-1824), author of the *Classical Dictionary* (1788), who was tutoring the Tracey children and William in French (*Four Generations*, II, 52).

[15] Another friend at Wem.

[16] I shall have enough money until you have an opportunity of sending some part to me.

Tuesday morning.

I have this morning gotten my French for tomorrow, and thirteen verses of the "Testament:" I have also written out the contractions, and can tell any of them. I said my lessons very well last night; I had only one word wrong in my fable, and not any one in my two verbs. I am to go to the concert to-night. I have written two verbs, and translated my French task. How ineffectual are all pleasures, except those which arise from a knowledge of having done, as far as one knew, that which was right, to make their possessors happy. The people who possess them, at night, lie down upon their beds, and after having spent a wearisome night, rise up in the morning to pursue the same "pleasures," or, more properly, vain shadows of pleasure, which, like Jacks with lanthorns, as they are called, under a fair outside, at last bring those people who are so foolish as to confide in them into destruction, which they cannot then escape. How different from them is a man who *wisely "in a time of peace, lays up arms, and such like necessaries in case of a war."* Mrs. Tracey desires me to give her respects.

[*Neither complimentary close nor signature given.*]

[53]

No. 6

To the Reverend William Hazlitt

MS. Yale.
Address: Revd. Mr. Hazlitt/Wem/Shropshire.

[July 1790]*
Dear Father,
I now sit down to spend a little time in an employment, the productions of which I know will give you pleasure; though I know that every minute, that I am employed in doing any thing, which will be advantageous to me, will give you pleasure. Happy, indeed unspeakably happy are those people, who, when at the point of Death, are able to say, with a satisfaction which none but themselves can have any idea of, I have done with this world, I shall now have no more of its temptations to struggle with, and praise be to God I have overcome them; now no more sorrow, now no more grief, but happiness for evermore! But, how unspeakably miserable is that man, who, when his pleasures are going to end, when his Lamp begins to grow dim, is compelled to say, Oh, that I had done my Duty to God, and man, oh that I had been wise, and spent that time, which was kindly given me by providence for a purpose quite contrary to that which I employed it to, as I should have done! but it is now gone; I cannot recal time, nor can I undo all my wicked actions. I cannot seek that mercy which I have so often despised. I have no hope remaining. I must do as well as I can; but, who can endure everlasting fire? Thus does the wicked man breathe his last, and without being able to rely upon his good; with his last breath, in the anguish of his soul, says, have mercy upon me a sinner, O God! After I had sealed up my last letter to

---

* W.C. Hazlitt assigned this letter to March (cf. *The Hazlitts,* p. 381), but internal evidence and a later recollection by Hazlitt himself, regarding attendance at his very first play, point to May. Cf. Letter 5, note 6. Cf. also *The Journal of Margaret Hazlitt,* editor, Ernest J. Moyne (Lawrence, Kansas: University of Kansas Press, 1967), pp. 21-22 and p. 128, n. 25. Present dating is Professor Sikes'.

you, George asked me if I were glad the Test Act was not repealed. I told him, no. Then he asked why and I told him, because I thought, that all the people who are inhabitants of a country, of whatsoever sect, or denominations, should have the same rights with others. But, says he, then they would try to get their religion established, or something to that purpose. Well, what if it should be so. He said that the church religion was an old one. Well, said I, popery is older than that. But then said he, the church religion is better than popery. And the presbyterian is better than that, said I. I told him, I thought so for certain reasons, not because I went to chapel. But at last when I had overpowered him with my arguments, he said, he wished he understood it as well as I did, for I was too high learned for him. I then went to the concert. But as I am now going with George to a Mrs. Cupham, I must defer the rest of my letter till another time. I have gotten to the 36th verse, 15C.

Monday morning.

I was very much pleased at the concert; but I think Meredith's singing was worth all the rest. When we came out of the concert which was about nine o'clock, we went to Mrs. Chilton's at whose house we slept. It rained the next morning, but I was not much wet coming home. George was very much wet, and the colour of his coat was almost spoiled. On Wednesday Mr. Clegg did not come as he was confined to his bed. On Wednesday evening Mr. Dolounghpryeé came to whom I was very attentive. I was sorry Mr. Clegg did not come on Saturday, but I hope he will come on Wednesday next. Saturday afternoon I and George with Miss Avis went to a Mrs. Barttons who appeared to be an unhospitable, English prim "Lady," if such she may be called. She asked us as if she were afraid we should accept it, if we would stay to tea. And at the other English person's, for I am sure she belongs to no other country than to England, I got such a surfeit of their ceremonial unsociality, that I could not help wishing myself in America—I had rather people would tell one to go out of the house than ask one to stay, and at the same time be trembling all over, for fear one should take a slice of meat, or a dish of tea, with them. Such as these require an Horace or a Shakespear to describe them. I have not yet learned the gamut perfectly, but I would have done it, if I could. I spent a very agreeable day yesterday, as I read 160 pages of Priestley,[1] and heard two good sermons. The best of which, in my opinion, was Mr. Lewin's, and the other Mr. Smith's. They both belong to Benn's Gardens Chapel.[2] Mr. Nicholls called last night, who informed me that he sent the note by his boy, who left it with the servant, and that when he went again Mr. Yates had not received it, so that I have not yet received the books, which I am very sorry for. I forgot to tell you, Winfield also all the other part of the family are very well, and that Mrs. Tracey said, I said my French task very well last Saturday. I am now almost at the end of my letter, and shall therefore answer all those questions in your letter, which I received this morning, which I have not already answered. And in the first place. I have not seen Mr. Kingston since. I am glad that you liked my letter to Jo, which I was afraid he had not received as you said nothing about it. Does he intend to answer me? Miss Shepherd [3] will go, on Monday I believe, and I shall go with her. I have not seen Mr. Yates since I wrote last. I do not converse in French, but I and Miss Tracey have a book, something like a vocabulary where we get the meanings of words. Miss Traceys never do accompts, but I take an hour or two every other day. I will follow your Greek precept.[4] Give my best love to mamma, and tell her I shall write to her next time, and hope she will write to me in answer to it. Give my respects to Mr. and Miss Cottons, and to every other inquirer, not forgetting Kynaston. I wish people made larger paper. I shall put this into the post-office to-night, Monday evening.

I am your affectionate son,
William Hazlitt.

---

[1] Joseph Priestley (1733-1804), Unitarian minister, democratic champion of the French Revolution and American independence, and discoverer of oxygen. William was probably reading the *Essay on the First Principles of Government* (1768), which influenced his second work, *Free Thoughts on Public Affairs* 1806).

[2] One of the most active congregations of Protestant Dissenters in Liverpool.

[3] Probably related to William Shepherd (1768-1847), Minister at Gateacre, and member of a prominent Unitarian family. Cf. Letter 28, n.7.

[4] The letter containing the precept is not known to have survived.

No. 7

To the Editor of the *Shrewsbury Chronicle*
Remains, I, xxiv-xxvii.

[Summer] 1791

Mr. Wood,[1]

'Tis really surprising that men—men, too, that aspire to the
character of Christians—should seem to take such pleasure in
endeavouring to load with infamy one of the best, one of the wisest,
and one of the greatest of men.

One of your late correspondents, under the signature of
ΟΨΔΕΙΣ, seems desirous of having Dr. Priestley in chains, and
indeed would not perhaps (from the gentleman's seemingly
charitable disposition) be greatly averse to seeing him in the flames
also.[2] This is the Christian!

This the mild spirit its great Master taught. Ah! Christianity,
how art thou debased! How am I grieved to see that universal
benevolence, that love to all mankind, that love even to our
enemies, and that compassion for the failings of our fellow-men,
that thou art contracted to promote, contracted and shrunk up
within the narrow limits that prejudice and bigotry mark out. But
to return;—supposing the gentleman's end to be intentionally good,
supposing him indeed to desire all this, in order to extirpate the
Doctor's supposedly impious and erroneous doctrines, and promote
the cause of truth; yet the means he would use are certainly wrong.
For may I be allowed to remind him of this (which prejudice has
hitherto apparently prevented him from seeing), that violence and
force can never promote the cause of truth, but reason and
argument of love, and whenever these fail, all other means are

---

[1] This letter, which Hazlitt's son called his "first literary production," was
written "in protest against the treatment accorded to Joseph Priestley at the
hands of the mob of Birmingham, on the occasion of the second anniversary of the
Fall of the Bastille" Howe, p. 11.

[2] Priestley's Meeting House was burned down.

vain, and ineffectual. And as the Doctor himself has said, in his letter to the inhabitants of Birmingham, "that if they destroyed him, ten others would arise, as able or abler than himself, and stand forth immediately to defend his principles; and that were these destroyed, an hundred would appear; for the God of truth will not suffer his cause to lie defenceless."[3]

This letter of the Doctor's also, though it throughout breathes the pure and genuine spirit of Christianity, is, by another of your correspondents, charged with sedition and heresy; but, indeed, if such sentiments as those which it contains be sedition and heresy, sedition and heresy would be an honour; for all their sedition is that fortitude that becomes the dignity of man, and the character of Christian: and their heresy, Christianity: the whole letter, indeed, far from being seditious, is peaceable and charitable, and far from being heretical, that is, in the usual acceptance of the word, furnishing proofs of that resignation so worthy of himself. And to be sensible of this, 'tis only necessary, that any one laying aside prejudice read the letter itself with candour. What, or who, then, is free from the calumniating pen of malice, malice concealed, perhaps, under the specious disguise of religion and a love of truth?

Religious persecution is the bane of all religion; and the friends of persecution are the worst enemies religion has; and of all persecutions, that of calumny is the most intolerable. Any other kind of persecution can affect our outward circumstances only, our properties, our lives; but this may affect our characters for ever. And this great man has not only had his goods spoiled, his habitation burned, and his life endangered, but is also calumniated, aspersed with the most malicious reflections, and charged with every thing bad, for which a misrepresentation of the truth and prejudice can give the least pretence. And why all this? To the shame of some one, let it be replied, merely on account of particular speculative opinions, and not any thing scandalous, shameful, or criminal in his moral character. "Where I see," says the great and admirable Robinson,[4] "a spirit of intolerance, I think

---

[3] *Familiar Letters Addressed to the Inhabitants of Birmingham in Refutation of Several Charges, Advanced against Dissenters* (1790).

[4] Anthony Robinson (1762-1827), prominent unitarian, author of *A Short History of the Persecution of Christians,* and defender of Priestley.

I see the great Devil." And 'tis certainly the worst of devils. And here I shall conclude, staying only to remind your anti-Priestlian correspondents, that when they presume to attack the character of Dr. Priestley, they do not so much resemble the wren pecking at the eagle, as the owl, attempting by the flap of her wings, to hurl Mount Etna into the ocean: and that while Dr. Priestley's name "shall flourish in immortal youth,"[5] and his memory be respected and revered by posterity, prejudice no longer blinding the understandings of men, their's will be forgotten in obscurity, or only remembered as the friends of bigotry and persecution, the most odious of all characters.

ΕΛΙΑΣΟΝ[6]

---

[5] Joseph Addison, *Cato,* V, i.
[6] Part of a petition in Church Liturgy meaning "Have mercy."

No. 8

To the Reverend William Hazlitt

Lamb and Hazlitt, 41-44.

London, Oct. 6th 1793

Dear father,[1],

I rec[d] your very kind letter yesterday evening. With respect to my past behaviour, I have often said, and I now assure you, that it did not proceed from any real disaffection, but merely from the nervous disorders to which, you well know, I was so much subject. This was really the case; however improbable it may appear. Nothing particular occurred from the time I wrote last, till the Saturday following. On the Wednesday before, C[orrie] [2] had given me a thesis. As it was not a subject suited to my genius, and from other causes, I had not written anything on it; so that I was [not] pleased to hear his bell on Saturday morning, which was the time for shewing our themes. When I came to him, he asked me whether I had prepared my theme. I told him I had not. You should have a very good reason, indeed, sir, says he, for neglecting it. Why really, sir, says I, I could not write it. Did you never write anything, then? says he. Yes, sir, I said, I have written some things. Very well, then, go along and write your theme immediately, said he. I accordingly went away, but did not make much progress in my theme an hour after, when his bell rang for another lecture. My eyes were much swollen, and I assumed as sullen a countenance as I could, intimating that he had not treated me well. After the lecture, as I was going away, he called me back, and asked me very

---

[1] From September 1793 to midsummer 1795 Hazlitt attended the Unitarian New College, Hackney, on a scholarship provided for the sons of ministers by the Presbyterian Fund. He left the College when "he declined pursuing his studies for the ministry." The following five letters were written at Hackney or at John Hazlitt's residence in London.

[2] John Corrie or Currie (1769-1839), classical tutor at Hackney and later a Fellow of the Royal Society.

mildly if I had never written anything. I answered, I had written several things. On which he desired me to let him see one of my compositions, if I had no objection. I immediately took him my essay on laws,[3] and gave it to him. When he had read it, he asked me a few questions on the subject, which I answered very satisfactorily, I believe. Well, sir, says he, I wish you'd write some more such things as this. Why, sir, said I, I intended to write several things, which I have planned, but that I could not write any of them in a week, or two or three weeks. What did you intend to write? says he. Among other things I told him that I intended to inlarge and improve the essay he had been reading. Aye, says he, I wish you would. Well! I will do it then, sir, said I. Do so, said he; take your own time now; I shall not ask for it; only write it as soon as you can, for I shall often be thinking of it, and very desirous of it. This he repeated once or twice. On this I wished him a good morning, and came away, very well pleased with the reception I had met.

My course [4] is as follows: on Monday at eleven I attend Dr. Rees on mathematics and algebra. This lecture lasts till twelve. At two I have a lecture, with several others, in shorthand, and one in Hebrew with Jo. Swanwick. These two detain us till dinner-time and we have another lecture in shorthand and another in Hebrew at eight at night. On Tuesday we have a lecture with Corrie, at eleven, in the classics, one week Greek, another Latin, which continues till twelve; and another lecture with Corrie, on Greek antiquities, from one to two. On Wednesday we have the same business as on Monday, on Thursday as on Tuesday, and so on.

The greek class which I have been in this week consists of two old students, J. Mason, [5] and myself. I think that I translate more

---

3 "Mr. Currie, my old tutor at Hackney, may still have the rough draught of this speculation, which I gave him with tears in my eyes, and which he good-naturedly accepted in lieu of the customary *themes* . . ." *Project for a New Theory of Civil and Criminal Legislation, Works,* XIX, 302-303.

4 In *William Hazlitt and Hackney College,* London, The Lindsey Press, 1930, H. W. Stephenson describes the liberal but thoroughly disciplined education of the College. Hazlitt's course of study may have been, as Augustine Birrell wrote, "a better *studium generale* than either Oxford or Cambridge at the same date" (Howe, p. 29).

5 James Mason (1779-1827) of Shrewsbury, author of political tracts, playwright, and translator of Virgil.

correctly and much better than any of them. The other day Mason was laughing at me, while I was translating a passage, on account of my way of speaking. Says Corrie to him, "Mr. Mason, you should be sure you can translate yours as well as Mr. Hazlitt does his, before you laugh at your neighbours."

I believe I am liked very well by the students in general. I am pretty well intimate with one of them, whose name is Tonson. J. Swanwick has been hitherto in a different class. But on applying to Corrie, he has been put into the same class with me. Farewell.

I am, your aff. son,
W. Hazlitt.

No. 9

To the Reverend William Hazlitt

Lamb and Hazlitt, 36-38.

Sunday Evening. [October 1793]*

Dear Father,

I rec^d your letter safely on Monday.

On the preceding Saturday, I finished the introduction to my essay on the political state of man, and shewed [it] to Corrie. He seemed very well pleased with it, desired me to proceed with my essay as quickly as I could. After a few definitions, I give the following sketch of my plan.

"In treating on the political state of man, I shall, first, endeavour to represent his natural political relations, and to deduce from these his natural political duties, and his natural political rights; and, secondly, to represent his artificial political relations, and to deduce from these his artificial political duties, and his artificial rights." This I think an excellent plan. I wish I could recite it to my own satisfaction. I hope, however, to do it tolerably by Christmas. I have already got the greatest part of the ideas necessary, though in a crude and undigested state; so that my principal business will [be] to correct and arrange them. But this will be a terrible labour, and I shall rejoice most heartily when I have finished it.

Corrie seemed much pleased with some of my translations this week.

I passed the Ass's Bridge [1] very safely, and very solitarily, on Friday. I like Dominie (that is the name Dr. Rees [2] gave him) and his lectures very much.

---

* Cf. Howe, pp. 15-17. for this and the following letters.

[1] Bridge of Asses, or *pons asinorum* (Euclid 1:15), the proposition that if a triangle has two of its sides equal, the angles opposite are also equal.

[2] Abraham Rees (1743-1825), Resident Tutor, author of *The New Cyclopedia* in forty-five volumes.

A young fellow, whose name is Reid,[3] is by much the cleverest of the students.

Since I wrote last, I have had seven more lectures in the week; and at a little after ten on Tuesday with Dr. Priestley on history, and one every morning at nine in the greek grammar with Corrie.

I have been in town to-day, as I generally go once a fortnight. J. Swanwick was with me. John and Mary[4] are very well. They are to come and drink tea with me on Saturday. Since I came here I have spent above eight guineas. You need not, however, be alarmed at this, as in future I shall not spend, or, at least, shall not spend more than five shillings a week. About a shilling a week for washing; about two for fire; another shilling for tea and sugar; and now another for candles, letters, etc. Books, furniture, and other necessaries have run away with a good deal, but these expenses are extraordinary.

J. S. [5] has had nine guineas from Mr. Lawrence, and being entirely stripped, he called at Lawrence's when we were in town to-day. When he had told him his errand, the little gentleman seemed very much surprized, and said that he must write to his father about it. But, sir, says Jo, I have a farthing, and I'd be glad if you'd let me have a guinea. Well, well, if you want it, you may. But, as he did not offer to get it and as we were rather in haste, I whispered to Jo, that I would lend him some money, till he could procure his; and so away we came, a good deal diverted with the citizen's prudence.

The weather here is charming. We had some of the clearest days last week I ever saw. My love to my mother and Peggy.

I am your affectionate son,
W. Hazlitt.

I have not read this letter; so you will correct any slips.

---

[3] John Reid (1776-1822) who became a licentiate of the College of Physicians in 1804.

[4] Mary Pearce Hazlitt, John Hazlitt's wife.

[5] Joseph Swanwick.

No. 10

To the Reverend William Hazlitt

Lamb and Hazlitt, 33-36.

[November 1793]

Dear father,

I rec^d your kind letter of Monday evening at five o'clock, the usual time. I was very much pleased you liked the plan of my essay. You need not fear for the execution of it, as I am sensible that, after I have made it as perfect as I can, it will have many imperfections, yet I know that I can finish in a manner equal to the introduction. I have made some progress, since I wrote last. The essay on laws will make a part of it. I will here give you an account of my studies, etc. On Monday I am preparing Damien's lectures from seven until half-past eight, except the quarter of an hour in which I say Corrie's grammar lecture, and from nine till ten. From ten till twelve we are with him. His lectures are Simpson's elements of gram. and Bonnycastle's algebra. By the bye, the Ass's bridge is the tenth proposition of the geometry. From twelve to two I am preparing Belsham['s] lectures in shorthand, and the Hebrew grammar, which I am saying till then. The shorthand is to write out eight verses, [of the] Bible. From half-past three till five I walk. From five to six, I have my g[reek] grammar for the morning. At liberty from six to seven. From seven to eight, preparing Belsham's evening lectures in L[atin] and Heb[rew]. With them from eight to nine. And from half after nine till eleven I am reading Dr. Price's lecture [1] for the next day. On Tuesday I am from seven till h.p. eight preparing Corrie's classical lecture, only the time that I am saying my grammar. And again from nine to h.p. ten, from which time to h.p. eleven I attend Dr. Priestley's lecture in history. From then till a little after twelve is C's classical lecture, which is

---

[1] In *A Review of the Principal Questions in Morals* by Richard Price, who died in 1791.

Sophocles one week and Quintilian the next. In the greek we have two of the old students, in the latin five. J[oseph S[wanwick] is now in my classes, at first he was not. But on his requesting it, he is now with me. You will take care not to mention this. From twelve till one, I am at Corrie's lecture in g[reek] antiquities. With him till half-past one. From which till three I study my essay. Walking as before. From five till six, preparing my evening lecture in geography with Corrie, and my g[reek] for the next day. And from seven to nine, except about half-an-hour at geography with Corrie, I again studying my essay. From half-past nine to eleven, reading David Hartley.[2] I go on in the same course [for the] rest of the week, except the difference that not having Dr. P[riestley]'s lecture makes, and that I now study after supper on Saturday night. On Sundays, too, I am always idle. I like Hebrew very well, the mathematics very much. They are very much suited to my genius. The Reid whom I mentioned is about eighteen, a Bristol lad, and a pupil of Mr. Eslin.[3] I was in town to-day. I was glad to hear of the increase of my yearly allowance, and of what Corrie told Rowmann.[4] They are very well. I am sorry to hear that my mother is poorly. My love to her and Peggy.
I am,

Your affectionate son,
W. Hazlitt.

I forgot to give you an account of my expenses, and, as I am tired, shall defer till next time. I have spent only 8s. since Thursday fortnight, though I have had everything I wanted. Adieu.

---

[2] Hazlitt later attempted to refute Hartley's materialistic theory of self-interest in *Some Remarks on the Systems of Hartley and Helvetius* added to *An Essay on the Principles of Human Action* (1805).

[3] John Prior Estlin (1747-1817), Unitarian lecturer of Bristol and friend of Coleridge and Southey.

[4] A trustee of the College Fund.

No. 11

To the Reverend William Hazlitt

Lamb and Hazlitt, 38-41.

[Late Autumn 1793]

Dear father.

I was very sorry to hear from your two last letters that you wish me to discontinue my essay, as I am very desirous of finishing it, and as I think it almost necessary to do so.[1] For I have already completed the two first prop. and the third I have planned and shall be able to finish in a very short time; the fourth prop., which will be the last, will consist only of a few lines. The first section you know I have done for some time; and the first, second, and fourth propositions are exactly similar to the first, second, and fourth of the second section, so that I have little else to do than to alter a few words. The third will consist principally of observations on government, laws, etc., most of which will be the same with what I have written before in my essay on laws. My chief reason for wishing to continue my observations is, that, by having a particular system of politics I shall be better able to judge of the truth or falsehood of any prevarication which I hear, or read, and of the justice, or the contrary, of any political transactions. Moreover, by comparing my own system with those of others, and with particular facts, I shall have it in my power to correct and improve it continually. But I can have neither of these advantages unless I have some standard by which to judge of, and of which to judge by, any ideas, or proceedings, which I may meet with. Besides, so far is my studying this subject from making me gloomy or low-spirited, that I am never so perfectly easy as when I am, or have been, studying it. With respect to theories, I really think them rather disserviceable than otherwise. I should not be able to make a

---

[1] Mr. Hazlitt had expressed his concern over William's characteristic intensity and concentration.

good oration from my essay. It is too abstruse and exact for that purpose. I shall endeavour to write one on providence, which will, I think, be a very good subject. I shall certainly make it my study to acquire as much politeness as I can. However, this is not the best place possible for acquiring it. I do not at all say that the fellows who are here do not know how to behave extremely well; but the behaviour which suits a set of young fellows, or boys, does not suit any other society. This disadvantage, however, if of very little consequence, as little else is necessary to politeness than care and a desire of pleasing.

I have nothing new to add. My lectures go on as usual. We began the lectures on logic on Friday last. These, I fancy, will be easy and entertaining, though the students who have gone through them say they are not. We have two lectures a week on logic, which are on Wednesday and Friday. I was in town this day week. My brother and sister were very well. But I suppose you have heard from him since that time. He has not been here to-day. I wrote to J. Wickstead Friday week.[2] Present my respects to Mr. Jenkins; also to Mr. Rowe.[3] Compliments to all inquirers. I hope my mother and P.[eggy] are quite well before this time. I long to see you. I wish they could come too.

I am, dear father,

Your aff. son,

W. Hazlitt

I forgot to tell you that Corrie has not returned me the first part of my essay.

---

[2] John Wicksteed of Shrewsbury, grandfather of Philip Henry Wicksteed, author and translator.

[3] Unitarian ministers at Shrewsbury and Whitchurch. In 1798 Coleridge "came to Shrewsbury to succeed Mr. Rowe in the spiritual charge of a Unitarian Congregation there" ("My First Acquaintance with Poets," *Works*, XVII, 106).

No. 12

To the Reverend William Hazlitt

Lamb and Hazlitt, 44-47.

[London], Sunday, Oct. 23rd. [1796][1]

My Dear Father

I write, not so much because I have anything particular to communicate, as because I know that you, and my mother, and Peggy will be glad to hear from me. I know well the pleasure with which you will recognise the characters of my hand, characters calling back to the mind with strong impression the idea of the person by whom they were traced, and in vivid and thick succession, all the ready associations clinging to that idea, and the impatience with which you will receive any news which I can give you of myself. I know these things: and I feel them. Amidst that repeated disappointment, and that long dejection, which have served to overcast and to throw into deep obscurity some of the best years of my life, years which the idle and illusive dreams of boyish expectation had presented glittering, and gay, and pros-

---

[1] W. Carew Hazlitt placed this letter after the one written on 6 October 1793; but it must have been written either in 1791 or 1796, the only two years in the decade in which October 23 fell on a Sunday. Although the somewhat pretentious moralizings are akin, in tone, to the earlier letters, the other details point to 1796. Hazlitt's biographers understand the musings on disappointment and dissatisfaction to refer to Hazlitt's departure from Hackney College, but there is no evidence to sustain Howe's assumption that Hazlitt returned to the College after leaving it in 1795. In the *Literary Remains* his son records that Hazlitt "returned home in the year 1795"; and H. W. Stephenson cites a letter from Dr. Andrew Kippis, Lecturer in History, to the Reverend Mr. Hazlitt, which convincingly states that "Hazlitt left the college in the Summer of 1795." There he seems to have lived in "long dejection," "much dissatisfaction and much sorrow," which obviously continued after he proceeded to London to stay with his brother. Exactly when he went there is not clear, but, inasmuch as he admits in this letter that he has not "anything particular to communicate," he must have arrived there well before October, 1796; moreover, he indicates that he has been engaged for some time in the composition of his essay, has "toiled long" and has reached "the midway of the steep." Cf. Howe, p. 18; also Baker, p. 28n.

perous, decked out in all the fairness and all the brightness of colouring, and crowded with fantastic forms of numerous hues of ever-varying pleasure,—amidst much dissatisfaction and much sorrow, the reflection that there are one or two persons in the world who are [not] quite indifferent towards me, nor altogether unanxious for my welfare, is that which is, perhaps, the most "soothing to my wounded spirit."

Monday.

We [2] have just received your letter. With respect to that part of it which concerns my brother's business, I have information to give you of one new 7 guinea picture. As to my essay, it goes on, or rather it moves backwards and forwards; however, it does not stand still. I have been chiefly employed hitherto in rendering my knowledge of my subject as clear and intimate as I could, and in the arrangement of my plan. I have done little else. I have proceeded some way in a delineation of the system, which founds the propriety of virtue on it's coincidence with the pursuit of private interest, and of the imperfections inseparable from it's scheme.[3] I have written in all about half a dozen pages of shorthand, and have composed one or two good passages, together with a number of scraps and fragments, some to make their appearance at the head of my essay, some to be affixed to the tail, some to be inserted in the middle, and some not at all. I know not whether I can augur certainly of ultimate success. I write more easily than I did. I hope for good. I have ventured to look at high things. I have toiled long and painfully to attain to some stand of eminence. It were hard to be thrown back from the mid-way of the steep to the lowest humiliation. I must conclude. You will not fail to give my love, and all our loves, to my mother and Peggy. Give my love to J. S. Remember me to Wicksteed and to Kynaston, when you see him. Compliments according to form. I am sorry Molly has been so ill. Farewell.

I am your affectionate son,
W. Hazlitt.

---

[2] I. e. Hazlitt and his brother John.

[3] This is clearly the thesis of *An Essay on the Principles of Human Action*, which was revised for publication in 1805.

No. 13

To the Reverend William Hazlitt

Four Generations, I, 79.

[10 June 1798] [1]

My dear Father,

I have just time to let you know, that I shall set out on my way home this evening. Mr. Coleridge is gone to Taunton to preach for Dr. Toulmin.[2] He is to meet me at Bridgewater, and we shall proceed from thence to Bristol to-morrow morning. You may expect to see me on Saturday, or, perhaps not till the next day. I received your letter on Friday. Farewell.

W.H.

---

[1] Written at Nether Stowey while visiting Coleridge, whom Hazlitt had met at Shrewsbury the preceding January. Cf. "My First Acquaintance with Poets," *Works,* XVII, 106. The date is provided by a letter from Coleridge to Thomas Pool, 16 June 1798 *(Collected Letters,* I, 413).

[2] Joshua Toulmin (1740-1815), Unitarian minister at Taunton and author of many biographies, including one of Socinus, 1777.

No. 14

To the Reverend William Hazlitt

MS. Pforzheimer, published by permission of The Carl H. Pforzheimer Library.
Address: Revd. Mr. Hazlitt/Wem/Shropshire.

Monday morning [1]
London (PM: DE 16/99/)

My dear Father,

I arrived here yesterday evening a little after five. I got to Shiffnal the day I left you in very good time, and without any fatigue. The next morning, I set off on foot about nine, and had walked seven miles, when the mail overtook me. I rode on the outside the rest of the way to Oxford, where I slept that night. I only stopt there to breakfast the next day, as I was too cold, and uncomfortable to have had any pleasure in looking at the buildings. I proceeded that day to Henley, which is 23 miles from Oxford, and I left Henley yesterday morning at half past 7. I walked 35 miles in 10 hours. My travelling expences in all amounted to 2 guineas, and a shilling. I paid 22 shillings for coach-hire. I dined the first day on my hard egg, and wigs.[2] I did not eat the pudding till the day after. I was very much shook on the coach box; and I wore out my gloves, and bruised my hands by the rubbing of the iron rail, which I was obliged to keep fast hold of, to prevent my being thrown from my seat. I rode inside from Woodstock to Oxford. I just now began Godwin's new novel, which I do not at present admire very much. It is called The Travels of St. Leon, a tale of the 16th century.[3] I do not know,

---

[1] The only letter that survives for the year 1799, written at the residence of John Hazlitt, 12 Rathbone Place. Howe's conjecture, that Hazlitt arrived in London in October to occupy "his brother's back painting room," is correct, except for the month. Cf. K. N. Cameron, *Shelley and His Circle,* I, 219-220.

[2] "A kind of bun or small cake made of fine flour" (O.E.D.).

[3] He later admired it very much: *"Caleb Williams* and *St. Leon* are two of the

whether I shall begin any thing this week as I have neither paints, nor brushes here. The little box with the clothes came yesterday. You will let us know, when you write, if you have not already, where to inquire for the other boxes, and when they are to arrive in London. John tells me, that he wrote on Friday, and gave you a letter full of all the news. I am in pretty good spirits. The weather is colder than it was, when I left Wem, and quite as dark. I shall give you another letter [4] when the pictures come, and I have begun to paint again. I saw two, or three little views on the road, which I shall endeavour to sketch out in some way, or other from memory.[5] The dinner is just coming up, and I can hardly see to write. You must give my love to my mother, and Peggy. I shall send the things I talked of as soon as I can. When I looked back on the road to the [Lea Hills(?)] [6] and saw how dim, and low they grew, and how small the objects upon them appeared, and recollected, that you were still farther off, I wondered at the distinct idea I had of you all: and yet I still recollect you as I saw you last in the parlour at breakfast. I am

your affectionate son
W. Hazlitt

---

most splendid and impressive works of the imagination that have appeared in our times" *(Spirit of the Age, Works,* XI, 24). Godwin (1756-1836) was the son of a Unitarian minister whom the Rev. William Hazlitt had succeeded at Wisbeach in 1764. The families enjoyed a long association. Hazlitt had probably met Godwin first in 1787, when, as a boy of nine, he had accompanied his father and brother John on the trip to London for the purpose of leaving John to study under Sir Joshua Reynolds (cf. Letter 2). John Hazlitt was often a guest of the Godwins during his student days, and, after his marriage to Mary Pearce in 1793, Godwin visited them at their house in Long Acre. In his journal for 17 September 1794 Godwin records having had tea with the Hazlitts and "Hazlitt junr." (Abinger Ms.) In spite of their similar backgrounds (both attended Unitarian academies and studied under Dr. Kippis and Dr. Rees) and their respect for each other's abilities, their disagreement over Hazlitt's *English Grammar* (published by Godwin in 1809) and *Memoirs of Holcroft* (cf. Letters 30, 31) caused a break in their friendship. Nevertheless, in 1825 Godwin praised the "admirable temper and fairness" of the *Spirit of the Age,* which contains the best contemporary appraisal of his influence upon the writers of the age. (Ms. letter to Henry Colburn, 22 November 1824, Victoria and Albert Museum.)

[4] Probably not extant.

[5] During this trip he probably saw for the first time many of the paintings later described in *Sketches of the Principal Picture-Galleries in England* (1824).

[6] The "first hills Hazlitt would pass on the road from Wem to Shrewbury were at Lea Hall" *(Shelley and his Circle,* I, 223).

No. 15

To the Reverend William Hazlitt [1]

Remains, I, xxxviii-xl.

16th October 1802

My Dear Father,

I arrived here yesterday. . . . Calais is a miserable place in itself, but the remains of the fortifications about it are very beautiful. There are several ranges of ramparts, and ditches one within another, "wall within wall, mural protection intricate." The hand of time is very evident upon both; the ditches are filled with reeds and long grass, and the walls are very much decayed, and grown very dark coloured. (I am so perplexed with French that I can hardly recollect a word of English.) The country till within a few miles of Paris was barren and miserable. There were great numbers of beggars at all the towns we passed through. The vineyards near this have a most delightful appearance; they look richer than any kind of agricultural production that we have in England, particularly the red vines with which many of the vineyards are covered. Paris is very dirty and disagreeable, except along the river side. Here it is much more splendid than any part of London. The Louvre is one of the buildings which overlook it. I went there this morning as soon as I had got my *card of security* from the police-office. I had some difficulty in getting admission to the Italian pictures, as the fellows who kept the doors make a trade of it, and I was condemned to the purgatory of the modern French gallery for

---

[1] This and the next five letters were written in Paris, where Hazlitt went to paint at the Louvre from October 1802 to February 1803. He took with him a commission from "a Mr. Railton of Liverpool for five copies from the old masters" (Howe, 53); for a list of Hazlitt's paintings cf. Howe, 395. Joseph Railton, Hazlitt's only patron, was a Liverpool merchant who had apparently been impressed with William's talents during his stay with the Traceys. Railton's daughter, Frances-Ann was one of Hazlitt's early loves. Two other members of the family distinguished themselves as artists: William, designer of the Nelson Memorial in Trafalgar Square, and Herbert, an illustrator of books.

some time. At last some one gave me a hint of what was expected, and I passed through. The pictures are admirable, particularly the historical pieces by Rubens. They are superior to anything I saw, except one picture by Raphael. The portraits are not so good as I expected. Titian's best portraits I did not see, as they were put by to be copied. The landscapes are for the most part exquisite. I intend to copy two out of the five I am to do for Railton. I promised Northcote [2] to copy Titian's portrait of Hippolito de Medici [3] for him. He had a print of it lying on the floor one morning when I called on him, and was saying that it was one of the finest pictures in the whole world; on which I told him that it was now at the Louvre, and that if he would give me leave, I would copy it for him as well as I could. He said I should delight him if I would, and was evidently excessively pleased. Holcroft [4] is in London. He gave me a letter to Mr. Merrimee, [5] the same painter to whom Freebairn's [6] letter was. I called on him this afternoon, and he is to go with me in the morning to obtain permission for me to copy any pictures which I like, and to assist me in procuring paints, canvasses etc. . . . I hope my mother is quite easy, as I hope to do very well. My love to her and Peggy.

I am your affectionate,
W. Hazlitt.

Paris, à l'Hôtel Coq Heron,
Rue Coq Heron, pres la Palais Royal.

---

[2] James Northcote, R. A. (1746-1831), student of Reynolds, author, and wit, encouraged both John and William Hazlitt in their careers as painters. In 1826 Hazlitt began to contribute the "Conversations of Northcote" under the title of "Boswell Redivivus" to the *New Monthly Magazine* and, subsequently, the *London Weekly Review, The Atlas,* and the *Court Journal* before collecting them for the *Conversations of James Northcote, Esq., R.A.* (1830). Cf. Letter 165.

[3] A favourite portrait, which he discusses in *Notes of a Journey Through France and Italy,* "Sir Joshua Reynolds's Discourses," and the "Fine Arts," *Works,* XVIII, 62ff; XVIII, 111ff respectively.

[4] Thomas Holcroft (1745-1809), playwright, novelist, and democrat, whose trial for treason was a *cause célèbre* in 1794. In 1816 Hazlitt published the *Memoirs of Thomas Holcroft.*

[5] J.F.L. Mérimée (1765-1836), painter, father of Prosper.

[6] Robert Freebairn (1765-1808), painter of landscapes and exhibitor at the Royal Academy from 1782 to 1808.

No. 16

To the Reverend William Hazlitt

Remains, I, xl-xliii.

Oct. 20th, 1802

My Dear Father,

I have begun to copy one of Titian's portraits. . . . I made a very complete sketch of the head in about three hours; and have been working upon it longer this morning; I hope to finish it next week. To-morrow and Saturday I can do nothing to it; there are only four days in the week in which one is allowed to, or at least able to, do anything. Friday is allotted to sweeping the rooms, and Saturday and Sunday are usually visiting days. There are great numbers of people in the rooms (most of them *English*) every day; and I was afraid at first that this would confuse and hinder me; but I found on beginning to copy that I was too occupied in my work to attend much to, or to care at all about what was passing around me; or if this had any effect upon me indirectly, it was to make me more attentive to what I was about. In order that I and my copy might not fall into contempt, I intend to employ the vacant days of the week in making duplicates of the copies which I do here, and in doing a picture of myself, in the same view as that of Hippolito de Medici, by Titian, which I intend to begin upon to-morrow. This, it is true, will occasion an increase in the expense, but I shall do them better here, at least the duplicates, than I could at home, and it will be necessary for me to have them as models to keep by me. The pictures I wish to copy are the following:—lst. Portrait of a young man in black, and very dark complexion, by Titian.[1] This is

---

[1] "The *ideal* is no less observable in the portraits than in the histories here [in the Louvre]. Look at the portrait of a man in black, by Titian. . . . There is a tongue in that eye, a brain beneath that forehead. It is still; but the hand seems to have been just placed on its side; it does not turn its head, but it looks towards you to ask, whether you recognise it or not? It was there to meet me, after an interval of years, as if I had parted with it the instant before. Its keen, steadfast glance staggered me like a blow. It was the same—how I was altered!" (*Notes of a Journey through France and Italy, Works,* X, 112).

the one I am doing. 2nd. Another portrait, by Titian.[2] 3rd. The portrait by Titian of Hippolito de Medicis.[3] 4th. Portrait of a lady, by Vandyke.[4] 5th. Portrait of the Cardinal Bentivoglio, by Vandyke also.[5] 6th. Leo X., by Raphael.[6] If I cannot get them removed into the room, either through the influence of Mr. Merrimee or by bribing the keepers, I shall substitute either Titian's Mistress, [7] or a head of a Sibyl, by Guercino, a very good painter, or two landscapes in the room. The finest picture in the collection is the Transfiguration [8] by Raphael. This is without any exception the finest picture I ever saw, I mean the human part of it, because the figure of Christ, and the angels, or whatever they are, that are flying to meet him in the air, are to the last degree contemptible. The picture of the Taking down from the Cross, by Rubens, which I have heard John describe, is here. It is a very fine one. One of the pictures is Reynolds' picture of the Marquis of Granby. Mr. Merrimee came to look at the [young man in] black and the old woman, which he liked very much, though they are contrary to the French style; on the other hand, without vanity be it spoken, they are very much in the style of the Flemish and Italian painters. I like them better, instead of worse, from comparing them with the pictures that are here. The modern French pictures are many of them excellent in many particulars,

---

[2] Possibly "The Young Man's Head, with a glove that used so much to delight" but which later disappointed Hazlitt (ibid.).

[3] "Among these ... is Titian's Hippolito di Medici ... with the spirit and breadth of history, and with the richness, finish, and glossiness of an enamel picture. I remember the first time I ever saw it, it stood on an easel which I had to pass, with its back to me, and as I turned and saw it with the boar-spear in its hand, and its keen glance bent upon me, it seemed 'a thing of life,' with supernatural force and grandeur" (ibid., 225). Cf. *The Plain Speaker, Works*, XII, 286.

[4] "... that charming portrait of an English lady with a little child ... sustained by sweetness and dignity, but with a mother's anxious thoughts passing slightly across her serene brow" (*Notes of a Journey*, ut sup., p. 111). The picture is more fully described in Essay XXV of *The Plain Speaker, Works*, XII, 280-281.

[5] "The Cardinal Bentivoglio (which I remember procuring especial permission to copy, and left untouched, because, after Titian's portraits, there was a want of interest in Vandyke's which I could not get over) ..." (*Notes of a Journey*, 111).

[6] "... that little portrait in a cap in the Louvre, muffled in thought and buried in a kind of mental *chiaroscuro*" ("The Vatican," *Works*, XVII, 150).

[7] "... she is a very fine servant-girl, conscious of her advantages, and willing to make the most of them" (*The Plain Speaker, Works*, XII, 282).

[8] "The Transfiguration is a wonderful collection of fine heads and figures ..." (*Notes of a Journey, Works*, X, 240).

though not in the most material. I find myself very comfortable here.

With my love to my mother, John, and Peggy, I am your
affectionate son,
W. Hazlitt.

I saw Bonaparte.[9]
Paris, at the Hôtel Coq-Heron,
rue Coq-Heron.

---

[9] "What a fine iron binding Buonaparte had round his face, as if it had been cased in steel! What sensibility about the mouth! What watchful penetration in the eye! What a smooth, unruffled forehead!" ["On Thought and Action" (1821), *Table-Talk, Works,* VIII, 109.]

No. 17

To the Reverend William Hazlitt

Remains, I, xliii-xliv.

Sunday, November 14th, 1802.

My Dear Father,

A fortnight ago to-morrow, I began a copy of a picture I had not seen before—the subject of which is described in the catalogue in this manner—"852, by Lodovic Lana, born at Modena, in 1597; died in 1646. The death of Clorinda.—Clorinda, having been mortally wounded in battle by Tancred, is seen lying at the foot of a tree, her bosom bare, discovering the place where she was wounded. On the point of expiring she desires to receive the baptismal sacrament; and while Tancred administers it to her with the water he has brought in his helmet from a neighbouring spring, she holds out her hand to him, in token of forgiveness, and breathes her last." It is in my mind the sweetest picture in the place.[1] My canvass is not so large as the other, but it includes both the figures, which are of the size of life. I have worked upon it forty hours, that is seven mornings: and am going over the whole of it again this week, by the end of which I intend to have it finished. I propose to complete the copy of Titian, which I began the week following, in five weeks from the time I got here. The three heads, which I shall then have to do, I shall, I think, be able to do in the same time, allowing three weeks for another portrait by Titian, and a head of Christ crowned with thorns, by Guido, and two more for Titian's Mistress, in which the neck and arms are seen. I shall then, if I have time, do a copy of the Cardinal Bentivoglio,

---

[1] In 1822 Hazlitt wrote: "As I look at my long-neglected copy of the Death of Clorinda, golden gleams play upon the canvas, as they used when I painted it. The flowers of Hope and Joy springing up in my mind, recall the time when they first bloomed there. The years that are fled knock at the door and enter. I am in the Louvre once more" ("On Great and Little Things," *Table-Talk, Works,* VIII, 237).

which is at present exhibited in the great room, and probably some others. But the first five I have mentioned, I have certainly fixed upon. I generally go to the Museum about half-past nine or ten o'clock, and continue there until half-past three or four. Charles Fox [2] was there two or three mornings. He talked a great deal, and was full of admiration. I have not yet seen Bonaparte near. He is not in Paris.

With love to all,
I am your affectionate son,
W. Hazlitt.

---

[2] Charles James Fox (1749-1806), statesman, was in Paris during the Treaty of Amiens (1802). Hazlitt later recalled Fox's interest in art: "I myself have heard Charles Fox engaged in familiar conversation. It was in the Louvre. He was describing the pictures to two persons that were with him. He spoke rapidly, but very unaffectedly. I remember his saying—'All those blues and greens and reds are the Guercinos; you may know them by the colours'" ["On Writing and Speaking" (1820), *The Plain Speaker, Works,* XII, 274].

No. 18

To the Reverend William Hazlitt

Remains, I, xlv-xlvi.

November 29th, 1802.

My Dear Father,

I received your letter on Sunday. I wrote to you, that day fortnight; I am, therefore, sorry that you did not receive my letter sooner. I there gave you an account of what pictures I had been doing; and of what I intended to do. The copy of the Death of Clorinda is as good as finished, though I shall have to go over the most of it again, when it is quite dry. The copy of Titian is also brought forward as much as it could be till it is dry; for, as the room is not kept very warm, the pictures do not dry fast enough to be done out and out. I have been working upon the portrait of Titian's Mistress, as it is called, these two last days. I intend to complete this the beginning of next week, if possible; the rest of that week and the two following, I shall devote to going over and completing the other two; if I succeed in this, which I am pretty confident of doing, I shall have done eight of my pictures in eight weeks, from the time I came here. But as one of them contains two whole figures, it may be reckoned equal to two; so that I shall have gone on at the rate of a portrait in a fortnight. I shall, therefore, have a month left to do the other two heads, which will make up the whole number. I intend to give an hour a day to copying a Holy Family, by Raphael, one of the most beautiful things in the world. Of this, and the Death of Clorinda, I shall probably be able to get prints taken in London, as this is frequently done; as my copies certainly contain all that is wanted for a print, which has nothing to do with colouring. I intend to write to Robinson [1] about

---

[1] Anthony Robinson, a friend mentioned in Letter 7, assisted Hazlitt in Paris and later encouraged Joseph Johnson to publish Hazlitt's first book, *An Essay on the Principles of Human Action* (1805).

it. I was introduced this morning to Mr. Cosway,[2] who is here, doing sketches of the pictures in the Louvre, by a Mr. Pellegrini,[3] whose pictures John knows very well, and whom I have seen with Mr. Merrimee. If Railton chooses, I will do a copy of a most divine landscape, by Rubens, for him; but it will take at least a fortnight to do it, most probably three weeks. I have heard from Loftus.[4] This is all I can recollect at present, except my love, etc.

Your affectionate son,
W. Hazlitt.

I would have written a longer letter, if I had had time.

---

[2] Richard Cosway, R. A. (1740-1821), is discussed in "On the Old Age of Artists," *The Plain Speaker, Works,* XII, 95-96.

[3] Domenico Pellegrini (1759-1840), Italian portrait painter.

[4] Tom Loftus, a maternal cousin, is "L" in "On Personal Character" who " 'doubled-down and dog-eared' " *Tristram Shandy* in the same places as Hazlitt (*Works,* XII, 233).

No. 19

To the Reverend William Hazlitt

Remains, I, xlvi-xlix.

December 10th, 1802.

My Dear Father,

I yesterday morning completed my copy of the picture called
The Death of Clorinda; I have been, in all, fifteen mornings about
it. It is a very good copy; when I say this, I mean that it has very
nearly all the effect of the picture, and will certainly make as great
a figure in R[ailton]'s parlour, as the original does in the Louvre. It
has been praised by some of the French painters. They have begun
of late to compliment me on my style of getting on; though, at first,
they were disposed to be very impertinent. This is the way of the
world; you are always sure of getting encouragement, when you do
not want it. After I had done my picture yesterday, I took a small
canvass, which I had in the place, and began a sketch of a head in
one of the large historical pictures, being very doubtful if I could;
not at all expecting to finish it, but merely to pass away the time;
however, in a couple of hours, I made a very fair copy, which I
intend to let remain as it is. It is a side face, a good deal like yours,
which was one reason of my doing it so rapidly. I got on in such a
rapid style, that an Englishman, who had a party with him, came
up, and told me, in French, that I was doing very well. Upon my
answering him in English, he seemed surprised, and said, "upon
my word, sir, you get on with great spirit and boldness; you do us
great credit, I am sure." He afterwards returned; and after asking
how long I had been about it, said he was the more satisfied with
his judgment, as he did not know I was a countryman. Another
wanted to know if I taught painting in oil. I told him that I stood
more in need of instruction myself; that that sort of rapid sketching
was what I did better than anything else; and that, after the first
hour or two, I generally made my pictures worse and worse, the
more pains I took with them. However, seriously, I was much

pleased with this kind of notice, as however confident I may be of the real merit of my work, it is not always so clear, that it is done in a way to please most other people. This same sketch is certainly a very singular thing, as I do not believe there are ten people in the world, who could do it in the same way. However, I have said enough on the subject. I shall go on with this business as I find it succeed. I intend to copy a composition of Rubens in this manner, which I can do at intervals, without interfering with my regular work. The copy of Titian's Mistress, and the other, which I began from him, I purpose finishing in the six following days; and another copy of Titian, in the six after that, which will be four out of the five, which I am doing for R[ailton]. I shall want another fortnight for the copy of Guido; and it will take another fortnight, if I do that for Northcote. This will make fourteen weeks: I have been here seven already. I will now enumerate the pictures I have done, or am doing: 1. The Death of Clorinda, completed; 2. Portrait of a Man in Black, by Titian, nearly finished; 3. Titian's Mistress; this will take four days more to finish it; 4. Portrait of another Man in black, by the same, not yet begun; 5. Christ Crowned with Thorns, by Guido, not begun; 6. Hippolito de Medici. As I have six hours to work every morning, from ten till four, I intend to give an hour to making rough copies for myself. In this way I shall make a sketch of the head I mentioned; and I propose doing a Holy Family, from Raphael (a very small picture), and a larger copy, from Rubens, in the same way. My love to all.

Your's affectionately,
W. Hazlitt.

No. 20

To the Reverend William Hazlitt

Remains, I, xlix-1.

Paris, January 7th, 1803.

My Dear Father,

I finished, as far as I intend, the copy of Hippolito de Medici, for Northcote, the day after I wrote to him; [1] and the day following I began a copy of a part of the Transfiguration, by Raphael, which had not been exhibited in the common or large room, till the week before. I have nearly done the head of the boy, who is supposed to see Christ in his Ascension from the Mount, and who is the principal figure in the piece. I shall paint it in another morning. It is the best copy I have done, though I have been only fifteen hours about it. There will be two other figures included in the canvass; this is 4 feet 8 inches high, and 10 feet 8 in breadth. You will easily get a distinct idea of the size of the picture, by measuring it on the parlour floor. Northcote's copy, and that of the Death of Clorinda are the same size. The Transfiguration itself is about three times as high, and three times as wide. It is by no means the largest, though it is the finest figure-picture in the place. I am about a second copy of the de Medici for Railton. I shall have done it in two or three days more. I have also finished, since I wrote last, the first copy which I began, from Titian.

I am, your affectionate son,

W. Hazlitt.

---

[1] This letter does not survive.

No. 21.

To William Godwin [1]

MS. Abinger.

Wem in Shropshire
December 29 [1804]

Dear Sir,

I should think it an essential service if you could procure me 3, or 4 pictures to do at 5 guineas each among any of your friends, or acquaintance in London. I am merely anxious about such a number as would clear my expences for board, and lodging for a month, or six weeks' stay in town. If you think there is any chance of this, and would let me know, I would send a picture of my father [2] which I was to send to my brother to town immediately, which you might either see there, or it could be left at your house. I remain your obliged friend and servant,

W. Hazlitt.

---

[1] The recipient is not named but the presence of this letter in Godwin's correspondence amongst the Abinger manuscripts indicates that it was addressed to him.

[2] Professor Baker assigns this letter to 29 December 1803 on the assumption "that the fiasco at the Lakes in the fall of 1803 had forced him back to Wem, and that he was eager to escape," and because Hazlitt's portrait of his father "was probably the one shown at the 1802 Royal Academy exhibition at Somerset House" (p. 140). However, in Letter 24 addressed to his father in January 1807 Hazlitt mentions having Christmas dinner and remembering that "it was much such a day as it was two years ago, when I was painting your picture." It is therefore highly probable that it is this portrait of his father which he is proposing to send to London and that the date he is writing is 29 December 1804. If he had intended to send the one which had been exhibited it is probable that he would have mentioned that fact.

No. 22

To Joseph Johnson

MS. Lockwood.

August 30 [1805] [1]

Dear Sir,

I have sent you the abridgement I have made of the two first volumes. The proportion in quantity is as near as I can guess about 210 pages to 790, that is considerably up than a third. I imagine, the 3 last volumes, though much larger, will not take more than the 2 first, and that the 3d and 4th will be about 400 pages, or perhaps more. If you should think this is too much in quantity, the sooner you let me know the better. I find that going on in the way I have done, I can insert almost everything that is worth remembering in the book, and give the amusing passages almost entire. In fact, I have done little more than leave out repetitions, and other things that might as well never have been in the book. But whether I have done it properly, or no, you will be able to determine better than I. I am with great respect, your obt servant,

W. Hazlitt.

If the first manuscript should be awkward to print from being written both ways, I could easily have it transcribed.[2]

109 Great Russell St.

---

[1] Howe (p. 86) assigns this letter to 1806.

[2] Hazlitt sometimes wrote vertically across what he had written horizontally on a page.

No. 23

To William Godwin [1]

MS. Cornell.

Wem, Jany. 5th, 1806

Dear Sir,

I inclose this for you in a parcel conveying to Johnson all that remains of Mr. Search [2] after the Caput mortuum is taken away. I have done my job quicker, and with less trouble than I expected, and moreover I have done it better than I expected. I have written a note [3] to Johnson giving him an account of my performance, but as I did not expect to get a letter or answer from him for some months to come, I did not request any: and my reason for troubling you at present is to request that you would, i.e. "at some convenient and leisure hour" by the time that you suppose Johnson has quite forgot the subject, just remind him of it; and if he is satisfied with what I have done, say something about the price. This, if you will give me leave, I will leave entirely to you. I should however be glad, as I imagine he will be in no hurry about the publication, if he could advance me half the money out of hand, or indeed I should have no objection to the whole, if this is not considered as contrary to order. As I suppose it will be expected that I should overlook the press, I shall either be in town myself time enough to do this, or get some one else. Will you favour me

---

[1] Godwin had helped interest Joseph Johnson (1738-1809), publisher and bookseller of St. Paul's Churchyard, in Hazlitt's *Abridgment of the Light of Nature Pursued* (1807), by Abraham Tucker (1705-1774). Johnson was the publisher of Mary Wollstonecraft Godwin, Priestley, Cowper, Erasmus Darwin, and Maria Edgeworth. In a letter of 15 January 1806, Lamb, who had met Hazlitt at Godwin's in 1804, reports: "Godwin went to Johnson's yesterday about your business" (*Letters*, I, 416).

[2] "Edward Search" was the pseudonym of Abraham Tucker.

[3] This note may refer to Letter No. 22.

with a line on the subject, when you have got through all delays and difficulties? With compliments to Mrs. Godwin, I remain

your obliged friend and servant,

W. Hazlitt.

If you should see Lamb,[4] will you tell him that I expected to have heard from him before this?

---

[4] Lamb wrote on 7 January 1806. The letter was discovered too late for inclusion in Mr. Lucas's edition but was printed in the *Spectator* of 5 August 1938. A portion of it follows:

I have been a long time without writing to you, but I don't know that it has deprived you of any valuable communications. You know Lord Nelson is dead. He is also to be buried. And the whole town is in a fever. Seats erecting, seats to be let, sold, lent etc. Customers crowding in to every shop between Whitehall and St. Pauls, and the tradesman and the customer changing parts, the latter being willing to become the obliged person, and the former assuming new airs of choice and selection. "A favour to beg of you Mr. Tape—to let my young ladies come and see the funeral procession on Thursday—my girls are come home from school, and young folks love sights"—Mr. Tape very grave "how many, maam?"—"O! there'll be only me, and my three daughters, and perhaps their cousin Betty, and two young men to escort them, unless my Cousin Elbowroom happens to come to town, then there'll be nine of us."

The streets are in a perfect fever. The whole town as unsettled as a young lady the day before being married. St. Paul's vergers making their hundred pounds a day in sixpences for letting people see the scaffolding inside, and the hole where he is to be let down; which money they under the Rose share with the Dean and Praecentors at night. . . . Just to get the Buzzing out of my head let me remember something vastly different—The American Farmer. I thank you for sending it to us, and am a little sorry that I cannot say so much in its praise as the usual compliments in these cases require. To shame the Devil, then, at once, it does appear to be a very stupid uninteresting Book. In what kind mood you pick'd it up I can't guess, or how Wordsworth also came to give his testimony for it, but to me it is perfectly disagreeable. Why should a book be pleasant to one, that if it were made into a Man (the binding a coat, the leaves a shirt with a frill, the etc., etc. make out the rest of the metamorphosis, I have no time, Lord Nelson etc one thing or other—my head's (dizzy) if the said book were a man and not a book, would be odious? A wretched purse-proud American Farmer with no virtue but industry and its ostentatious concomitant charity, no ideas but of clearing land and setting the poor to work (damn him for that if I was a lousy Beggar happy in the sun) calling Ladies young women and praising them for decent mirth and needle work and possibilities of being notable mothers: things too tradesman-quaker-like (quakers the worst of tradesmen) to come into that agreeable book the young man's best companion or the Apprentices Guide: cold and chill & barren as Dr Franklin's Golden rules or Poor John's Thoughts in an

No. 24

To the Reverend William Hazlitt

Four Generations, I, 97-99.
Address: Revd. Mr. Hazlitt/Wem, Salop.

Tuesday. [Early in January 1807] *

My Dear Father,

I have just seen Tom Loftus, who told me to my surprize that he left you last Friday. He called last night; but I was out. I was rather surprized, because, though I knew of his going into Wales, I did not think of his going your way. He seems much pleased with his reception and with his journey altogether. He has brought home some Welch mutton with him, which I am going to eat a part of to-night. He stopped a whole day at Oxford, which he thinks a finer place than Wem or even Shrewsbury. I have just finished the cheeks which I had dressed last Friday for my dinner after I had taken a walk around Hampstead and Highgate. I never made a better dinner in my life. T. Loftus came to help me off with them on Saturday, and we attacked them again at night, after going to the Opera, where I went for the first time and probably for the last. The fowls I took to Lamb's the night I received them, and the pickled port. They were very good. But I found only one tongue in the basket, whereas you seem to speak of two.

American almanac. Thou that has read Romeo and Juliet and Midsummers Nights Dream, to feed on the garbage and husk of dried leaves of ledgers and journals and swallow ploughs and harrows! If I didn't like it as you expected, it might be in part (principally, no doubt, its own stupidity) in part because we had just read thro' Bruce's Travels with infinite delight where all is alive and novel, and about Kings and Queens and fabulous Heads of Rivers, and Abyssinian wars and the Line of Solomon and he's a fine dashing fellow and intrigues with Empresses and gets into Harams of Black Women, and was himself descended from Kings of Scotland: not farmers and mechanics and Industry—.

* Cf. Howe, p. 80; Wardle, p. 96.

The book [1] I took to John's yesterday. The preface to Search is finished and printed to my great comfort. It is very long, and for what I know very tiresome. I am going on with my criticisms,[2] and have very nearly done Burke. I do not think I have done it so well as Chatham's. I showed the one I did of him to Anth. Robinson, who I understand since was quite delighted with it, and thinks it a very fine piece of composition. I have only Fox's to do of any consequence. Pitt's I shall take out of my pamphlet,[3] which will be no trouble. I am to settle with Budd to-morrow, but I doubt my profits will be small. These four viz. Burke, Chatham, Fox, Pitt, with Sir R. Walpole's, will be the chief articles of the work, and if I am not mistaken confounded good ones. I am only afraid they will be too good, that is, that they will contain more good things, than are exactly proper for the occasion. Have you seen it [4] in any of the papers? It was in the *M. Chronicle*. It is a pretty good one. I might if I was lazy take it, and save myself the trouble of writing one myself. I supped at Godwin's on New Year's Day, and at Holcroft's on Sunday.

I am going to dinner at Hume's [5] to-morrow, where I also was on Christmas day, and had a pleasant time enough. It was much such a day as it was two years ago, when I was painting your picture. Tempus preterlabitur.[6] I am afraid I shall never do such another. But all in good time: I have done what I wanted in writing and I hope I may in painting.

My mother I suppose was much pleased to see T. Loftus. He said that he intended returning the same day, having no time to spare, but that you pressed him so much to stop. Did not you think him a good deal like me? He intends calling on John to say that he has seen you.

I can think of nothing more but my best love to my mother and Peggy, and that I am Your affectionate son,

W. Hazlitt.

---

[1] Mr. Hazlitt's *Sermons*, which Johnson published in 1808.

[2] For *The Eloquence of the British Senate* (1807).

[3] *Free Thoughts on Public Affairs* (1806), which J. Budd published.

[4] Godwin's *Character of Fox* in the *Morning Chronicle* of 22 November 1806 served as a model for Hazlitt's characters.

[5] Joseph Hume, a member of Lamb's "Wednesday Evenings." Cf. the "Suicide Joke," Letter 27.

[6] Time glides by.

No. 25

To Joseph Johnson

MS. Lockwood.

[July 1807]

Dear Sir,

I have had a letter from my father, in which he is anxious to know what progress is made in the proof sheets.[1] Would you have the goodness to let me have one soon?—If you would fix on some day to sit for the picture [2] I spoke of, you would also confer a favour on your much obliged, humble servant,

W. Hazlitt.

Tuesday morning
34 Southampton Buildings,
Holborn.

---

[1] Of the *Sermons.*
[2] The portrait does not survive.

No. 26

To William Godwin

MS. Abinger.

(PM: 6 August 1807)

Dear Sir,

I am sorry I inserted the passage you object to.[1] For my own part I looked upon it as a joke, and thought you would do the same. As to any serious offence, it was so far from my thoughts, that I brought the manuscript one day in my pocket to read, but was prevented by somebody's being there. I think if you recollect all circumstances, you will find that the passage in question clenches the attack upon Malthus, and that I could not [have] taken the advantage I have done of his expressions, without glancing at you. You stood a little in my way, but I was determined not to lose my blow at him. This was the vow I made when I began the work, and I have performed it as well as I could. When you recollect that the whole book is written on your side of the question as far as the present controversy was concerned, and when I add farther that my spleen against Malthus, and the bitterness with which I have treated him arose originally from the unfair and uncandid use which was made of some unguarded expressions you let fall on this very subject, you will perhaps find that a single sentence may be passed over as no very great matter. It was not in my power to remove an unjust aspersion; except in the very way that I have done it, and with which you find so much fault, viz. by bringing Malthus into the same scrape. This is the best excuse I can make, and as you will see a very sincere one.

I am, Dear Sir, yours very truly,
W. Hazlitt.

---

[1] Comparing Godwin and Malthus in *A Reply to the Essay on Population* (1807), Hazlitt had written: "This is something like Mr. Godwin's saying, he does not regard a new-born infant with any peculiar complacency" (*Works*, I, 340n.).

P.S. No one has ever been more ready than I have to take part with my friends on all occasions. I have committed four or five riots in my zeal for the reputation of Coleridge and Wordsworth: and all the thanks I ever got for this, my zeal in their favour was some of the last indignities that can be put upon any person.[2] In my list of friends it has always been my good luck to come in like the tail of an etc. and to subsist only upon sufferance. —I called this morning, but you were out.

---

[2] Hazlitt had not yet discussed either Wordsworth or Coleridge in print, although he had praised Coleridge's "masterly and unanswerable essay" on Pitt in *Free Thoughts on Public Affairs* (1806), and in *The Eloquence of the British Senate* (1807) had quoted from memory without giving the source a line which he heard Wordsworth recite during a short, unhappy visit to the Lakes in 1803. *Works,* I, 112, 147. Hazlitt's "riots" refer primarily to his conversations with other young authors and friends, such as Crabb Robinson, who recorded in his diary that Hazlitt in 1799 had introduced him to "the Lyrical Ballads and the poems generally" of Wordsworth and Coleridge. Hazlitt's relationship with the two poets is, like their own association, far too complex to summarize. As his letters and essays show, Hazlitt expected more assistance from Coleridge than the latter was either able or willing to give. Their intellectual, political, and religious differences were too great for a lasting friendship. The episode of Hazlitt's attempt to seduce a girl in the Lake District in 1803 and Wordsworth's account of it to Lamb and Crabb Robinson twelve years later as the reason for Hazlitt's "malignant attack" on *The Excursion* helped to keep them estranged. Nevertheless, two years before his death Hazlitt wrote: "Till I began to paint, or till I became acquainted with the author of *The Ancient Mariner,* I could neither write nor speak. He encouraged me to write a book, which I did according to the original bent of my own mind." Cf. "On the Causes of Popular Opinion," *Works,* XVII, 312.

On Coleridge and Wordsworth, the following are the most important: "My First Acquaintance with Poets," *Works,* XVII, 106-122; "On the Living Poets," *Works,* XI, 5-184; "Lectures on the English Poets," *Works,* V, 1-168; "Mr. Coleridge" (pp. 28-38) in "The Spirit of the Age," *Works,* XIX, 9-25.

No. 27

To Joseph Hume [1]

MS. Lockwood.
Address: Joseph Hume, Esq./Victualling Office/Somerset Place.

(PM: January 11, 1808) *

The humble petition and remonstrance of William Hazlitt,—— †
now residing at No. 34, Southampton Buildings, in the parish of
St. Ann's, Holborn, shewing that he is not dead, as has been
pretended by some malicious persons, calling themselves his *friends*
(the better to conceal their base purposes), and praying that his
funeral, for which he understands a paltry subscription has been
entered into may not take place as was intended.

† N.B.—A blank is here left which the modesty of the writer would
not permit him to fill up. Perhaps he belonged to the class of *non-
descripts* rather than any other. The opinion of the world was
divided: some persons being inclined to regard him as a gentleman,
and others looking upon him as a low fellow. It is hard to say
whether he ought to be considered as an author, or a pourtrait-
painter. It is certain that he never painted any pictures but those of
persons that he hired to sit for him, and though he wrote a number
of books, it does not appear they were ever read by any body.

---

* Cf. *Lamb and Hazlitt* (London, 1900): "Dated Sunday the 10th of Jany. 1808,"
p. 75. "The post-mark is: '12 o'clock, Ja. 11, 1808,' " p.76

[1] This letter forms a part of the "Suicide Joke" perpetrated by Lamb and
Hume, another friend, a purchasing agent at the Victualling Office. They
pretended that Hazlitt's "unfortunate passion" (i.e., forthcoming marriage) had
caused him to "put an end to his existence" (*Letters,* II, 41). This "humble
petition" is Hazlitt's retaliation.

This petition sheweth that the best way of proving clearly that a man is not dead is by setting forth his manner of life, and, first, that he, the said W. Hazlitt, has regularly for the last month rang the bell at eleven at night, which was considered as a sign for the girl to warm his bed, and this being done, he has gone to bed, and slept soundly for the next twelve or fourteen hours. Secondly, that every day about twelve or 1 o'clock he has got up, put on his clothes, drank his tea, and eat two plate-fulls of buttered toast, of which he had taken care to have the hard edges pared off as hurtful to the mouth and gums, and he has then sat for some hours with his eyes steadfastly fixed upon the fire, like a person in a state of deep thought, but doing nothing.

Thirdly, that not a day has passed in which he has not eat and drank like other people. For instance, he has swallowed eight dozen of pills, nine boluses, and as many purgative draughts of a most unsavoury quality. What he has fed on with the most relish has been a mess of chicken-broth, and he has sent out once or twice for a paper of almonds and raisins. His general diet is soup-meagre with bread and milk for supper. —That it is true that the petitioner has abstained both from gross feeding and from all kinds of intoxicating liquors; a circumstance, he conceives, so far from denoting a natural decay and loss of his faculties, that on the contrary it shews more wisdom than he was always possessed of.

Fourthly, that in regard to decency he has been known to walk out at least once a week to get himself shaved.

Fifthly, that growing tired of his sedentary posture, he has occasionally got up from his chair and walked across the room (not as an *automaton* or a dead man pulled with wires might be supposed to do, but with an evident attention to his manner of rising, and an inequality in his gait, resembling a limp). At one time he turned the front of his great picture [2] to the light, but finding the subject painful to him he presently turned it to the wall again. Also, that he has twice attempted to read some of his own works, but has fallen asleep over them.

---

[2] Probably "A Nymph and Satyr."

Sixthly, that the said W. H. has, it being Christmas time, received several invitations to entertainments and parties of pleasure, which he politely declined; but that on such occasions he has generally about the hour of four in the afternoon been tormented with the apparition of a fat goose or a sirloin of beef.

Seventhly, that in compliment to the season, and to shew a fellow-feeling with his absent friends, he has ordered a wine-glass and a decanter of water to be set upon the table, and has drank off a glass or two, making a shew as if it were port or sherry, but that he desisted from this practice after a few trials, not finding it answer.

Eighthly, be it known that the person, concerning whom such idle reports are prevalent, has actually within the given time written a number of love-letters, and that a man must be dead indeed, if he is not alive when engaged in that agreeable employment. And lest it should be suggested that these epistles resemble Mrs. Rowe's *Letters from the Dead to the Living,*[3] being just such vapid, lifeless compositions, it may be proper to state, by way of counteracting any such calumny, that on the contrary they are full of nothing but ingenious conceits and *double entendres,* without a single *grave* remark or sickly sentiment from beginning to end. Farther that they had some life in them, he is assured by the quickness of the answers, which he received with that sort of pleasing titillation and gentle palpitation common to flesh and blood, reading them with alternate smiles and sighs, and once letting fall a tear at a description given by the lady of the ruinous state of a cottage [4] or tenement, which he hopes one day to call his own.

It should also be especially noted that within the last three weeks he has borrowed money of his friends, which was at all times his constant custom.

Again, that he has held more than one argument which nobody could understand but himself. Indeed his ideas seemed so thin and attenuated that they might be thought not unlike the notions of a

---

3 Elizabeth Row (1674-1737), *Friendship in Death, in Twenty Letters from the Dead to the Living* (1728).

4 Sarah Stoddart's cottage at Winterslow, Wiltshire, which Hazlitt liked.

disembodied spirit. But it should be remembered that his conversation was in general of that kind that it was difficult to make head or tail of it.

That he has made several good resolutions to be put in practice as soon as he recovers, which he hopes shortly to do without undergoing the ancient ceremony of sacrificing a Cock to Aesculapius: [5] as namely to live better than he has lately done, not to refuse an invitation to a haunch of venison, nor to decline drinking to a lady's health, to pay a greater attention to cleanliness, and to leave off w-nching, as injurious both to the health and morals.

That as it is possible he may not after all be able to defeat the arts of his calumniators, who may persuade the young lady before alluded to that the petitioner is a dead man, not able to go through the ordinary functions of life, that he has therefore formed divers plans for his future maintenance and creditable appearance in the world, as writing a tragedy, setting up quack-doctor, or entering into holy orders.

That as the most effectual means of suppressing such insinuations for the future, and to prevent his friends from persevering in their misrepresentations, it may be proper to inform them that they will get nothing by his death, whenever it happens.

Lastly as there are some appearances against him, and as he is aware that almost every thing goes by appearances, in case it should be determined that he is a dead man and that he must be buried against his will, he submits to this decision but with two provisos, first, that he shall be allowed to appear as chief mourner at his own funeral, secondly that he shall have liberty to appoint Joseph Hume, Esq. of the Victualling Office, his executor and administrator of his effects, as a man of prudence and discretion,

---

[5] In Plato's *Phaedo,* Socrates' last request of Crito was the sacrifice of a cock to the god of healing.

well-looked on in the world, and as the only person he knows, who will not be witty on the occasion! *

The said effects and valuables should be principally appropriated to pay his apothecary's and washer-women's bills.

Here follows a schedule of those of the greatest account.

1. A picture of an old woman, painted in strong shadow, nearly invisible. Valued at 5 pounds.

2. Sketch of a large picture of Count Ugolino, the canvass as good as new. Valued at 15s.

3. A Nymph and Satyr. —As there is something indecent in the subject, it is suggested that, if a prosecution could be procured against it by the Society for the suppression of vice, it might then be disposed of by raffle to great advantage.

4. Three heads of the father of Dr. Stoddart, in naval uniform, done from description. It is supposed they will do equally well for any other naval officer, deceased, who has left behind him pious relatives. Their value will depend on the fancy of the purchaser.

5. A parcel of rubbishly copies of old masters. —It is proposed that Mr. Tickell [7] should have the refusal of these, as he will easily be able to dispose of them as originals. The price to be left to his generosity.

6. A bundle of manuscripts, exceedingly abstruse and unintelligible. It is hoped they may occasion great disputes among the learned. If they are refused by the booksellers, they may be offered

---

* Alas, vain are the hopes of man! How are we deceived to the very last! It is plain the writer had not at this time seen a burlesque account of his last illness and miserable exit written by this very friend in whom he trusted in a vein of irony and humour, shewing a turn for satirical description, but reflecting little credit on the feelings of his heart.

6 Hume continued the joke in further letters to Lamb (*Lamb and Hazlitt,* 83-96).
7 A fraudulent art dealer.

to the British Museum for a trifling sum, which if not advanced they may be deposited there for the inspection of the curious.

7, and lastly, a small Claude Lorraine mirror, which Mr. Lamb the other evening secretly purloined after a pretended visit of condolence to his sick friend; and which will doubtless be found shamelessly hung up in the chambers of the fraudulent possessor as a final trophy and insult over the memory of the deceased. It is probable that when charged with this irregular transfer of property he will say that it was won at a game at cribbage. But this is an entirely false pretence. With all the sincerity of a man doubtful between life and death, the petitioner declares that he looks upon the said Charles Lamb as the ring-leader in this unjust conspiracy against him, and as the sole cause and author of the jeopardy he is in: but that as losers have leave to speak, he must say, that, if it were not for a poem he wrote on tobacco[8] about two years ago, a farce called Mr. H—he brought out last winter with more wit than discretion in it, some prologues and epilogues he has since written with good success, and some lively notes he is at present writing on dead authors,[9] he sees no reason why he should not be considered as much a dead man as himself, and the undertaker spoken to accordingly.

A true copy.
W. Hazlitt.

Dated Sunday the 10th of Jany.

1808.

P. S. Whereas it is scandalously and falsely asserted in a written paper circulated at the expence of the above-named W. H. that he has been heard to spout amourous verses,[10] and sing licentious ditties and burthens of old songs with his latest breath, a number of penny ballads and verses being also strewed about his room in an indecent manner, he begs leave to state that the only song he

---

[8] "Farewell to Tobacco" (1805).

[9] Lamb was at work on the *Specimens of English Dramatic Poets Who Lived about the Time of Shakespeare* (1808).

[10] In the letter to Hume cited above Lamb claimed that Hazlitt "had written some pretty things in prose and verse."

has once thought of of late is the Cuckoo Song, but that this has run a good deal in his head, and that he has often broken out into the following verse,

"Mocks married men from tree to tree." [11]

Also once, upon receiving some expressions of tender concern and anxious inquiries into the cause of his illness from a person that shall be nameless, he sung in a faint manner the following parody on two lines in the Beggar's Opera:

"For on the pill that cures my dear,
Depends poor Polly's life!" [12]

---

[11] *Love's Labour's Lost,* V, ii, 905. "The cuckoo then on every tree, Mocks married men; for thus sings he, 'Cuckoo! Cuckoo, cuckoo!' " "When Daisies Pied" was set to music by Thomas Arne.

[12] Air XII.

For on the rope that hangs my dear
Depends poor Polly's life.

No. 28

To Sarah Stoddart [1]

MS. Lockwood.
Address: Miss Stoddart/Winterslow/near Salisbury.

Tuesday night
[January, 1808] *

My dear love,

Above a week has passed and I have received no letter—not one of those letters "in which I live, or have no life at all." [2] What is become of you? Are you married, hearing that I was dead (for so it has been reported) [3] or are you gone into a nunnery? Or are you fallen in love with some of the amorous heroes in Boccacio? [sic] Which of them is it? Is it with Chynon who was transformed from a clown into a lover, and learned to spell, by the force of beauty? Or with Lorenzo, the lover of Isabella whom her three brethren hated (as your brother does me) [4] who was a merchant's-clerk? Or with Frederigo Alberighi,[5] an honest gentleman who ran through his fortune, and won his mistress by cooking a fair falcon for her

---

* Cf. Howe, p. 97; Baker, p. 168; Wardle, p. 108.
[1] Hazlitt's first wife (c. 1775-1842) of Winterslow, Wiltshire. Because her father, a retired officer of the Royal Navy, was dead at this date and her mother had recently lost her sanity, Sarah's brother, John Stoddart (1773-1856), King's Advocate of Malta from 1803 to 1808, was her legal guardian. The Stoddarts were friends of John Hazlitt and, through him, of the Lambs. Sarah had spent two years on Malta while Coleridge was there and her letters to Mary Lamb contain much information about him. Returning to Winterslow in 1806, Sarah was disappointed in several matrimonial prospects which she also reveals in her letters to Miss Lamb. In response, the Lambs began to look among their friends for a suitable husband. On 2 June 1806 Mary writes: "William Hazlitt, the brother of him you know, is in town. I believe you have heard us say we like him?" (*Letters*, II, 10). On 26 June 1806 Charles writes to Wordsworth describing Hazlitt's shyness among girls: "W. Hazlitt is in Town. I took him to see a very pretty girl professedly, where there were two young girls—the very head and sum of the Girlery was two young girls—they neither laughed nor sneered nor giggled nor whispered—but they were young girls—and he sat and frowned blacker and blacker, indignant that there should be such a thing as Youth and Beauty, till he tore me away before supper in perfect misery and owned he could not bear young

dinner, though it was the only means he had left of getting a dinner for himself? This last is the man: and I am the more persuaded of it, because I think I won your good liking myself by giving you an entertainment—of sausages, when I had no money to buy them with. Nay now, never deny it, for did not I ask your consent that very night after, and did not you give it? Well, I should be confoundedly jealous of those fine gallants, if I did not know that a living dog is better than a dead lion: though now I think of it Boccacio [sic] does not in general make much of his lovers: it is his women who are so delicious.[6] I almost wish I had lived in those times, and had been a little *more amiable*. Now if a woman had written the book, it would not have had this effect upon me: the men would have been heroes and angels, and the

---

girls. They drove him mad. So I took him home to my old Nurse, where he recover'd perfect tranquillity. Independent of this, and as I am not a young girl myself, he is a great acquisition to us" (*Letters*, II, 15). Since Sarah herself was no longer young or pretty, and was as forthright and practical as Hazlitt was withdrawn and self-conscious, they must have seemed a perfect match to the Lambs. Throughout 1806 they are told a good deal about each other in a most subtle and charming way. The introduction probably took place at Christmas of that year when Sarah came up to London for a visit. The courtship was nearly over before Miss Lamb writes again to Sarah requesting her to preserve her letters "that I may one day have the pleasure of seeing how Mr. Hazlitt treats of love," and adding, "if I were sure you would not be quite starved to death, nor beaten to a mummy, I should like to see Hazlitt and you come together, if (as Charles observes) it were only for the joke's sake" (*Letters*, II, 38-39). However, this is the only love letter from Hazlitt to his first wife that has survived. On 1 May 1808 a "treaty of marriage," as Lamb called it, took place between William Hazlitt and Sarah Stoddart at St. Andrew's Church, Holborn. Miss Lamb was the brides-maid.

[2] *Othello*, IV, ii, 58.

[3] Cf. Letter 27.

[4] John Stoddart had returned to England in 1808 and was a leader writer on *The Times* from 1812 to 1816. In 1817 he founded the *New Times* as a rival to it. He disapproved of the marriage because of Hazlitt's poor financial and social position, and disliked his admiration of Napoleon. William Hone satirized Stoddart's excessive flattery of Tory statesmen in *A Slap at Slop* (1820). In 1826 Stoddart returned to Malta as Chief Justice and on 27 July he was knighted by George IV.

[5] Hazlitt was very fond of this "divine story of the hawk" from the *Decameron* (Fifth Day, Novel IX), and later used it as an illustration in several works, including, "Why the Arts are not Progressive—A Fragment, "*The Round Table, Works*, IV, 160, 163-164; *Characters of Shakespear's Plays: Works*, IV, 331; and *Lectures on the English Poets, Works*, V, 82.

[6] For a continuation of this theme cf. the essay."Why the Heroes of Romances are Insipid," *Works*, XVII, 246.

women nothing at all. Isn't there some truth in that? Talking of departed loves, I met my old flame [7] the other day in the street. I did dream of her *one* night since and only one: every other night I have had the same dream I have had for these two months past. Now if you are at all reasonable, this will satisfy you.

Thursday morning. The book is come. When I saw it, I thought that you had sent it back in a *huff,* tired out by my sauciness and *coldness* and delays and were going to keep an account of dimities and sayes, or to salt pork and chronicle small beer as the dutiful wife of some fresh looking rural swain: so that you cannot think how surprized and pleased I was to find them all done.[8] I liked your note as well or better than the extracts: it is just such a note as such a nice rogue as you ought to write after the *provocation* you had received. I would not give a pin for a girl "whose cheeks never tingle," nor for myself if I could not make them tingle sometimes. Now though I am always writing to you about "lips and noses" and such sort of stuff, yet as I sit by my fireside (which I do generally 8 or 10 hours aday) [9] I oftener think of you in a serious, sober light. For indeed I never love you so well as when I think of sitting down with you to dinner over a boiled scrag-end of mutton, and hot potatoes. You please my fancy more then than when I think of you in—.[10] No, you would never forgive me if I were to finish the sentence. Now I think of it, what do you mean to be dressed in when we are married? But—it does not much matter! I wish you would let your hair grow, though perhaps nothing will be better than "the same air and look, with which at first my heart was took." But now to business. I mean soon to call upon your

---

[7] In the *Journal* that Sarah kept during the *Liber Amoris* episode she wrote in reference to Sarah Walker: "I told him it was like his frenzy for Sally Shepherd; he said *that* was but a fleabite, nothing at all to this, for she had never pretended to love him, but all along declared she did not, but this was the only person who ever really seemed and professed to be fond of him" (pp. 247-248). "Here," as Howe wrote, "we have the name of Hazlitt's 'old flame,'" but nothing more about her. She may have been the Miss Shepherd of Liverpool mentioned in Letter 6, n. 3 but not a daughter of Dr. Shepherd of Gateacre, as W. C. Hazlitt thought, who was Hazlitt's senior by only ten years.

[8] Since he was now preparing a "History of English Philosophy," it is possible that Sarah had offered to transcribe "extracts" for him.

[9] He had recently suffered a stomach disorder and was still confined to his rooms in Southampton Buildings.

[10] "Your" and an illegible word crossed out.

brother *in form,* namely, as soon as I get quite well, which I hope to do in about another *fortnight.* And then I hope you will come up by the coach as fast as the horses can carry you; for I long mightily to be in your ladyship's presence—to vindicate my character. I think you had better sell the small house,[11] I mean that at 4.10, and I will borrow a 100£. So that we shall set off merrily, in spite of all the prudence of Edinburgh.

Goodbye, little Dear.

W. H.

---

[11] She had inherited two houses in Salisbury, one of which she sold, and owned also a cottage at Winterslow. These were settled upon her only, much to Hazlitt's annoyance, at her brother's instigation.

No. 29

To the Right Honorable William Windham,[1] M.P.

MS. British Library.
Address: The Right Honourable Will. Windham, M.P./Pall-Mall/London.

15 February 1809

Sir,

I take the liberty to offer to your notice the enclosed Prospectus.[2] I have no other excuse to make for this intrusion than that I believe the design of the work is such as may meet with your approbation,—and the natural wish of every one that what has employed many years of his life and many anxious thoughts may not be entirely lost. My principal view in it would be to chastise the presumption of modern philosophy.[3] The advocates of this system, however, by an exclusive and constant claim to the privilege of reason, have so completely satisfied themselves, and so very nearly persuaded others to believe that they are the only rational persons in the world, that any attempt to disprove their doctrines is looked upon as flying in the face of reason itself and an attack upon first principles. An attempt like the present must therefore I believe fail of success, without some particular support; and my object in soliciting the names of a few persons distinguished for liberal knowledge, and elevated powers of mind as subscribers to the work, was to shew that an opposition to the fashionable paradoxes was not the same thing as formally declaring one's self on the side of ignorance and error. I know of no name, Sir, that would

---

[1] (1750-1810). Secretary for War throughout Pitt's administration. Hazlitt may have written to Windham at the suggestion of his friend William Cobbett (1762-1835), whom Windham had helped to found the *Political Register*. Both Hazlitt and Windham were boxing enthusiasts, which Hazlitt remembered in "The Fight."

[2] "Prospectus of a History of English Philosophy." The work was not completed. Cf. *Works*, II, 113-119.

[3] Cf. *Lectures on English Philosophy, Works*, II, 123-284.

contribute to this end more than you own; [4] the permission to make use of which would be thankfully and proudly acknowledged by, Sir, your obedient, very humble servant,

W. Hazlitt.

Winterslow, near Salisbury.

---

[4] No evidence of Windham's support has been found.

No. 30

To William Godwin

MS. Abinger.

[Latter part of June 1809] *

Dear Sir,

I was not at all offended, but a good deal vexed at the contents of your former letter, having had three books which I have written suppressed,[1] and as I had taken some trouble with the grammar,[2] I thought it might answer the purpose, and as you seemed to approve of what I had done to it, I was sorry to be dashed in pieces against the dulness of schoolmasters. I do not much like the style and title of *Mr. W. Hazlitt;* it looks like one of a firm of ushers; otherwise I can have no objection to the matter. I send you Crombie,[3] and the revised grammar, and remain, Dear Sir,

yours truly,

W. Hazlitt.

The Lambs will be down here in the beginning of July.[4] I can only say that the woods and walks will be then green, and that the sherry is not all drank up.

Friday

[Winterslow]

---

* Cf. Baker, p. 171n.

[1] He is referring to *Free Thoughts on Public Affairs, Addressed to a Member of the Old Opposition* (1806), a pamphlet published at his own expense, denouncing the peace negotiations of the Treaty of Amiens and the continuation of the war with France; the attacks upon *Letters in Answer to Malthus* which appeared in Cobbett's *Political Register* before being published as *A Reply to the Essay on Population* (1807); and a proposed "History of English Philosophy," which gained no support, only the "Prospectus" being printed in 1809.

[2] In November 1809 Godwin published Hazlitt's *New and Improved Grammar of the English Tongue, Works,* II, 5-110

No. 31

To William Godwin

MS. Abinger.

[Late Summer of 1809] *

Dear Sir,
   I am forced to trouble you with the following questions [1]
which I shall be much obliged to you to answer as well as you
can.

1. At what time H[olcroft] lived with Granville Sharp [2]
whether before or after he turned actor, and whether the scene
described in Alwyn [3] as the occasion why Hilkirk (*i.e.* himself
in the subsequent part) went on the stage, really took place
between Sharp and Holcroft, I mean the one where Seddon
discovers his apprentice at a sporting club in the character of
Macbeth?

---

[3] Alexander Crombie's *The Etymology and Syntax of the English Language Explained
and Illustrated,* 1802.
   [4] Because Mary Lamb was taken ill this month and the Hazlitt's first child, a
son (born 15 January 1809) died on 5 July 1809, the visit was postponed until
October. Cf. Letter 32.

---

* Cf. Wardle, pp. 115-116; Baker, p. 172 and p. 492, n. 26.
   [1] Hazlitt was at work on the *Memoirs of the Late Thomas Holcroft* based upon
material given him by Holcroft's widow. Although he finished the book in
January 1810, it was not published until 1816 because of Godwin's opposition to
it. In a letter to Mrs. Holcroft, Godwin protested "with the strongest feelings of
disapprobation" against Hazlitt's inclusion of a few mild references to him taken
from Holcroft's Diary. These were omitted from the published text, but Godwin's
objection ended arrangements for having the book appear in 1810.
   [2] (1735-1813). Abolitionist and author of *The Law of Retribution, or a Serious
Warning to Great Britain and her Colonies—of God's Temporal Vengeance against Tyrants,
Slaveholders, and Oppressors* (1776).
   [3] *Alwyn, or the Gentleman Comedian* (1780), the first of many novels by Holcroft
(1745-1809), was based upon his own adventures as a strolling actor described in
the character of Hilkirk.

[109]

2. What was the maiden name of Mrs. Sparks? [4]

I received yours of the second yesterday. As to the attack upon Murray,[5] I have hit at him several times, and whenever there is a question of a blunder, "his name is not far off." Perhaps it would look like jealousy to make a formal set at him. Besides, I am already noted by the Reviewers for want of liberality, and an undisciplined moral sense.[6] I have ordered Taylor [7] to leave out the second table of sounds, viz. the fifth appendix, but the first ap. must stand as there is a particular reference to it in the text body of the Grammar. —It will be easy if you think proper to insert the additional remarks on H.T.[8] at the end of the preface as a note to p.—, or as a P.S. in between brackets, for there is I think a blank leaf left. The whole will then be comprised in the regular sheet, *teres et rotundus.*[9]

With respect to the Guide,[10] I can only say I was very much pleased with the plan which seemed to me very simple and ingenious. But the truth is I know very little about the matter, and I am besides sick of the subject of grammar. As to the manner in which you speak of the plan, it seemed to me more in the way of business than anything of your own in the same manner. I was (if you will allow me to say so) rather hurt to find you lay so much apparent stress upon the matter as you do in your last sentence; for assuredly the works of William Godwin do not stand in need of

---

[4] An actress; like Holcroft, a member of Booth's Company at Drury Lane in 1773. She was "the youngest daughter of Mills, the late manager" of Drury Lane (*Memoirs of Holcroft, Works,* III, 78).

[5] Lindley Murray (1745-1826), whose *Short Introduction to English Grammar* (1795) went into fifty editions before 1816. Hazlitt disagreed with many of Murray's definitions and examples.

[6] A reference to Horace Twiss's review of *A Reply to the Essay on Population* in the May 1809 *London Review.*

[7] Richard Taylor (1781-1858), the printer of the book and editor of *The Philosophical Magazine.*

[8] John Horne Tooke (1736-1812), philologist and politician whose "etymological system" was included in Hazlitt's *Grammar.* Cf. Letter 160.

[9] Smooth and polished.

[10] Godwin's *New Guide to the English Tongue* was added to the *Grammar,* although Hazlitt disliked some parts of it.

[110]

those of E. Baldwin for vouchers or supporters.[11] The latter (let them be as good as they will) are but the dust in the balance as compared with the former. Coleridge talks out of the Revelations of somebody's "new name from heaven": [12] for my own part, if I were you, I should not wish for any but my old one. —I am, dear Sir, very faithfully and affectionately yours,

W. Hazlitt.

I send this in a parcel, because it will arrive a day sooner than by the post. Will you send me down a copy of the Grammar when you write again, by the same conveyance? As for the postage of the proof-sheets, it will not be more nor so much as the extra expence of corrections in the printing, occasioned by blurred paper in the author. It may therefore be *set off*.

---

[11] Godwin had published several works under the pseudonym of Edward Baldwin. Hazlitt implies that his criticism of the *Guide* should not have been regarded so seriously, and that Godwin should publish the work under his own name.

[12] *The Friend: A Series of Essays,* edited by Henry Nelson Coleridge (New York, 1878), "Essay XIV."

No. 32

To the Reverend William Hazlitt

MS. Boston.
Address: Revd. W. Hazlitt/Wem/Shropshire.

Sunday, 5 of November [1809]

My dear Father,
I received your last letter about a week ago. I was very glad to hear that my mother was got so much better and I hope she will now continue so. The weather here has undergone a change in the last week, which I find agrees with me, but I suppose it will not have the same effect on her. It is today very wet and rainy. The Lambs went on Friday week.[1] The whole of the time they were here was very fine; we had many long, and some pleasant walks, to Stonehenge, Salisbury, Wilton, etc. and in the woods near our own house. We are I find just on the borders of Hampshire, and that part of the country which lies on the Hampshire side is as woody and pleasant as the Wilts side is bleak and desert.[2] I suppose this

---

[1] Charles and Mary had spent the month of October with the Hazlitts at Winterslow. On 30 October Lamb wrote to Coleridge: "I have been with Mary on a visit to Hazlitt. The journey has been of infinite service to her. We have had sunshiny days and daily walks from eight to twenty miles a-day; have seen Wilton, Salisbury, Stonehenge, etc. Her illness lasted but six weeks; it left her weak, but the country has made us whole" (Letters, II, 83). Mary expressed her appreciation to Sarah Hazlitt: "The dear, quiet, lazy, delicious month we spent with you is remembered by me with such regret, that I feel quite discontent and Winterslow-sick. I assure you, I never passed such a pleasant time in the country in my life, both in the house and out of it, the card playing quarrels, and a few gaspings for breath after your swift footsteps up the high hills excepted, and those drawbacks are not unpleasant in the recollection" (Letters, II, 85).

[2] The woods figure prominently in many of Hazlitt's writings. For example, in a later description of the Bois de Boulogne, he wrote: "Some of the woods on the borders of Wiltshire and Hampshire present exactly the same appearance, with the same delightful sylvan paths through them, and are covered in summer with hyacinths and primroses, sweetening the air, enamelling the ground, and with nightingales loading every bough with rich music" [Notes of a Journey through France and Italy (1826), Works, X, 158].

was the origin of the two names, Hants, i.e. Haunts, and Wilts, i.e. Wilds. Miss Lamb continued in perfect health and spirits while she staid, and I hope the journey will be of service to her, as well as to him, for he neither smoked nor drank any thing but tea and small beer, while he was here. Phillips,[3] a friend of Lamb's, and a very good-natured card-playing fellow, came down for the last ten days. He shot us a hare and a pheasant, having been formerly an old sportsman, and an Oxonian of idle renown. He is one of those kind of people who are always very much pleased with every thing, and it is therefore pleasant to be with him. Since they went, I have set to pretty hard at Holcroft's Life,[4] and have written (*above:* in the evenings for I paint in the day time) 35 pages in the last week, in addition to near a hundred which I had before transcribed from his own narrative which comes down to his fifteenth year. This will be the best part of the work but I hope to make the rest out tolerably well from memorandums, anecdotes, his own writings, criticisms etc. etc. I shall finish it, I hope, by Christmass, and certainly it will not be a hard job. His own narrative will comprise about 80 quarto pages, in which size it will be printed, a diary which he left for the years 1798 and 99, and which is almost as amusing as Boswell's Life, will take up about 50 more — 130, what I shall write will be about 170 pages, making 300 of the Life, and there will be another 150 pages of Letters to and from his friends; in all about 450 pages. Above half the volume will therefore be mere strait forward transcription, and the rest will be merely picking out memorandums etc. from different places, and bringing them together, except such few reflections as I shall have to make, which will not be very long or deep. The Grammar [5] is printed, and will I suppose be published very shortly. Remember me to J. Swanwick when you see him. I think you had better not enter into a contest with old Swanwick,[6] unless you are quite sure of success,

---

[3] Edward Phillips, secretary to John Rickman, and, after 1814, his successor as secretary to the Speaker of the House. Both were favourites at Lamb's "Wednesday evenings," and Phillips figures "as a masterful cribbage player in Hazlitt's essay "On the Conversation of Authors," *Works,* XII, 37. Phillips is also "P—, who was deep in a game of piquet at the other end of the room" in "Of Persons One Would Wish to Have Seen" (*Works,* XVII, 129).

[4] Cf. Letter 31.

[5] Cf. Letter 31.

[6] Friends of the family at Wem. Cf. Letter 4.

particularly as he seems not likely to live very long. We heard from Peggy since she went.[7] I have not had any letter from John lately. I have written a pretty long letter and shall conclude with mine and Sarah's best love to you and my mother.

W. H.

---

[7] Probably on a short visit with relatives or friends.

No. 33

To Henry Crabb Robinson

MS. Dr. Williams.

Sunday Afternoon
3 December 1809 *

Dear Robinson,

—I did not receive your friendly letter till this morning. There is sometimes a delay of one or two days in the post, and I shall therefore send you this in a parcel by the coach, so that you will have it tomorrow. I am obliged to you for thinking of me for the coadjutor in the Review; [1] and I am willing to try what I can do in the way you proposed to the editor.[2] I am only afraid I shall disgrace your recommendation and shew that you have more good nature than discretion in your opinions of your friends. I shall have done Holcroft's Life in a fortnight when I shall bring it up to town, and it will then be time enough to talk of the book or books to be reviewed. With respect to Opie's Lectures,[3] I suppose you know that they are transcribed with little variation from Fuseli's [4] printed ones, and that the delivery of them was what nobody but Opie would have undertaken, and that nobody but Mrs. Opie would have thought of their publication. However, there is good scope for criticism in them, and there being a mixture of scandal in it would not perhaps be the worse; but of this, as of all other questions of what may or may not answer I am quite ignorant. Be

---

* The editors are indebted to John Creasey, Librarian of Dr. Williams' Library, for the correct dating of this letter. Cf. Howe (p. 111) for Robinson's dating.

[1] Crabb Robinson (1775-1867) was acting editor of a short-lived quarterly, the *London Review,* and had invited Hazlitt to contribute to it.

[2] The editor was Richard Cumberland (1732-1811), author of *The West Indian* and other plays; but no issue of the *London Review* appeared after this letter.

[3] John Opie (1761-1807), the painter, whose *Lectures on Painting, With a Memoir by His Wife,* Amelia Opie, was published in 1809.

[4] Henry Fuseli (or Fuessli) (1741-1825), historical painter and illustrator. His *Lectures on Painting Delivered at the Royal Academy* appeared between 1801 and 1820.

it remarked that I have at the same time a good opinion of Opie. There is only one way in which the Life of Holcroft can interfere with the review, which is that there are in a Diary of his, which is to be put in as an Appendix, one or two most excellent stories about Cumberland, which I should be loth to leave out, but which Cumberland, without being the most irritable man in the world, might be disposed to complain of.[5] Indeed I am afraid I shall get into more than one scrape of this kind, in consequence of the philosophical and philanthropical studies of my author on his acquaintance in the above-named Diary. I am sorry Miss Lamb looked so low, but I hope it was only the effect of the Wednesday nights smoking, and sitting up. I am pushing hard to get Holcroft done (all but correcting and Heaven knows there will be enough of that wanted) by Tuesday, and I must therefore return to a most pathetic account of his being blown up by aquafortis in 1800.[6] I am tired to death of the work, having been at it unceasingly the last fortnight, and I hope you will therefore excuse brevity and stupidity. I am glad to hear you see A. Robinson [7] often, when you do again, make my best respects to him. I received a very friendly, I may say affectionate, letter from him in the summer. I believe I have said all that was necessary about the Review. With Mrs. H's compliments, I am yours truly,

W. Hazlitt.

My reason for not calling when in town was the fear of not finding you at home, and my being in the country makes me more *nervous*, as they call it, than I generally am.

---

[5] The "two most excellent stories" about Cumberland in Holcroft's Diary concern his play *Tiberius* which was "cheerfully received till the title was read, then immediately returned," and his parsimony. His guests were always served "bread and cheese and small beer" (*Works,* III, 197). These were included in the *Memoirs* because Cumberland had died before the book was published.

[6] This account of Holcroft's accident is given toward the end of the book (*Works,* III, 231).

[7] Anthony Robinson. Cf. Letter 18.

No. 34

To Henry Crabb Robinson

MS. Dr. Williams.

Winterslow, near Salisbury
Feb. 26 [1810] *

Dear Robinson,

Yesterday as soon as you were gone, it occurred to me that I had forgot to mention a circumstance which might perhaps turn to account. Mrs. Holcroft [1] when I was there the other day was shewing me and praising a work called the Martyrs by the famous Chateau Briand, which I believe has not been translated. It was published 1809. It is in 3 vols. and is as far as I understand from her account and what I read a sort of poetical romance (in prose) founded on the persecutions against the Christian Religion, something in the style of the death of Abel,[2] or more properly in his own style, if you are acquainted with it. I was thinking that a translation might sell, and that it would possibly be in Tipper's [3] way to engage in such a work. The subject is orthodox, and the style as fine as can be. If you could take the trouble to mention it to him, and he thought the plan feasible, I should be glad to attempt it at any rate you could procure for me, 2½ guineas, 2, or 1½ per sheet. One more push I must make, and then I hope to be afloat, at least for a good while to come. I had also before this last project started up, thought of turning the History of E. Philosophy [4] into a

---

* Cf. Howe, p. 113.

[1] Louisa Mercier Holcroft, Holcroft's fourth wife, was the daughter of Louis-Sébastien Mercier (1740-1814), dramatist, and author of *L'An deux mille quatre cent quarante* (1770) Londres, Nouvelle édition, 1785).

[2] *The Death of Abel* (1762) by Salomon Gessner, which Coleridge had mentioned to Hazlitt. Cf. "My First Acquaintance with Poets," *Works,* XVII, 120.

[3] Samuel Tipper, publisher of the *London Review.* Hazlitt did not proceed with a translation of *Les Martyrs.*

[4] The "History of English Philosophy," which was not completed, although the articles for it formed the "Lectures on English Philosophy" which Hazlitt delivered at the Russell Institution, Russell Square, from January to April 1812.

volume of Essays on the subjects mentioned in the prospectus, making the history subservient to the philosophy, which I believe is what I should do best, but I suspect that this is a subject to which Tipper would not very seriously incline his ear. I have in short many plots and projects in my head, but I am afraid none of them good ones. Such as they are, you will I hope excuse my troubling you with them, and believe me to be yours affectionately,

W. Hazlitt.

No. 35

To Sarah Stoddart Hazlitt

MS. Houghton Library.
Address: Mr. Lamb/India House/London.

Sunday evening
(PM: April) [1810]*

My dear Sarah,[1]
I begin on a large sheet of paper though I have nothing new to fill a half one. Both parcels of prints came safe, and I need hardly say that I was glad to see them, and that I thank you exceedingly for getting them for me. I am much obliged to you for your trouble in this as well as about the pictures. Your last letter but one I did not receive in time to have come up to see them before Friday (the day then fixed for the sale) and though I got your letter on Friday time enough to have been with you yesterday morning, I did not feel disposed to set out. The day was wet and uncomfortable, and the catalogue did not tempt me so much as I expected. There were a parcel of Metzus and Terburghs [2] and boors smoking and ladies at harpsichords which seemed to take up as much room as the St. Cecilia, the Pan and St. George, the Danae and the Ariadne in Naxos.[3] Did Lamb go to the sale, and what is the report of the pictures? But I have got my complete set of Cartoons,[4] "here I sit with my doxies surrounded," [5] and so never mind. I just took out my little copy of Rembrandt to look at and was so pleased with it I

---

* Cf. *Lamb and Hazlitt* (London, 1900), p. 99; Howe, p. 114n.; Baker, pp. 170 and p. 491, n. 23

[1] Mrs. Hazlitt was visiting the Lambs in London; Hazlitt remained at Winterslow painting and writing.

[2] Gerard Terborch (1617-81) and Gabriel Metzu (1615-58), Dutch painters. Metzu's work is discussed in "The Marquis of Stafford's Gallery," *Works*, X, 27.

[3] Various paintings of these subjects, such as Raphael's "St. Cecilia" are discussed in *Sketches of the Principal Picture Galleries in England*, *Works*, X, 206.

[4] A copy of Raphael's "Cartoons, Commentary on the Scriptures," a favorite work.

[5] *The Beggar's Opera*, III, xvii.

had almost a mind to send it up, and try whether it might not fetch two or three guineas. But I am not at present much in the humour to incur any certain expence for an uncertain profit. With respect to my painting, I go on something like Satan, through moist and dry,[6] something glazing and sometimes scumbling as it happens, now on the wrong side of the canvas, and now on the right, but still persuading myself that I have at last found out the true secret of Titian's golden hue and the oleaginous touches of Claude Lorraine.[7] I have got in a pretty good background, and a *conception* of the ladder which I learned from the upping stone on the down,[8] only making the stone into gold, and a few other improvements. I have no doubt there was such another on the field of Luz, and that an upping stone is the genuine Jacob's ladder.[9] But where are the angels to come from? That's another question, which I am not yet able to solve. My dear Sarah, I am too tired and too dull to be witty, and therefore I will not attempt it. I did not see the superscription of the wrapping paper till this morning, for which I thank you as much as for the prints. You are a good girl, and I must be a good boy. I have not been very good lately. I do not wish you to overstay your month, but rather to set off on the Friday. You will I hope tell me in your next about Mrs. Holcroft and the books.[10] If the sale had been the 23rd I intended to have come up, and brought them with me. Our new neighbour arrived the day after you went. I have heard nothing of her but that her name is Armstead, nor seen anything of her till yesterday and the day before on one of which days she passed by our house in a blue pelisse and on the other in a scarlet one. She is a strapper, I assure you. Little Robert and his wife still continue in the house.[11] They returned the coals, but I sent them back thinking they would be

---

6 *Paradise Lost,* III, 1, 652.

7 Hazlitt wrote frequently about both artists. For criticism of their paintings see "Fine Arts," *Works,* XVIII, 111-124, among others.

8 A tall stone used for mounting at the foot of Shotover Hill, Wiltshire.

9 Hazlitt's painting of Jacob, suggested by Rembrandt's "Jacob's Dream," was not completed. Of the latter, he wrote: "No one else could ever grapple with this subject, or stamp it on the willing canvass in its gorgeous obscurity but Rembrandt!" "The Dulwich Gallery," *Works,* X, 21.

10 While arranging the *Memoirs* for publication, Hazlitt had used Holcroft's books.

11 Tenants in one of Sarah's houses at Salisbury.

badly off perhaps. But yesterday they walked out together, he as smart as a buck, and she skipping and light as a doe. It is supper time, my dear, I have been painting all day, and all day yesterday, and all the day before, and am very, very tired, and so I hope you will let me leave off here, and bid you good night. I inclose a 1£ note to Lamb. If you want another, say so. But I hope your partnership concern with Mr. Phillips [12] will have answered the same purpose. I am ever your affectionate,

W. Hazlitt.

Before you come away, get Lamb to fix the precise time of their coming down here.[13]

---

[12] Ned Phillips, her partner at cribbage. Cf. Letter 32.

[13] Charles and Mary chose July for their holiday at Winterslow. On the 12th, Lamb wrote to Basil Montagu: "my head has received such a shock by an all-night journey on the top of the coach, that I shall have enough to do to nurse it into its natural pace before I go home. I must devote myself to imbecility. I must be gloriously useless while I stay here" (*Letters,* II, 101). At Winterslow, Lamb ordered a "pair of brown or snuff-coloured breeches" from the tailor of a neighbouring village— "instead of which the pragmatical old gentleman (having an opinion of his own) brought him home a pair of 'lively Lincoln-green,' in which I remember he rode in triumph in Johnny Tremain's cross-country caravan through Newberry, and entered Oxford, 'fearing no colours,' the abstract idea of the jest of the thing prevailing in his mind (as it always does) over the sense of personal dignity" ("Character of the Country People," *Works,* XVII, 66-67).

No. 36

To William Cobbett [1]

The Political Register, 24 November 1810.
Sir,

The title-page of a pamphlet which I published some time ago, and part of which appeared in the Political Register [2] in answer to the Essay on Population, having been lately prefixed to an article in the Edinburgh Review as a pretence for making a formal eulogy on that work, I take the liberty to request your insertion of a few queries, which may perhaps bring the dispute between Mr. Malthus's admirers and his opponents, to some sort of issue. It will, however, first of all be proper to say something of the article in the Review. The writer of the article accuses the "anonymous" writer of the reply to the Essay, of misrepresenting and misunderstanding his author, and undertakes to give a statement of the real principles of Mr. Malthus's work. He at the same time informs us for whom this statement is intended, namely, for those who are not likely even to read the work itself, and who take their opinions on all subjects moral, political, and religious, from the periodical reports of the Edinburgh Review. For my own part, what I have to say will be addressed to those who have read Mr. Malthus's work, and who may be disposed to form some opinion of their own on the subject. The most remarkable circumstance in the Review is, that it is a complete confession of the force of the arguments which have been brought against the Essay. The defence here set up of it may indeed be regarded as the euthanasia of that performance. For in what does this defence consist but in an adoption, point by point, of the principal objections and limitations, which have been offered to Mr. Malthus's system; and which being thus ingeniously

---

[1] Published under the heading of "Mr. Malthus and the Edinburgh Reviewers," this letter is Hazlitt's answer to the Reviewer in that journal who had written a notice of his *Reply to Malthus,* three years after its publication, in the August 1810 number.

[2] The first three "Letters" of the *Reply* had appeared in *The Political Register* between March and May 1807.

applied to gloss its defects, the Reviewer charges those who had pointed them out with misrepresenting and vilifying the author? In fact, the advocates of this celebrated work do not at present defend its doctrines, but deny them. The only resource left them is that of screening its fallacies from the notice of the public by raising a cry of misrepresentation against those who attempt to expose them, and by holding a mask of flimsy affectation over the real and distinguishing features of the work. Scarcely a glimpse remains of the striking peculiarities of Mr. Malthus's reasoning, his bold paradoxes dwindle by refined gradations into mere harmless commonplaces, and what is still more extraordinary, an almost entire coincidence of sentiment is found to subsist between the author of the essay and his most zealous opponents, if the ignorance and prejudices of the latter would but allow them to see it. Indeed the Edinburgh Reviewer gives pretty broad hints that neither friends nor foes have ever understood much of the matter, and kindly presents his readers, for the first time, with the true key to this much admired production. He accordingly proceeds with considerable self-complacency to translate the language of the essay into the dialect of the Scotch school of economy, to put quite on one side the author's geometrical and arithmetical ratios, which had wrought such wonders, to state that Mr. Malthus never pretended to make any new discovery, and to quote a passage from Adam Smith, which suggested the plan of his work; to shew that this far-famed work which has been so idly magnified, and so unjustly decried as overturning all the commonly received axioms of political philosophy, proves absolutely nothing with respect to the prospects of mankind or the means of social improvement, that the sole hopes either of the present or of future generations do not centre (strange to tell!) in the continuance of vice and misery, but in the gradual removal of these, by diffusing rational views of things and motives of action, and particularly by ameliorating the condition, securing the independence, and raising the spirit, of the lower classes of society; and finally that both the extent of population, and the degree of happiness enjoyed by the people of any country depend very much upon, and, as far as there is any difference observable between one country or state of society and another, are wholly regulated by political institutions, a good or bad government, moral habits, the state of civilization, commerce,

[123]

or agriculture, the improvements in art or science, and a variety of other causes quite distinct from the sole mechanical principle of population. And this, Sir, is what the Reviewer imposes on his unsuspecting readers as the sum and substance, the true scope and effect of Mr. Malthus's reasoning. It is in truth an almost literal recapitulation of the chief topics insisted on in the Reply to the Essay, which the Reviewer seems silently to regard as a kind of necessary supplement to that work. In this account it is evident, both that Mr. Malthus's pretensions as an original discoverer are given up by the Reviewer, and that his obnoxious and extravagant conclusions are carefully suppressed. Now with regard to the general principle of the disproportion between the power of increase in population, and in the means of subsistence, and the necessity of providing some checks, moral or physical, to the former, in order to keep it on a level with the means of subsistence, I have never in any instance called in question either of "these important and radical facts," which it is the business of Mr. M.'s work to illustrate. All that I undertook in the Reply to the Essay was to disprove Mr. Malthus's claim to the discovery of these facts, and to shew that he had drawn some very false and sophistical conclusions from them, which do not appear in the article in the Review. As far therefore as relates to the Edinburgh Reviewers, and their readers, I might consider my aim as accomplished, and leave Mr. Malthus's system and pretensions in the hands of these friendly critics, who will hardly set the seal of their authority on either one or the other, till they have reduced both to something like their own ordinary standard. But against this I have several reasons. First, as I never looked upon Mr. Malthus as "a man of no mark or likelihood," I should be sorry to see him dandled into insignificance, and made a mere puppet in the hands of the Reviewers. Secondly, I in some measure owe it to myself to prove that the objections I have brought against his system are not the phantoms of my own imagination. Thirdly, Mr. Malthus's work cannot be considered as entirely superseded by the account of it in the Review, as there are, no doubt, many persons who will still take their opinion of Mr. Malthus's doctrines from his own writings, and abide by what they find in the text as good authority and sound argument, though not sanctioned in the Commentary. I will therefore proceed to put the questions I at first proposed as the best means I can devise for determining, both what the contents of Mr. Malthus's work really are, and to what degree of credit they are entitled, or how far they are true or false, original or borrowed.[3]

Query 1. Whether the real source of Mr. Malthus's Essay is not to be found in the long extract from Wallace's "Various Prospects of Mankind," [4] quoted in the second letter of the Reply to the Essay. Or whether this writer has not both stated the principle of the disproportion between the unlimited power of increase in population, and the limited power of increase in the means of subsistence, which principle is the corner-stone of the Essay; and whether he has not drawn the very same inference from it that Mr. Malthus has done, *viz.* that vice and misery are necessary to keep population down to the level of the means of subsistence?

2. Whether the chapter in Wallace, written expressly to prove these two points (or in other words, to shew that the principle of population is necessarily incompatible with any great degree of improvement in government or morals) does not throw considerably more light on the history of Mr. Malthus's work, the first edition of which was written expressly to prove the same points, than the passage from Adam Smith, which the Reviewer says *he has heard* first gave rise to the Essay, but which Mr. M. might have read a hundred times over, without once dreaming either of his principle or his conclusion.

3. Whether the idea of an arithmetical and geometrical series by which Mr. Malthus has been thought to have furnished the precise rule or *calculus* of the disproportion between food and population, is not, strictly speaking, inapplicable to the subject; inasmuch as in new and lately occupied countries, the quantity of food may be made to increase nearly in the same proportion as population, and in all old and well cultivated countries must be stationary, or

---

[3] The "Queries" which follow were slightly expanded and published in *The Examiner,* 29 October 1815, as No. 23 of the Round Table Series *(Works,* VII, 357-361).

[4] Robert Wallace (1697-1771), published his *Various Prospects of Mankind, Nature and Providence* in 1761. For the extract which Hazlitt had quoted, cf. *Works,* I, 190-194.

nearly so? Whether, therefore, this mode of viewing the subject has not tended as much to embarrass as to illustrate the question, and to divert the mind from the real source of the only necessary distinction between food and population, namely, the want of sufficient room for the former to grow in; a grain of corn, as long as it has room to increase and multiply, in fact propagating its species much faster even than a man?

4. Whether the argument borrowed from Wallace, and constituting the chief scope and tenor of the first edition of the Essay, which professed to overturn all schemes of human perfectibility and Utopian forms of government from the sole principle of population, does not involve a plain contradiction; both these authors, first of all, supposing or taking for granted a state of society in which the most perfect order, wisdom, virtue, and happiness shall prevail, and then endeavouring to shew that all these advantages would only hasten their own ruin, and end in famine, confusion, and unexampled wretchedness, in consequence of taking away the only possible checks to population, *vice* and *misery?* Whether this objection does not suppose mankind in a state of the most perfect reason, to be utterly blind to the consequences of the unrestrained indulgence of their appetites, and with the most perfect wisdom and virtue regulating all their actions, not to have the slightest command over their animal passions? There is nothing in any of the visionary schemes of human perfection so idle as this objection brought against them, which has no more to do with the reasonings of Godwin, Condorcet, &c. (against which Mr. Malthus's first Essay was directed) than with the prophecies of the Millennium!

5. Whether, in order to give some colour of plausibility to his argument, and to prove that the highest conceivable degree of wisdom and virtue could be of no avail in keeping down the principle of population, Mr. Malthus did not at first set out with representing this principle, to wit, the impulse to propagate the species, as a law of the same order and cogency as that of satisfying the cravings of hunger; so that reason having no power over it, vice and misery must be the necessary consequences, and only possible checks to population?

[126]

6. Whether this original view of the subject did not unavoidably lead to the most extravagant conclusions, not only by representing the total removal of all vice and misery as the greatest evil that could happen to the world, but (what is of more consequence than this speculative paradox) by throwing a suspicion and a stigma on all subordinate improvements or plans of reform, as so many clauses or sections of the same general principle? Whether the quantity of vice and misery necessary to keep population down to the level of the means of subsistence, being left quite undetermined by the author, the old barriers between vice and virtue, good and evil, were not broken down, and a perfect latitude of choice allowed between forms of government and modes of society, according to the temper of the times, or the taste of individuals; only that vice and misery being always the *safe side,* the presumption would naturally be in favour of the most barbarous, ignorant, enslaved, and profligate? Whether the stumbling-block thus thrown in the way of those who aimed at any amendment in social institutions, does not obviously account for the alarm and opposition which Mr. Malthus's work excited on the one hand, and for the cordiality and triumph with which it was hailed on the other?

7. Whether this view of the question, which is all in which the Essay differs fundamentally from the most commonplace disquisition on the subject, is not palpably, and by the author's own confession, false, sophistical, and unfounded?

8. Whether the additional principle of *moral restraint,* inserted in the second and following editions of the Essay as one effectual, and as the only desirable means of checking population, does not at once overturn all the paradoxical conclusions of the author respecting the state of man in society, and whether nearly all these conclusions do not stand as they originally stood. Whether, indeed, it was likely, that Mr. Malthus would give up the sweeping conclusions of his first Essay, the fruits of his industry and the pledges of his success, without great reluctance; or in such a manner as not to leave the general plan of his work full of contradictions and almost unintelligible?

9. Whether, for example, in treating of the durability of a perfect

form of government, Mr. Malthus has not "sicklied over the subject with the same pale and jaundiced cast of thought," [5] by supposing vice and misery to be the only effectual checks to population; and in his tenacity on this his old and favourite doctrine, whether he has not formally challenged his opponents to point out any other, "except indeed" (he adds, recollecting himself) "moral restraint," which however he considers as of no effect at all?

10. Whether, consistently with this verbal acknowledgment and virtual rejection of the influence of moral causes, the general tendency of Mr. M's system is not to represent the actual state of man in society as nothing better than a blind struggle between vice, misery, and the principle of population, the effects of which are just as mechanical as the ebbing and flowing of the tide, and to bury all other principles, all knowledge, or virtue, or liberty, under a heap of misapplied facts?

11. Whether, instead of accounting for the different degrees of happiness, plenty, populousness, &c. in different countries, or in the same country at different periods, from good or bad government, from the vicissitudes of manners, civilization, and knowledge, according to the statement in the Edinburgh Review, Mr. Malthus does not expressly and repeatedly declare that political institutions are but as the dust in the balance compared with the inevitable consequences of the principle of population; and whether he does not treat with the utmost contempt all those, who not being in the secret of "the grinding law of necessity," had like the Edinburgh Reviewer, superficially concluded that moral, political, religious, and other positive causes were of considerable weight in determining the happiness or misery of mankind? It were to be wished that the author, instead of tampering with his subject, and alternately holding out concessions, and then recalling them, had made one bold and honest effort to get rid of the bewildering effects of his original system, by affording his readers some clue to determine, both in what manner and to what extent other causes, independent of the principle of population, actually combine with that principle (no longer pretended to be absolute and uncontrollable) to vary the face of nature and society, under the same general

---

[5] Cf. *Hamlet,* III, i, 85.

law, and had not left this most important *desideratum* in his work, to be apocryphally supplied by the ingenuity and zeal of the Reviewer?

12. Whether Mr. Malthus does not uniformly discourage every plan for extending the limits of population, and consequently the sphere of human enjoyment, either by cultivating new tracts of soil, or improving the old ones, by repeating on all occasions the same stale, senseless objection, that, *after all,* the principle of population will press as much as ever on the means of subsistence; or in other words, that though the means of subsistence and comfort will be increased, there will be a proportionable increase in the number of those who are to partake of it? Or whether Mr. Malthus's panic fear on this subject has not subsided into an equally unphilosophical indifference?

13. Whether the principle of moral restraint, formerly recognized in Mr. Malthus's latter writings, and in reality turning all his paradoxes into mere impertinence, does not remain a dead letter, which he never calls into action, except for the single purpose of torturing the poor under pretence of reforming their morals?

14. Whether the avowed basis of the author's system on the poor laws, is not the following: that by the laws of God and nature, the rich have a right to starve the poor whenever they (the poor) cannot maintain themselves; and whether the deliberate sophistry by which this right is attempted to be made out, is not as gross an insult on the understanding as on the feelings of the public? Or whether this reasoning does not consist in a trite truism and a wilful contradiction; the truism being, that whenever the earth cannot maintain all its inhabitants, that then, by the laws of God and nature, or the physical constitution of things, some of them must perish; and the contradiction being, that the right of the rich to withhold a morsel of bread from the poor, while they themselves roll in abundance, is a law of God and nature, founded on the same physical necessity or absolute deficiency in the means of subsistence?

15. Whether the Edinburgh Reviewers have not fallen into the same unwarrantable mode of reasoning, by confounding the real

funds for the maintenance of labour, *i.e.* the actual produce of the soil, with the scanty pittance allowed out of it for the maintenance of the labourer (after the demands of luxury and idleness are satisfied) by the positive, varying laws of every country, or by the caprice of individuals?

16. Whether these two things are not fundamentally distinct in themselves, and ought not to be kept so, in a question of such importance, as the right of the rich to starve the poor by system?

17. Whether Mr. Malthus has not been too much disposed to consider the rich as a sort of Gods upon earth, who were merely employed in distributing the goods of nature and fortune among the poor, who themselves neither ate nor drank, "neither married nor were given in marriage," [6] and consequently were altogether unconcerned in the limited extent of the means of subsistence, and the unlimited increase of population?

18. Lastly, whether the whole of the reverend author's management of the principle of population and of the necessity of moral restraint, does not seem to have been copied from the prudent Friar's advice in Chaucer?

> Beware therefore with lordes for to play,
> Singeth Placebo:
> To a poor man men should his vices tell,
> But not to a lord, though he should go to hell.[7]

Nov. 21, 1810.

---

6 Matthew, XXII, 30.
7 *The Canterbury Tales,* "The Somnour's Tale," 2074-2077.

No. 37

To Thomas Hardy [1]

Hazlitts, 448-449.
Address: Mr. Hardy/Boot-Maker/Fleet Street, London.

Sunday evening
[May or June 1811] *

Dear Sir,

I was obliged to leave London without discharging my promise,[2] the reason of which was that I was myself disappointed in not receiving £20 which was due to me, £10 for a picture,[3] and £10 for revising a manuscript.[4] I am at present actually without money in the house. If you can defer it till October, when I shall be in London to deliver some Lectures,[5] by which I shall pick up some money, I shall esteem it a favour, and shall be glad to pay you the interest from the time I was in London last. Hoping this delay will be no particular inconvenience, and that you will think it unavoidable on my part, I remain, yours respectfully,

W. Hazlitt.

Winterslow, Salisbury

---

* Cf. Howe, p. 124n.

[1] (1752-1832). Political reformer and bootmaker who had been tried for high treason in 1794 with Holcroft and Horne Tooke, but acquitted.

[2] To pay for his boots.

[3] Of an unidentified "handsome young man" which "had been sent home with an abusive letter by the mother," according to Crabb Robinson *(Diary,* 15 April 1811, I, 30).

[4] He may still have hoped to publish his *History of English Philosophy.*

[5] The Lectures on English Philosophy which, however, were not delivered until January-April 1812. Cf. Letter 34.

No. 38

To Thomas Robinson

MS. Dr. Williams.

July 18, 1811 *

Dear Sir,

I was quite ashamed to receive your letter, and know not what to answer. I have the picture by me, and brought it down with a full intention to set about improving it immediately.[1] I have however put it off from day to day and week to week first from an unfortunate habit that what I ought to do, I seldom do, and secondly from a fear of doing away what likeness there is without mending the picture. I will however do what I can to it before I come to town in October, and will then leave it with your brother. Till then I do not forget that I am your debtor.

I am glad to hear that Mr. Clarkson's [2] picture is thought like, and only wish that it were what it should be. Hoping you will excuse this lame answer, and with respects to Mrs. Robinson, I remain, Dear Sir, your obliged humble servant,

W. Hazlitt.

Winterslow.

---

* The editors are indebted to John Creasey, Librarian of Dr. Williams' Library for the correct dating of this letter.

[1] Hazlitt was still working on the picture of Crabb Robinson's brother in the following year: "24 Dec. 1812. Called late on Charles Lamb. The party there. Hazlitt, I was gratified by finding in high spirits; he finds his engagement with Perry as Parliamentary reporter very easy, and the four guineas per week keep his head above water. He seems quite happy. I therefore ventured to ask about my brother's picture which he promises me; and I believe I shall get it" (Diary, I, 116).

[2] Thomas Clarkson (1760-1846) of Bury St. Edmunds, antislavery agitator and friend of the Robinsons and the Hazlitts.

No. 39

To Henry Crabb Robinson

MS. Dr. Williams.

October 29, 1811

Dear Robinson,

One of the things which I meant to do on coming to town was to call upon you: which I suppose was the reason, that is to say, cause I did not. In truth I was held in durance vile all the time I was there by one of the greatest miseries of human life, I mean a tight pair of boots, which made it impossible for me to move a step without being put in pain and out of humour, so that after a journey of a mile, I should not have had spirits left to open my case, which is briefly this. That I am going (in spite of the muse that presides over eloquence, I do not know her name) to deliver lectures, that I have got 30 subscribers, and want ten or a dozen more if I can possibly get them.[1] If therefore you could assist me by picking up one or two names, I can only say I shall be much obliged to you, and that the lectures will be as good as I can make them. The subjects of them will be nearly as follows. I have written 6. Lecture 1. On Hobbes's writings with a general view of philosophy since his time, shewing that succeeding writers have done little more than expand, illustrate, and apply the metaphysical principles distinctly laid down by him. Lect. 2. On Locke's Essay on the Human Understanding, or on the nature of *ideas,* shewing that all ideas necessarily imply a power for which

---

[1] Crabb Robinson records his attendance at the Lectures in his *Diary* entries for 14 and 21 January, 4 and 11 February. The first, "On Hobbes," was "delivered . . . in a low monotonous voice, with his eyes fixed intently on his book, not once daring to look on his audience," but by the second, "On Locke," he "delivered himself well . . . and was interrupted by applause several times." Hazlitt gave six lectures before the rest were cancelled. A "defective text" of nine lectures survives and is included in *Works,* II, 123-284. The last, "On Natural Religion," is missing.

sensation or simple perception does not account, *viz.* an understanding or comprehending faculty.

Lect. 3. On Berkeley's Principles of human knowledge, and on abstract ideas. In these two lectures I should attempt to prove in opposition to the modern opinion that we can have no complex or abstract ideas, that there are in reality no others, i.e. none which do not imply a power, to a certain extent, both of comprehension and abstraction.

Lect. 4. On self-love and benevolence.

Lect. 5. On Helvetius's doctrine on the same subject, and on Hartley's attempt to resolve all our affections and faculties into association of ideas.

6. On Bishop Butler's theory of the mind, or an account of the different original springs which move that various machine, such as sensibility, understanding, will, or the love of pleasure, the love of truth, and the love of action.

7. On the controversy between Price and Priestley or on materialism and necessity.

8. The same subject continued.

9. On Tooke's Diversions of Purley—theory of language and nature. 10. An argument on natural religion.

The price to each subscriber is two guineas, and they will be delivered about January. I remain, Dear Robinson, yours sincerely,

W. Hazlitt.

Winterslow, near Salisbury.

No. 40

To James Perry [1]

MS. Mr. and Mrs. Donald F. Hyde.

[August 1813] *

Dear Sir,

I have several papers of this kind by me, if they can be made of any use, such as—on classical education [2]—on advantages and disadvantages of education in general—on love of posthumous fame—on taste and seeing—on love of nature—on patriotism—causes of methodism—on envy among artists—characters of writers, painters, actors, &c. [3] I am

very respectfully your obedient
humble servant.
W. Hazlitt

Saturday

I should be very glad to write an answer to the Russian paper of 21st July as from a foreign journal. [4]

James Perry Esq.

---

* Cf. Baker, p. 193n.

[1] (1756-1821). Editor of the *Morning Chronicle*. In 1812, Hazlitt began his career in journalism as a reporter in the Press Gallery of the House of Commons. In 1813 Perry appointed him drama critic on the *Morning Chronicle*.

[2] Hazlitt's emergence as an essayist began in the *Morning Chronicle* for September of this year with the appearance of his first "Common-places"—*On the Love of Life* and *On Classical Education*.

[3] "On Posthumous Fame," *The Examiner* (22 May 1814), and *The Round Table*.
"Thoughts on Taste," *The Edinburgh Magazine* (October 1818 and July 1819).
"On Patriotism," *The Morning Chronicle* (5 January 1814) and *The Round Table*.
"On the Causes of Methodism," *The Examiner* (22 October 1815) and *The Round Table*.
"On Envy (A Dialogue)" *The Plain Speaker*.
"On the Literary Character," *Morning Chronicle* (28 October 1813) and *The Round Table*.
"On Actors and Acting," *The Examiner* (5 January 1817) and *The Round Table*.

No. 41

To the Curator, Lucien Bonaparte Collection

Hazlitts, 475.

[January 1815]

Dear Sir,

I will be much obliged to you if you will let me know the name and subject of Guerin's picture [1] at Lucien Buonaparte's.

Yours truly,
W. Hazlitt.

---

[4] A report from the "St. Petersburgh Papers" of 21 July, which appeared in the *Morning Chronicle* Foreign Affairs Section of 18 August 1813, recounted the attack of Napoleon's troops upon the "free corps" of infantry, cavalry, and Tirolese marksmen organized by the Prussian general Adolph Lutzow (1782-1834). During the Battle of Leipzig, the whole Corps, much outnumbered and already retreating, was completely annihilated. In the article, Napoleon is described as one "guided by irreligiousness and a covetousness for their neighbour's property," who "turned to his own use all vices and spread his influence over the whole continent of Europe," reducing "all nations to slavery," and bent upon "the destruction of the world." Hazlitt's offer of a reply "as from a foreign journal" must have been rejected, since none appeared in the *Chronicle.* This and Letter 41 are examples of his constant interest in Napoleon.

---

[1] Pierre Narcise Guerin's "Return of Marcus Sextus" is discussed along with other paintings in the article on "Lucien Buonaparte's Collection" in the *Champion* of 22 January 1815 (*Works,* XVIII, 87). The collection was sold at Buchanan's Gallery on 6 February 1815.

No. 42

To Francis Jeffrey [1]

MS. Yale.
Address: Francis Jeffrey, Esq./Edinburgh.

Feb.ry 15, 1815

Dear Sir,

You need hardly be assured of the gratification I have felt in receiving your very obliging letter. You have however quite misunderstood what I said about *a beginning*. What I meant was a beginning for the Review, and not to write any more about the Wanderer.[2] I meant to have done with it at once. Perhaps however in that case, it ends too abruptly and cavalierly. If so, an extract or two might be added.[3] I return you my thanks for your obliging expressions respecting the article. As to the rest, it is entirely in your hands, if you will be at the trouble of pruning its excrescencies. I had only calculated on its making a sheet and a half. The note about the Duke of Wellington I give up beforehand, but I confess I should like to see his Majesty mounted *con amore*.[4] But I

---

[1] (1773-1850), one of the founders of the *Edinburgh Review* and its first editor from 1802 to 1829. Upon being elected Dean of the Faculty of Advocates, Jeffrey resigned the editorship and was succeeded by Macvey Napier. In 1834 he was appointed a judge in the Court of Session, Edinburgh, and became Lord Jeffrey.

[2] Hazlitt's first contribution to the *Edinburgh Review* of February 1815 was an appraisal of Fanny Burney's novel *The Wanderer*. Because he was "compelled to speak so disadvantageously of the work of an excellent and favourite writer," he devoted most of the article to a criticism of the English novel and called it "Standard Novels and Romances." His just remarks about *The Wanderer* prompted a reproachful letter from Fanny's brother Martin, who "must consider it [the review] as the termination of our acquaintance." Howe, p. 167.

[3] Jeffrey did not, however, add any extracts from *The Wanderer* lest they detract from Hazlitt's criticism.

[4] No "note" on the Duke appeared in the *Edinburgh Review*, but he figures prominently in *Political Essays* and the *Life of Napoleon*. Hazlitt regarded Wellington as an over-ambitious egotist but appreciated his skillful and strong military leadership.

know that I am somewhat "splenetive and rash" [5] and submit the whole to your decision. I will get Sismondi [6] immediately. I should be glad to know whether you wish it for the next number of the review after the present one is out.

I remain, Dear Sir, very respectfully your obliged humble servant,

W. Hazlitt.

19 York Street
Westminster.

P.S. Sir James Mackintosh [7] is I understand in town, and I should have been happy to have conveyed your message, but I have not the honour of a personal acquaintance with him.

---

[5] *Hamlet,* V, i, 283.

[6] J.C.L. Simonde de Sismondi, *De la Littérature du Midi de l'Europe* (1813).

[7] Hazlitt had read Mackintosh's *Vindiciae Gallicae* (1791), an answer to Burke's *Reflections on the Revolution in France,* while at the New College, and had attended Mackintosh's lectures. In *The Spirit of the Age* he refers to him as "a political and philosophical juggler." In 1814 Crabb Robinson records that Hazlitt "is become an *Edinburgh Reviewer* through the recommendation of Lady Mackintosh," who had been so impressed with his articles on art in the *Champion* that she had praised him to the editor, John Scott, and had described Hazlitt as a "clever writer" to Jeffrey. But Hazlitt did not know Sir James personally. For further information on this point, see Professor Stanley Jones' comment that "this recommendation is likely to have been more Hazlitt's idea than her own." He then cites "An unpublished letter of 16 November 1814 from Sir James in Paris to his wife in London . . ." in support of his view. Cf. "Nine New Hazlitt Letters and Some Others," *Etudes Anglaises, Année 19, no. 3* (juillet-sept. 1966), p. 264.

No. 43

To Francis Jeffrey

MS. Yale.
Address: Francis Jeffrey, Esq./Edinburgh.

(PM February 19, 1815)

Dear Sir,

I ought to have mentioned yesterday that I think myself the part in the beginning after "Parson Adams sitting over his ale in Sir T. Booby's kitchen," on to a "sneaking fellow" might be omitted by adding an, etc. after kitchen.[1] Also the note about Defoe and the Duke of Wellington. Also for the names of Mrs. Opie and Miss Hamilton [2] might be substituted "certain writers," and the mention of Mrs. Radcliffe and Mrs. Inchbald (both favourites of mine) might be omitted altogether. The coach is setting off, and I am going into the country for a few days to repose on the satisfaction which your letter has given me.[3]

I am Dear Sir, your most obliged humble
servt.,
W. Hazlitt.

---

[1] "Standard Novels and Romances," *Works,* XVI, 5-24, was revised according to the changes suggested in this letter.

[2] Elizabeth Hamilton (1758-1816), Scottish novelist, author of *The Cottagers of Glenburnie.* For criticism of Amelia Opie's *Father and Daughter* see *A View of the English Stage, Works,* V, 268. For Mrs. Ann Radcliffe and Mrs. Elizabeth Inchbald, cf. "On the English Novelists," *Works,* VI, 123, 162, and *passim.*

[3] Jeffrey's praise of "Standard Novels and Romances."

No. 44

To Francis Jeffrey

MS. Yale.
Address: Francis Jeffrey, Esq./Edinburgh.

April 20, 1815

Dear Sir,

I received your obliging favour of the 17th this morning.[1] I have
not yet seen the Review, but I am quite satisfied of the propriety of
the alterations (for I am very sensible of my want of discretion in
these matters) and I am very glad to have got off so well in my first
adventure. I intend to do better before long. I will send you the
Sismondi in about six weeks, if that will do, and shall attend to
your suggestions in manufacturing it.[2] I think I may also make out
a short article about Rousseau and perhaps a comparison between
him and Voltaire, as well as I am able.[3] I have been reading
Spursheim,[4] and think I could "carve him like a dish fit for the
Gods," unless this has been already done to your hands. Between
ourselves, would you have any objection to let me loose on Lord
Castlereagh and the Congress in a political article? [5] I am not very

---

[1] Payment for "Standard Novels and Romances."

[2] The review of Sismondi's *Literature of the South* appeared in June 1815.

[3] No article on them was published in the *Edinburgh Review,* although Hazlitt
did contribute "On the Character of Rousseau" to *The Examiner* for 14 April 1816.

[4] J. G. Spurzheim, phrenologist, whose *Physiognomical System, founded on an
Anatomical and Physiological Examination of the Nervous System in general, and of the Brain
in particular* appeared in this year and interested both Coleridge and Hazlitt. The
latter devoted his essay "On Dreams" to a consideration of somnambulism and its
effect on the mind as related by Spurzheim. A review, "The Doctrines of Gall and
Spurzheim" was included in the June 1815 issue. The *Wellesley Index* (I, 454)
attributes it to John Gordon, and possibly others.

[5] Castlereagh represented England at the Congress of Chatillon (February and
March 1814) where, according to Hazlitt, he hindered the achievement of peace
between England and France. Cf. "On the Courier and Times Newspapers," the
leading article in *The Morning Chronicle* for 21 January 1814, *Works,* VII, 34. No
article appeared on the subject in the *Edinburgh Review.*

well read in the modern novelists: for in truth I hate to read new books, and my general rule is never to read a book that I have not read before. Of this practice I begin however to repent. By the bye, I am deep in Rousseau, Werter, Mrs. Inchbald, Mrs. Radcliffe & the Princess of Cleves.[6] The immediate question in your letter you will find answered by the signature at the end of this.[7] I am sorry to hear you have been unwell, and hope that by this time you are perfectly recovered. I need not say I am sure that I shall be both proud and happy to see you when you visit London. I have only to thank you once more for the frankness and liberality of your very obliging letter, and to subscribe myself, Dear Sir, very sincerely and respectfully, your obliged servt.,

[Signature removed]

19 York Street
Westminster

---

[6] A passage from Goethe's *The Sorrows of Werther* is used as an illustration in "On Beauty," *The Examiner,* 4 February 1816 *(Works,* IV, 70). For his criticism of the novels of Mrs. Inchbald and Mrs. Radcliffe cf. "On the English Novelists," *Works,* VI, 125-129. Hazlitt may have been reading *The Princess of Cleves* (1679) by Marie Madeleine Motier, Countess de la Fayette, in Elizabeth Griffith's translation, *A Collection of Novels,* 1777.

[7] Because Hazlitt nearly always signed his first name with the initial "W.," and his contributions to periodicals are either signed "W. H.," or left unsigned, Jeffrey had asked for his full name, which probably accounts for the signature having been torn out of this letter.

No. 45

To Francis Jeffrey

MS. Yale.
Address: Francis Jeffrey, Esq./Edinburgh.

May 1, 1815.

Dear Sir,

I wrote in answer to your favour of the 17th last Thursday week.[1] I begin to be apprehensive that some accident may have happened to the letter, which I gave to another person to put in thè post. The points in it (in case you have not received it) were that my christian name is William. Thàt Sismondi will be ready in five weeks from this time, or sooner if you require it,[2] and that if Spursheim is not done by any one else, I think I could make a hash of it. There is very good scope in it for speculations on character, physiognomy, and general metaphysics. I have seen the review,[3] and am proud of having required so few corrections.

I remain, Dear Sir, your obliged & very
respectful humble servant,
Wm. Hazlitt.

P.S. Perhaps Schlegel would make a future article.[4] I intend in Sismondi to collate the Italian and English poets.[5] In Schlegel there might be a comparison between Shakespeare and the French and german drama.[6] I am afraid you will begin to think me an *undertaker* more than a critic!

---

[1] Cf. the preceding letter.

[2] It appeared sooner—in the June 1815 issue.

[3] "Standard Novels and Romances," February 1815.

[4] August Wilhelm von Schlegel (1767-1845) delivered in Vienna in 1808, lectures on *Literature* and *Dramatic Art,* primarily on Shakespeare. They were published between 1809 and 1811; then translated (1815) into English by John Black, former colleague of Hazlitt on the *Morning Chronicle.* Hazlitt discussed the lectures in an article for the *Edinburgh Review* for February, 1816.

[5] Since Hazlitt knew little Italian, Leigh Hunt probably provided the translations and was "perhaps called into consultation over the review in general" (Notes, *Works,* XVI, 422).

[6] Cf. the last part of the review, *Works,* XVI, 90-99.

No. 46

To Charles Ollier [1]

Four Generations, I, 115-116.

19 York Street, Westminster
Saturday morning.
[May 1815] [2]

Dear Sir,

I feel myself exceedingly obliged by your kind attention with respect to your musical treat. I am afraid from unavoidable circumstances I shall not be able to avail myself of it. I have to get something done by the end of next week, which obliges me to practise a great deal more self-denial than I like. If I do not pay my respects to Corelli,[3] it is because I am held fast by half-a-dozen of his countrymen. If I can, however, I will escape from them. I am, Dear Sir, Your obliged very humble servant,

W. Hazlitt.

---

[1] (1788-1859), Publisher of Keats's *Poems,* 1817 and Hazlitt's *Characters of Shakespear's Plays* in the same year.

[2] W. C. Hazlitt's date, PM 4 October 1815, is incorrect. The article which Hazlitt was writing on Sismondi's *Literature of the South* and referred to here—"held fast by half-a-dozen of his countrymen"—appeared in the June 1815 *Edinburgh Review.* Cf. Howe, pp. 167-168.

[3] Archangelo Corelli (1653-1713), Italian violinist and composer. Hazlitt was either invited to a concert of Corelli's music or he has confused him with Domenico Corri (1746-1825) a member of a well-known musical family that had settled in London.

No. 47

To Francis Jeffrey

MS. Yale.
Address: Francis Jeffrey, Esq./Edinburgh.

[Spring 1815] *
Dear Sir,
I wished very much to have your approbation for doing between this and Christmas two articles, one of Scott's edition of Swift,[1] containing a view of the literature of Queen Anne, and the other of Buhle's history of modern philosophy, a subject to which I have paid some attention.[2] The work seems learned and able. My friend Mr. Hunt has desired me to communicate to you a wish on his part to contribute an occasional article to the Edinburgh Review, and mentioned as a work which he thought himself competent to handle, Nott's reprint of Lord Surrey's poems.[3]

I am Dear Sir respectfully and truly your
obliged humble servant,
W. Hazlitt.

P.S. I propose to send the conclusion of Sismondi in time for the next number, if you do not countermand it.

---

* Cf. Baker, p. 209.

[1] Jeffrey reviewed the edition in September, 1816.

[2] Hazlitt was not encouraged to review the French translation *(Histoire de la Philosophie Moderne)* of the *Geschichte der neuren Philosophie* by Johann G. Bühle (1763-1821).

[3] Hunt was released from prison in February 1815 after serving two years for printing remarks about the Prince Regent's morals in *The Examiner*. Although a review of Nott's *Surrey* appeared in the *Edinburgh Review* for December 1816, there is no evidence that Hunt wrote it.

No. 48

To Francis Jeffrey

MS. Yale.
Address: Francis Jeffrey, Esq./Edinburgh.

July 18, 1815

Dear Sir,

I should be much obliged to you to make the following corrections in the article on Sismondi.[1]

In the beginning of the account of Dante for "the external image" read "external appearance."

Imagery the French certainly have not, which the word image would imply. What I mean is that all their ideas are positive and definite or formal.

The other is a mistake of fact. The description of Celleno in Spenser is in the Cave of Mammon, and not in the Cave of Despair.[2] I was much obliged by your indulgence to me this time, and hope to stand less in need of it in future.

I remain Dear Sir very respectfully
your obliged humble servant,
Wm. Hazlitt

---

[1] This letter arrived too late to enable the revisions, and the article appeared as Hazlitt had first written it.

[2] The correction was not made and the review contains the error *(Works,* XVI, 54).

No. 49

To the Editor of *The Examiner*

The Examiner, October 29, 1815.

Sir,

You some time ago inserted in your Paper a letter from *A Mechanic,*[1] who seemed strangely puzzled by a learned friend of his, who thwarts him in all his notions, political, moral, domestic and economical, by interrogatories put to him out of Mr. Malthus's *Essay on Population.* I do not know whether your Correspondent has got rid of his troublesome acquaintance; but if he has not, I think he will be able to do it by putting to him the following questions as to the merits of Mr. Malthus and his work, which I met with in the course of my reading this morning, and which it appears to me to be incumbent on the admirers of that gentleman to answer, Aye or No.

[*Here follow* "*Queries Relating to the Essay on Population.*" *Cf. Letter 36* .]

Thus far, Sir, my author. The drift of these questions will be sufficiently intelligible to the adepts in the system; or if they should require a commentary, I shall be happy to supply it in any other part of your Paper, but the Round Table.

I am, Sir, your obedient servant,

Estesi.[2]

---

[1] Round Table No. 26, *Examiner* (15 February 1815).

[2] An English spelling of ΕΣΤΝΣΕ, meaning "He hath stood," taken from Coleridge who used it to sign his poems published in the *Morning Post* (1802-1803). As Coleridge explained to William Sotheby, "it is in truth no more than S. T. C. written in Greek. Es tee see (Greek ees-tay-see) cf Note 2" *(Collected Letters,* II, 867). Coleridge and Hazlitt shared similar views of Malthus's "falsely worded" truisms. Writing to Josiah Wedgwood on 21 May 1799 Coleridge expresses his opinion of the *Essay on Population* as "exceedingly illogical" and notes Wallace's precedence. Hazlitt no doubt took some of his points about Malthus from conversations with Coleridge prior to 1805.

No. 50

To Francis Jeffrey

MS. Yale.
Address: Francis Jeffrey, Esq./Edinburgh.

Nov. 20, 1815.

Dear Sir,

I am exceedingly sorry it has so happened that I could not get the Review of Schlegel ready in time.[1] But circumstances absolutely prevented me.[2] I hope to send it you in a fortnight or three weeks' time, so that it will be early for the next, if it should be approved of by you. I am afraid it will make three sheets. I received your bill for 45£ for which however you are not indebted to me. You sent me 25£ in the spring for the novels and romances. If you will let me know what it is your intention to allow for Sismondi, I will remit you the balance in your favour. I recollect nothing to add but to express my obligations to your kindness, and that I am, Dear Sir, your very respectful humble servant

W. Hazlitt.

P.S. The chief topics of the Review[3] I am about will be the differences between the classical and modern style, and a review of the Greek and French theatres, and Shakespeare. The work has only been out a few days. I had the copy from the Translator.[4]
19 York Street, Westminster.

---

[1] It did not appear until February 1816.

[2] The defeat of Napoleon and his "captivity in St. Helena" had "prostrated" Hazlitt who also had to contribute a dramatic article every week to *The Examiner* as well as a Round Table essay.

[3] Of Schlegel.

[4] John Black (1783-1855), a former colleague of the Press Gallery on the *Morning Chronicle;* he succeeded Perry as Editor of the *Morning Chronicle* in 1817.

No. 51 [1]

To Archibald Constable [2]

MS. Edinburgh.
Address: A. Constable, Esq. Walker's Hotel, 10 Bridge Street,
Blackfriars.

Dec. 18 19 York Street, Westminster
(endorsed: 1815)

Dear Sir,
I inclose what I suppose will be sufficient for our purpose. If it should not be so, and if you will send me the proper form, I will copy it out. When I said I could not let you have the manuscript, I meant that I could let you have it *in print,*[3] which I imagine will do as well. I will forward down to you half of the collection the latter end of the week. Might I add (as a poor author) that it would be a convenience to me to have a bill at half a year, when the publication is complete? This would probably be *(above:* the) same thing to you and Messrs. Longmans. I have only to add the expression of my thanks for your friendly assistance in this undertaking and that

I am Dear Sir your obliged humble servant,
W. Hazlitt

---

[1] This letter and the six following letters (all to Archibald Constable) and one to James Balfour were first published by Professor Stanley Jones of the University of Glasgow in the *Etudes Anglaises, Année* 19, no. 3 (juillet-sept. 1966), pp. 266-277.

[2] It may be surmised that Hazlitt's business relations with Archibald Constable, publisher of the *Edinburgh Review,* began towards the end of 1815 when Constable, who had acquired the *Encyclopaedia Britannica,* was on a visit to London. Whether on advice from Constable or from Jeffrey or on his own initiative, Constable's editor Macvey Napier authorized a new article on the Fine Arts from Hazlitt for the proposed *Supplement* to the *Encyclopaedia.* Then either Constable made an offer to Hazlitt or the latter was emboldened to approach Constable for the republication in book form of specified "Round Table" essays which had already attracted attention in Hunt's *Examiner.* Although the two-volume edition (in small 8vo) did not appear until February of 1817, this letter apparently marks the formal beginning of the transaction.

[3] The first twenty-four subjects of the series had already appeared in print.

I agree to give Mr. Constable and Messrs. Longman and Co. the right to print one edition of a thousand copies of a work to be entitled The Round Table, or a collection of miscellaneous Essays, in consideration of Fifty Pounds to be paid in half a year after the publication, *(above:* the price of) any other edition remaining to be arranged afterwards, and the copy *(above:* right) remaining with the authors.

Wm. Hazlitt

The subjects to be as follows, or nearly so.[4]

1. Introduction.	L. Hunt
2. On the love of life.	
3. On classical education.	
4. On character of women.	L. Hunt
5. On egotism.	L.H.
6. On the Tatler by Steele.	
7. On the imagination.	
8. On the passions.	
9. On the character of Iago.	
10. On *(above:* decline) of modern comedy.	
11. On the literary character.	
12. On a country life.	
13. On patriotism.	
14. On Milton's Lycidas.	
15. On Milton's general character as a poet.	
16. On importance of manner.	
17. On Chaucer's Squire's Tale.	L.H.
18. On Dissenters.	
19. Character of John Buncle, a theological romance.	
20. On causes of Methodism.	
21. On poetical character.	L.H.
22. On means of making a sick-bed comfortable.	L.H.
23. On Midsummer Night's Dream.	
24. On the Beggar's Opera.	
25-8.On Sir Joshua Reynolds' Discourses and pictures.	
29. On posthumous fame.	

---

[4] For an interesting commentary on the differences between the proposed subjects and titles, and those which eventually made up the published *Round Table,* cf. Prof. Jones, ibid., pp. 266-269. Especial note is taken of Hazlitt's having discarded essays on philosophical topics.

30. On religious hypocrisy
31.-2. On Mr. Wordsworth's Excursion.
33. On Hogarth's marriage a la mode.
34-6. A day by the fireside   L.H.
37. Whether public institutions promote the fine arts.
38. On taste.
39. On beauty
40. Comparison between Henry VI and Richard II.
41. On pleasure derived from tragedy.
42. On dramatic illusion.
43. On merit.
44-6. On modern philosophy.
47. On good-nature.
48. On commonplace people.   L.H.
49. On commonsense.
50. On acting, and actors.

No. 52

To Macvey Napier [1]

MS. British Library.

January 10, 1816.

Sir,

I received your obliging letter about a fortnight ago, and have to apologise for not answering it sooner. I mentioned to Mr. Constable that I would do such an article as you require by the middle of February, if I could possibly. I am now pretty sure of being able to do it by that time. I shall endeavour to supply what is wanting on the subject of the Fine Arts in the original article in the Encyclopedia Britannica. I suppose it will not be necessary to repeat the same things over again.

I remain, Sir, your very obliged obedient servant
W. Hazlitt.

---

[1] (1776-1847). Editor of the *Supplement* to the *Encyclopaedia Britannica* which Archibald Constable was publishing. Napier succeeded Jeffrey as editor of the *Edinburgh Review* and served from 1829 to 1847. Hazlitt's article on the Fine Arts appeared in the first volume of the *Supplement,* 1816, and was reprinted in 1824. Cf. *Works,* XVIII, 111-124.

No. 53

To Macvey Napier

MS. British Library.

19 York Street, Westminster
9 Feb. 1816.

Sir,

I received your obliging letter this day, and am glad of the additional time you give me. I hope to be ready then without fail. The Report you speak of to the French Institute [1] must be very curious, and I should be happy to see it, if you will send it me up. I propose to make the article [2] turn on the style of the different great works of art, on the causes that have produced them, and on the prospect of their revival at the present period. If you see any fault in this idea, you would oblige me by suggesting any alteration. I am Sir

very truly your obliged
humble servt.
W. Hazlitt

---

[1] The Institute was a group of scientists and men of letters which replaced the French Academy during the Revolution. The Report Napier had mentioned was one which Napoleon had directed the Institute to prepare on Kant's philosophy. Hazlitt read it and remembered it in 1825 when he referred to it in a note to "Old English Writers and Speakers," and added: "It is difficult for an Englishman to understand Kant; for a Frenchman impossible" (*The Plain Speaker, Works*, XII, 324).

[2] "On the Fine Arts."

No. 54

To Leigh Hunt

London Mercury, March, 1923.
Address: Leigh Hunt, Esq./Vale of Health/Hampstead
Heath.

Feb. 15, 1816

Dear Sir,

I have read the story of Rimini [1] with extreme satisfaction. It is full of beautiful and affecting passages. You have I think perfectly succeeded. I like the description of the death of Francesca better than any. *This will do.*[2] You are very metaphysical in the character and passion, but we will not say a word of this to the ladies. I am, Dear Sir, Your obliged friend and servant,

W. Hazlitt.

I hope to come up on Sunday.
I like the line—

Formed in the very poetry of nature [3]

exceedingly.
The following appear to me among the most elegant—

And she became companion of his thought
Silence her gentleness before him brought,
Society her sense, reading her books,

---

[1] Although six years younger than Hazlitt, Leigh Hunt (1784-1859) was already a successful author when Lamb introduced them to each other in 1812. Except for the argument recorded in Letter 84, they remained friends until Hazlitt's death. In the *Edinburgh Review* of June 1816 Hazlitt reviewed Hunt's "Rimini," but it "was so heavily over-written by Jeffrey as to be regarded as his own" *(Works,* XVI, 420).

[2] An echo of Jeffrey's famous "This will never do" in his review of Wordsworth's *Excursion,* November 1814.

[3] Canto II, line 47

Music her voice, every sweet thing her
looks.[4]

Then for the philosophy I mean these—

And looking round her with a *new-born eye.*[5]

As if to seem so, was to be, secure.[6]

Again—

And most from feeling the bare contemplation
Give them fresh need of mutual consolation.[7]

The character of the two lovers improves on repetition. The effect
of the whole is equal to the particular passages.[8]

---

[4] Canto III, lines 247-250
[5] Canto III, line 525
[6] Canto III, line 588
[7] Canto III, lines 348-349. In his *Select British Poets* (1824), pp. 736-742, Hazlitt
included the whole of the Third Canto.
[8] One wonders whether, amidst the compliments of this letter, there is some
touch of hidden irony. Hazlitt tells us that he thinks the death of Francesca the
supreme poetic achievement of the poem; we are surprised to find at the climax of
that scene the following literally pedestrian description of the death agony:

> "She ceased, and turning slowly towards the wall,
> They saw her tremble sharply, feet and all.-"
>   Canto IV, lines 407-408

No. 55

To Archibald Constable

MS. Edinburgh.
Address: Archibald Constable Esq, Edinburgh.

19 York Street
Westminster.
Feb. 19, 1816
(Postmark FE 20 1816)

Dear Sir,

I sent off the first half of the Round Table some weeks ago, and I begin to fear some accident has happened to it or that you do not approve of the contents. Neither have I heard of the Review [1] from Mr. Jeffrey, so that I am getting *blue-devilish* on that score also. You would oblige me by letting me know at your leisure whether anything has been done with the Essays, and whether I shall send off the remainder. I had a letter from Mr. Napier this day giving me till the middle of March for the article on the Fine Arts, a respite which was very agreeable to me. I will send off the copy from here on the twelfth, if possible.[2]

I am Dear Sir your obliged very humble servant
W. Hazlitt

[1] A review of "Lectures on Dramatic Literature" by August Wilhelm von Schlegel and translated by John Black. The article may have suggested or at any rate encouraged his own *Characters of Shakespear.* The article appeared early in May in the delayed February issue of the *Edinburgh Review.*

[2] It was sent on March 18.

No. 56

To Macvey Napier

MS. British Library.

[March 20, 1816] *

Dear Sir,

I enclose the remainder of the article, [1] and am anxious to know
your opinion of it. It contains the best part of what I know about
art. As to political innuendos, [2] and one or two other things
relating to proposed articles, you can omit or retain them at your
pleasure. I could make I think an original article on the subject of
the *Ideal,* but the engraving and architecture had better I conceive
be done by somebody else.[3] The account of Wilson [4] might be
shortened by adding immediately after "his [5]— landscapes are the
best"—in first page of the account of him—the concluding passage,
"Besides aerial perspective, he had a great—etc. of local colouring,"
or to that purpose. The whole is about 30 columns. I suppose I
could not have a proof in case you put what I have written to press.
I am Sir yours respectfully,

W. Hazlitt.

P.S. Please, Sir, to dele after "Parthenon" the words "and the
temple of Theseus," in the first Ms.

---

* The Ms letter is not dated by Hazlitt; in the *Athenaeum* (August 8, 1919) on
page 712, Howe says, "No date, Endorsed by recipient March 20, 1816." Cf.
Howe also, p. 178.

[1] "On the Fine Arts."

[2] The only political reference is to "red coats at Waterloo."

[3] There is no evidence that he wrote this article.

[4] Richard Wilson, R. A. (1714-1782), whose painting Hazlitt admired. Cf.
"Wilson's Landscapes at the British Institution," *Works,* XVIII, 24-28.

[5]. A word here is illegible.

No. 57

To Archibald Constable

MS. Edinburgh.
Address: Archibald Constable Esq., Edinburgh.

March 19, 1816
19 York Street. Westmr.
(PM: MAR 23 1816 BM)

Dear Sir,

I yesterday sent off the conclusion of the article on the Fine Arts to Mr. Napier. I wrote to you about a fortnight ago respecting the Round Table, as I began to be apprehensive from my not having heard anything repsecting it that some objection or difficulty had occurred. I should hope that is not the case, but I should be obliged if you could let me know shortly how the work stands. I should not trouble you about it but that just at present my affairs press, and I am anxious to know as nearly as possible what my resources are. I can send the remainder of the Essays whenever you wish. I would make any alteration you might suggest as to particular passages that might require to be softened. But I cannot help thinking the work would answer at least sufficiently to pay expenses and trouble, as I know they are talked of in London, and the Examiner has received several inquiries to know if it was not intended to collect them into a separate publication. I suppose the Edinburgh will soon be out to which I shall look with some anxiety.[1] I am, Dear Sir, your obliged humble servant

W. Hazlitt

---

[1] Hazlitt's review of Schlegel did not appear until early May when the belated February issue of the *Edinburgh Review* was published. However a letter from Constable to Hazlitt (MS Edinburgh) dated "Edinburgh (*crossed out:* April) 27 March 1816." may have brought Hazlitt some reassurance. It reads in part:

With this I have the pleasure of sending you proofs of the four first sheets of the Round Table which you will be so kind as revise and return as soon as possible. . . . The printing will proceed regularly and I should hope may be

No. 58

To Macvey Napier

MS. British Library.

34 Southampton Buildings
Holborn. [April 2, 1816] *

Dear Sir,
I was exceedingly gratified by the receipt of your very flattering letter of last week. I daresay that your objections to several of the observations are well-founded. I confess I am apt to be paradoxical in stating an extreme opinion when I think the prevailing one not quite correct. I believe however this way of writing answers with most readers better than the logical. I tried for some years to express the truth and nothing but the truth, till I found it would not do. The opinions themselves I believe to be true, but like all abstract principles, they require deductions, which it is often best to leave the public to find out. If you could let me have a proof, ¹ I would return it by the next day's mail: otherwise I should be obliged by your letting me have a copy at your convenience. The immediate purport of my writing was the following, which your

---

finished in (*crossed out:* April) May . . . I have not overlooked your work on the Philosophy of the Human Mind. I hope to be able to get you a few subscribers in this quarter.

I am with respect
Dear Sir,
Yours most truly
Archibald Constable

[For interesting speculation concerning the closing reference to Hazlitt's philosophical work, see Professor Stanley Jones' comments in *Etudes Anglaises* (previously referred to) pp. 271-272. For a different interpretation, see Professor Ralph Wardle's *Hazlitt*, p. 165.]

---

* Date written on envelope.
¹ Of the article "On the Fine Arts."

candour will excuse. I understood you to state in a former letter as the bookseller's arrangement that the money for any article would be paid when the article was printed. I suppose you will have nearly got through this so as to know the general size of it by this time. I have, Sir, a bill to take up tomorrow week, April 10, and if you could possibly transmit me fifteen pounds by that time, it would be a great assistance to me. The stagnation of money matters in this town is such that it is impossible to procure either by loan or anticipation, a single sixpence. I find this circumstance press particularly hard upon me at a time when I am clearing off the arrears into which my affairs had fallen owing to the aforesaid *logical way of writing*.[2] With every apology for this intrusion, I am, Dear Sir, with respect, your obliged humble servant.

W.H.

P.S. I received the proofs of the Round Table from Mr. Constable,[3] and shall return them tomorrow, or next day. I was thinking just now that the words *Colouring, Drawing, Ideal and Picturesque*[4] would make proper articles under the head of the Fine Arts, the metaphysics of which is in a very confused state at this day.

---

[2] His earnings from writing had to be increased in order to support his wife and two children; the younger, born in November 1815, died 19 June 1816.

3 Constable was negotiating for a collection in book form of the *Round Table* essays, which he published in 1817.

[4] "On the Picturesque and Ideal" was later written for *Table-Talk* (1821), *Works, VIII,* 317-320.

No. 59

To Macvey Napier

MS. British Library.

[Endorsed by recipient, July 17, 1816]

Dear Sir,

I write to ask you for directions about any article you might wish me to write for the next volume of the Encyclopedia. The last I find is very well spoken of by the artists here. I forgot in the hurry of my last to mention the receipt of the 15£ you were so obliging as to advance me upon it. I believe the whole would amount to 23£ at the rate I understood you to mention per column. Might I so far intrude upon your patience again as to solicit a remittance from you of whatever you deem the balance.[1] I believe I mentioned before that I thought the subject of Beauty [2] would make a good subject for an article. If you think proper, I would set about it immediately.

I am Dear Sir very respectfully your much obliged humble servant

W. Hazlitt.

P. S. If you see Mr. Jeffrey, would you be so good as to mention to him that I received his letter. I would have acknowledged the receipt of it immediately, but I have been waiting for another from him.

---

[1] Napier replied on 19 July: "I am quite ashamed at having so long delayed the small remittance which I now enclose as the balance for your excellent article" [On the Fine Arts] (MS. Letter, Edinburgh).

[2] The article on beauty in the *Supplement* was written by Jeffrey. For Hazlitt's treatment of the subject, cf. "On Beauty," *Works*, IV, 68.

No. 60

To Macvey Napier

MS. British Library.

22nd July 1816

Dear Sir,

The post is at the door and I have only time to return you my thanks for yours which I received this morning, with a note enclosed, and to say that I will get the articles you mentioned ready by the time.[1]

I am, dear Sir, your much obliged
humble servant
Wm. Hazlitt.

19 York St. West.

---

[1] Although Napier's letter does not survive, he had asked Hazlitt to write the articles on Barry, Basedow, Beckmann, Bettinelli, Bilfinger, and Bürger for the *Supplement.* Cf. Letter 66.

No. 61

To Archibald Constable

MS. Edinburgh.
Address: Archibald Constable Esq., Walker's Hotel, 10 Bridge
Street. Blackfriars.

July 24
19 York Street
(PM: 12 o'clock 25.JY.1816)

Dear Sir,

May I hope to see some more *Round Tables* before I die? I have
been and am exceedingly ill, but I think it would do me good, in
several respects, to have these volumes out. I have heard from Mr.
Napier *(above:* with a remittance.)

I am, Dear Sir, very respectfully,
your obliged humble servant,
W. Hazlitt

P.S. I can send the whole of the second volume.

No. 62

To Archibald Constable

MS. Edinburgh.
Address: Archibald Constable Esq., Walker's Hotel, 10 Bridge
Street, Blackfriars.

July 29.
19 York Street.
Westminster.
(PM: 29 JY 1816)

Dear Sir,

I shall be happy to see you on Wednesday at 2 oclock *(above:* in
Bridge Street). I shall also be proud to see you here any time before
you go out of town. I received the Round Tables, and will bring
them with me on Wednesday.

I am, Dear Sir, very truly
your much obliged humble
servant
W. Hazlitt

No. 63

To Francis Jeffrey

MS. Edinburgh.
Address: Francis Jeffrey/Edinburgh/North Britain.

3rd Jany 1817

Dear Sir,

I have been exceedingly unwell, or I should have answered your former letter before, and have got something for the Review. I cannot get either of the long articles done which I spoke of, on literature, and philosophy [1] for the present number, but I will attempt an article, which you shall have by the twenty-first, on Mr Coleridge's Lay Sermon, [2] if I do not hear from you to the contrary, it will be about a sheet, and enter into the skirts of the Kantean philosophy.

I am, dear Sir, yours faithfully
W. Hazlitt

---

[1] The letter containing the subjects of these articles has not been found. It is possible that he sent to Jeffrey early drafts of essays which were either published later (cf., "Self-Love and Benevolence," *Works,* XX, 419), or have not been identified as his.

[2] Hazlitt had already written for *The Examiner* two short "notices" of Coleridge's "Lay Sermon" *(The Statesman's Manual)* based upon the extensive advertisements of the book. On January 12, 1817 his "Literary Notice" of "Mr. Coleridge's Lay Sermon" appeared as a Letter to the Editor of *The Examiner* and is probably the article he here offers to Jeffrey, containing the germ of "My First Acquaintance with Poets" (1823). The long essay in the *Edinburgh Review* of December 1816 contains no reference to Kant and seems either to have been written entirely by Jeffrey or heavily overwritten by him. Cf. Letter 64.

No. 64

To the Editor of the Examiner [1]

Political Essays, London, 1819, 137-139 (reprinted).

Jan. 12, 1817

Sir,

Your last Sunday's "Literary Notice" has given me some uneasiness on two points.

It was in January, 1798, just 19 years ago, that I got up one morning before day-light to walk 10 miles in the mud, and went to hear a poet and a philosopher preach. It was the author of the "Lay-Sermon." Never, Sir, the longest day I have to live, shall I have such another walk as this cold, raw, comfortless one in the winter of the year 1798. Mr. Examiner, *Il y a des impressions que ni le tems ni les circonstances peuvent effacer. Dusse-je vivre des siècles entiers, le doux tems de ma jeunesse ne peut renaitre pour moi, ni s'effacer jamais dans ma mémoire.* [2] When I got there, Sir, the organ was playing the 100th psalm, and when it was done, Mr. C. rose and gave out his text, "And he went up into the mountain to pray, HIMSELF, ALONE." [3] As he gave out this text, his voice "rose like a steam of rich distill'd perfumes," [4] and when he came to the last two words, which he pronounced loud, deep, and distinct, it seemed to me, Sir, who was then young, as if the sounds had echoed from the bottom of the human heart, and as if that prayer might have floated in solemn silence through the universe. The idea of St. John came into my mind, "of one crying in the wilderness, who had his loins

---

[1] This letter, appearing originally in the *Examiner* for 12 January 1817 and bearing the caption "Mr. Coleridge's Lay-Sermon," is the seminal form of the essay entitled "My First Acquaintance with Poets," which Hazlitt contributed to the third number of Leigh Hunt's *The Liberal* in the spring of 1823.

[2] Cf. Rousseau's *Confessions.*

[3] Cf. St. John vi: 15.

[4] Cf. Milton's *Comus,* line 556.

girt about, and whose food was locusts and wild honey." [5] The preacher then launched into his subject, like an eagle dallying with the wind. *That* sermon, like *this* Sermon, was upon peace and war; upon church and state—not their alliance, but their separation—on the spirit of the world and the spirit of Christianity, not as the same, but as opposed to one another. He talked of those who had "inscribed the cross of Christ on banners dripping with human gore." He made a poetical and pastoral excursion,—and to shew the fatal effects of war, drew a striking contrast between the simple shepherd boy, driving his team afield, or sitting under the hawthorn, piping to his flock, as though he should never be old, and the same poor country-lad, crimped, kidnapped, brought into town, made drunk at an alehouse, turned into a wretched drummer-boy, with his hair sticking on end with powder and pomatum, a long cue at his back, and tricked out in the loathsome finery of the profession of blood.

> "Such were the notes our once-lov'd poet sung." [6]

And for myself, Sir, I could not have been more delighted if I had heard the music of the spheres. Poetry and Philosophy had met together, Truth and Genius had embraced, under the eye and with the sanction of Religion. This was even beyond my hopes. I returned home well satisfied. The sun that was still labouring pale and wan through the sky, obscured by thick mists, seemed an emblem of the *good cause:* and the cold dank drops of dew that hung half melted on the beard of the thistle, had something genial and refreshing in them; for there was a spirit of hope and youth in all nature, that turned every thing into good. The face of nature had not then the brand of JUS DIVINUM on it;

> "Like to that sanguine flower inscrib'd with woe." [7]

Now, Sir, what I have to complain of is this, that from reading your account of the "Lay-Sermon," I begin to suspect that my

---

[5] Cf. St. Matthew, iii: 3-4.
[6] Cf. Pope's *Epistle* to Robert, Earl of Oxford, line 1.
[7] Cf. Milton's *Lycidas,* line 106.

notions formerly must have been little better than a deception: that my faith in Mr. Coleridge's great powers must have been a vision of my youth, that, like other such visions, must pass away from me; and that all his genius and eloquence is *vox et preterea nihil:* for otherwise how is it so lost to all common sense upon paper?

Again, Sir, I ask Mr. Coleridge, why, having preached such a sermon as I have described, he has published such a sermon as you have described? What right, Sir, has he or any man to make a fool of me or any man? I am naturally, Sir, a man of a plain, dull, dry understanding, without flights or fancies, and can just contrive to plod on, if left to myself: what right then has Mr. C., who is just going to ascend in a balloon, to offer me a seat in the parachute, only to throw me from the height of his career upon the ground, and dash me to pieces? Or again, what right has he to invite me to a feast of poets and philosophers, fruits and flowers intermixed,— immortal fruits and amaranthine flowers,—and then to tell me it is all vapour, and, like *Timon,* to throw his empty dishes in my face? [8] No, Sir, I must and will say it is hard. I hope, between ourselves, there is no breach of confidence in all this; nor do I well understand how men's opinions on moral, political, or religious subjects can be kept a secret, except by putting them in *The Correspondent.*[9]

SEMPER EGO AUDITOR.

---

[8] Cf. *Timon of Athens,* III, vi.

[9] *The Correspondent:* consisting of letters, moral, political, and literary, between eminent writers in France and England. Dr. Stoddart arranged the English articles.

No. 65

To Francis Jeffrey

MS. Keynes.
Address: Francis Jeffrey, Esq./Edinburgh.

(PM: 4 March 1817)
Dear Sir,
I propose next week with your approbation to commence an article (taking Bühle or some other work, as a text) on the principles of modern philosophy.[1] It will run above two sheets of original matter, and will contain a view (I believe somewhat novel) of most of the disputed topics in metaphysics, such as the nature of an Idea, abstraction, association, language, self-interest, the love of pleasure, of truth, etc. I hope, if you approve of it, it will be no discredit to the Review; at least no greater than what I have been already guilty of. I would also be happy to bring down the account of novels and romances to the present time in the following number, if you have no objection. Perhaps Mr. Godwin's new novel would be a good opportunity.[2] If you let me know at your convenience whether the article on philosophical opinions would be acceptable, and when it would be necessary to have it ready, I would attend punctually to your wishes.[3]

I remain Dear Sir, your obliged and very faithful servant,

W. Hazlitt.

P.S. The volumes of the Round Table are out. Would you accept

---

[1] An article on Johann Buhle's *Histoire de la Philosophie Moderne,* Paris, translated by A.J.L. Jourdan, 6 vols. (1816), was written and forwarded to Jeffrey, but it did not appear in the *Edinburgh Review* and has not been found. Cf. Letter 63.

[2] None of these proposed articles appeared in the *Edinburgh Review.* Godwin's "new novel" was *Mandeville.*

[3] In a later essay, "On the Causes of Popular Opinion" (1828) *(Works,* XVII, 308-313), Hazlitt wrote: "When I wished to unburthen my mind in the *Edinburgh* by an article on English (not Scotch) metaphysics, J[effrey]. . . said he preferred what I wrote for effect, and was afraid of its being thought heavy—by the side of Macculloch!"

of a copy in my name from Mr. Constable?—If you see Mr. Napier, might I request you to tell him that I received his letter enclosing 15£ and should have answered it long ago, but that I have been so ill as to be unable to do almost anything.[4] What do you think of Wat Tyler for a flying article? [5]—W. H.

---

[4] Nevertheless, he had continued the dramatic criticism and political articles in *The Examiner,* and had recently completed his *Characters of Shakespear's Plays* for publication in the following month.

[5] Jeffrey reviewed Southey's *Wat Tyler;* Hazlitt's only contribution to the *Edinburgh Review* of this year was his review of *Biographia Literaria* in August, *Works,* XVI, 115-138.

No. 66

To Macvey Napier

MS. British Library.

March 13, 1817.

Dear Sir,

I conceive that nobody has been to blame in this business but myself. In fact, I have been very ill all the winter, and have had more to do than I could have got through properly, if I had been well. I will send you Burger [1] in the course of next week, and shall be happy at any time to do what I can for the Supplement. But I would have you to understand at first that I am a very unscientific person, and am therefore always liable to blunder on such matters.[2] All that I know anything about (except things of amusement) is metaphysics, and I know more of my own metaphysics than anybody else's. I should think that the article on Buonarotti [sic] might be made something of, a little different from the Biography.

I am, Dear Sir, very respectfully your obliged humble servant,

W. Hazlitt.

---

[1] The article on G. A. Bürger, German poet, was the last of seven contributions to the *Supplement*.

[2] He had also written the articles on J. B. Basedow, German educational reformer, and John Beckmann, German technologist, which had been based upon translations.

No. 67

To Francis Jeffrey

MS. Yale.
Address: Francis Jeffrey, Esq./Edinburg.

April 20, 1817

Dear Sir,
I take the liberty of troubling you with a copy of a work I have just finished relating to Shakespear. I thought perhaps if you approved of it you might take a brief notice of it in the Edinburgh Review.[1] I should not make this abrupt proposition, but from the necessity of circumstances. My friends may praise what I write, but I do not find that the public read it, and without that, I cannot live. If I could dispose of the copyright of the Round Table and of this last work,[2] I could find means to finish my work on Metaphysics,[3] instead of writing for three newspapers[4] at a time to the ruin of my health and without any progress in my finances. A single word from you would settle the question, and make what I write a marketable commodity.[5] The booksellers have kept me in a hole for the last ten years: do, Dear Sir, extend a friendly hand to

---

[1] Jeffrey wrote an enthusiastic and just appraisal of the *Characters of Shakespear's Plays* in the August 1817 *Edinburgh Review.*

[2] In January Constable had published *The Round Table,* a collection of forty essays by Hazlitt and twelve by Leigh Hunt. The book was not reprinted until 1841. *Characters of Shakespear's Plays,* "the first of Hazlitt's books to achieve immediate success" *(Bibliography,* 24), was published by Charles and James Ollier, but the second edition of 1818 was brought out by Taylor and Hessey.

[3] The "History of English Philosophy," the "Prospectus" having been printed in 1809.

[4] *The Examiner, The Morning Chronicle,* and *The Times.*

[5] Jeffrey's review no doubt had a good deal to do with the success of the first edition of the *Characters,* but the attack on it in *The Quarterly Review* appeared in June 1818: "Taylor and Hessey told me that they had sold nearly two editions of the *Characters of Shakespear's Plays* in about three months, but that after the Quarterly Review of them came out, they never sold another copy" ("On Living to One's Self," *Works,* VIII, 99).

help me out of it. I would not ask such a favour for myself, if I thought the mere notice of either of the trifles above alluded to would be any discredit to the high character of your Journal. I have had to write a new Preface to the Characters (a very bad one, as it usually happens in such cases) which has prevented me from sending the article on modern philosophy. But I will finish and send it off as soon as possible,—I hope in time for the next number, if it is admissible in other respects.[6] I remain, Dear Sir, with every apology for the contents of this letter, your obliged and respectful humble servant,

W. Hazlitt

---

[6] If Hazlitt did write an article on modern philosophy, as it would seem from this and Letter 65, it did not appear in the *Edinburgh Review*. However, from 1815 to 1817 he contributed several occasional pieces on philosophy to *The Examiner,* such as "Mind and Motive," "On the Doctrine of Philosophical Necessity," and "Mr. Locke a Great Plagiarist." The article which he here mentions was probably "On the Principle of Self-Love"—a theory which he had developed of "the Natural Disinterestedness of the Human Mind" in *An Essay on the Principles of Human Action* in order to refute the modern philosophers' overemphasis on the sensations and to refute likewise utilitarian self-interest. After Jeffrey's rejection, Hazlitt revised the article, changed the title to "Self-Love and Benevolence," and published it in *The New Monthly Magazine* in October, 1828. It is reprinted in *Works,* XX, 162-186. A comment by Patmore helps to explain the tone of this letter: "To think was and ever had been the business and the pleasure of his intellectual life."

No. 68

To Archibald Constable

MS. Edinburgh
Address: Archibald Constable, Esq., Edinburgh.

(PM: JUN 1 1817 BM)

Dear Sir,

I some time ago sent Mr. Jeffrey a volume which I have written for a friend, who wishes to dispose of the edition of 1000 copies for 200 guineas. Perhaps you might be willing to purchase it! [1] I do not know what Mr. Jeffrey's opinion [2] of it is, but I enclose you an extract from the Times newspaper, which may have some weight with it. I am afraid to ask after the Round Table: but I hope it will find its way. Would you favour me with a line in reply at your earliest convenience?

> I remain, Dear Sir, your much obliged
> faithful servant
> W. Hazlitt

May 29th

[*Attached to the sheet is a newspaper clipping, reading as follows:*]

Shakespeare: The lovers of the drama, and more particularly of the great master of it, may derive, we apprehend, considerable pleasure from a work written by Mr. W. Hazlitt entitled "Charac-

---

[1] Constable declined the offer. The work was printed by C.H. Reynell (possibly the "friend" referred to in the beginning of the letter) and sold finally by R. Hunter, and C. and J. Ollier. For discussion of printers and booksellers, see Jones, "Nine New Hazlitt Letters and Some Others," *Etudes Anglaise,* XIX, Année *19, No. 3,* Juillet-Sept., 1966, pp. 274-275.

[2] Jeffrey's opinion, complimentary in the main, appeared in the *Edinburgh Review,* No. LVI for August, appearing tardily on September 17, 1817.

ters of Shakespear's Plays." The observations have much of the ingenuity and depth of the famous German commentator Schlegel, without his efforts at system. We have not room for more than the following short passage; which we insert as a criterion of the justice of our eulogium:—"This is that *Hamlet* the Dane . . ."

[*Then follows an excerpt from the section on Hamlet.*]

No. 69

To Francis Jeffrey

MS. Yale.

June 13, 1817
19 York Street
Westminster

Dear Sir,

I received your obliging and very friendly letter this morning. I will set about finishing the article on philosophy immediately, and let you have it in a fortnight from this time.[1] With respect to what you say of my writing, I have no other objection to make than that it is too favourable. I confess to all the faults. I am sorry to say in reference to your very friendly suggestion that I am afraid I am unfit for almost any other profession than that of an author: but I hope soon to get out of my difficulties. Indeed, the obliging remittance you speak of will very nearly clear me of my old arrears, and at present my immediate receipts are greater than my outgoings. With respect to the Shakespear, I shall be satisfied if you find any thing to praise in it. I know it has plenty of faults. There was an eulogium and an extract from it in the *Times* the other day.[2] You may see by this that the politics of this great city are a little changed.

I am Dear Sir very respectfully your obliged and faithful servant,

W. Hazlitt.

---

[1] Cf. Letter 65.
[2] *The Times* of 28 May 1817; cf. Letter 68.

No. 70

To Francis Jeffrey

MS. Yale.
Address: Francis Jeffrey, Esq./Edinburgh.

(PM: 12 August 1817)

Dear Sir,

I sent off yesterday by the Edinburgh Mail an article or package on the Literary Life and Opinions.[1] It is I am afraid very long and desultory. But there are some things in it which I hope may tell. I shall send you a short article on a miscellaneous subject next week. I wish you could at your leisure favour me with a line to say whether you think the article will do, and also whether you think it likely you can *insinuate* The Shakespear Characters in the next no.[2] The book does very well, I understand, and your notice would at once lift me from the character of a disappointed author to that of a successful one. I have to thank you for your remittance of £50. Perhaps if you like my Biographical article *very much,* I might apply in *forma pauperis* for one of 30£ in advance for the one which I meditate on modern novels.[3] You have read the apothecary's speech in Romeo and Juliet, "My poverty," [4] etc. and will I hope excuse these renewed applications from Dear Sir, your obliged humble servant,

W. Hazlitt.

---

[1] "Coleridge's Literary Life," a review of the *Biographia Literaria,* appeared in the August issue.

[2] Cf. Letter 69.

[3] If completed, the article was not published in the *Edinburgh Review;* however, it may have formed part of "On the English Novelists" in *Lectures on the English Comic Writers, Works,* VI, 106-132.

[4] "My poverty but not my will consents," *Romeo and Juliet,* V, i, 75.

No. 71

To B. W. Procter [1]

MS. Unknown. Keynes (copy).

[April 1817]

Dear Procter,

Mr. Stodart [2] wishes me to ask you to dine with him today (at half past four) to meet Mr. Farren, [3] Mr. W. Irvine [4] and one or two others. Can you come? I shall start from St. Martin's Street, at 4 o'clock.

Yours ever, W. H.

---

[1] Bryan Waller Procter ("Barry Cornwall") (1787-1874), barrister, author, and friend of poets. Under the influence of Leigh Hunt, Procter wrote the poetical dramas *Marcian Colonna* (1820) and *A Sicilian Story* (1821) as well as a successful tragedy, *Mirandola,* in which Charles Kemble acted the part of Guido at Covent Garden in January 1821. He met Hazlitt at Lamb's in 1816 and saw much of him as a fellow contributor to the *London Magazine.* The first of Hazlitt's friends to write about him after his death, Procter's "Recollections" in the *New Monthly Magazine* for November 1830 are also the most perceptive of those that followed. As he wrote, Hazlitt was "a first-rate critic in matters connected with art and the theatres" and "was characterized as an acute and profound thinker."

[2] Publisher of *A View of the English Stage.*

[3] William Farren the actor, whose interpretation of Lord Ogleby in Garrick's *The Clandestine Marriage* Hazlitt admired.

[4] Washington Irving (1783-1859), whose visit to England is described in "American Literature—Dr. Channing," *Works,* XVI, 318 and in *The Spirit of the Age, Works,* XI, 183.

No. 72

To Archibald Constable [1]

MS. Edinburgh.

[January or February 1818]

Dear Sir,

I have taken the liberty of sending the bearer in case you should be able to assist me this morning.

I am, Dear Sir,
Your truly obliged
W. Hazlitt.

Saturday.

---

[1] Publisher of the *Edinburgh Review* and head of Constable and Company until his death in 1827, partly caused by his famous bankruptcy in 1826, which with his partner, James Ballantyne, involved Sir Walter Scott in enormous debts. Constable was at this time negotiating with Hazlitt for the publication of *Lectures on the English Poets,* but because they failed to reach a satisfactory agreement the book was brought out by Taylor and Hessey in April 1818.

No. 73

To Archibald Constable

MS. Edinburgh.

[January or February 1818]

Dear Sir,

I enclose a note of hand for 40£. I saw Mr. Reynolds [1] last night, and we arranged about the lectures. I remain, Dear Sir, your much obliged humble servant,

W. Hazlitt.

---

[1] John Hamilton Reynolds (1796-1852), a regular contributor to Constable's *Edinburgh Magazine,* represented the publisher in his negotiations with Hazlitt mentioned in the preceding letter. Wardle, p. 227n., offers a different explanation, making reference to an *Edinburgh Magazine* review of Hazlitt's *Lectures* by Reynolds and suggesting a later date.

No. 74

To Archibald Constable

MS. Edinburgh.

[January or February 1818]

Dear Sir,

I will do myself the pleasure of waiting on you in the morning at half past nine. I am, Dear Sir, your obliged, etc.

W. Hazlitt.

No. 75

To P. G. Patmore [1]

Hazlitts, 445.

[March, 1818]

Dear Sir,

I am very well satisfied with the article, [2] and obliged to you for it. I am afraid the censure is truer than the praise. It will be of great service, if they insert it entire, which, however, I hope.

Your obliged,
W. Hazlitt

---

[1] Peter George Patmore (1786-1855), father of Coventry Patmore, author and journalist, was at this time secretary of the Surrey Institution, a cultural group established by a "body of respectable persons in the middle classes of life," and London correspondent to *Blackwood's Edinburgh Magazine.* Patmore and Hazlitt met in February 1818 when Hazlitt delivered his "Lectures on the English Poets" at the Surrey Institution, and from this time until his death Patmore was one of Hazlitt's closest and most loyal friends, his confidant and the recipient of the famous letters written during the affair with Sarah Walker. In 1854 Patmore published *My Friends and Acquaintance,* a vivid record of his friendship with Hazlitt, Lamb, and other literary men.

[2] Patmore had shown him the MS. of his "Notice of Hazlitt's Lectures on English Poetry" published in *Blackwood's Magazine* for April, 1818.

No. 76

To Francis Jeffrey[1]

MS. Yale.
Address: Francis Jeffrey, Esq./Edinburgh.

May 12, 1818

My dear Sir,

I ought to have answered your friendly letter before, which I received in due course, with the 100£ draught inclosed. I hope it will set me on my legs again, as I shall pass the summer in the country, doing little, & thinking less. I purpose however among other nothings to send you two pretty long reviews, which may I fear tire ·your patience. I took the liberty to inclose to Mr. Henderson for you a copy of my Lectures.[2] You will see by that that there is an end of the question which I troubled you about in my letter.[3] I got in all (Lectures and copyright included) 200 guineas for them, which is very well for ten weeks work. I imagine I have to ask your pardon for some things in them. I have some thoughts of making an article on Drake's book,[4] taking the amusing anecdotes, and adding a little speculation on the age of Elizabeth, Protestantism, the Bible, translations from the classics, etc. I shall however send the metaphysics first—that there may be

---

[1] A reply to a letter from Jeffrey of 3 May 1818 which stated: "We cannot let a man of genius suffer . . . I take the liberty of enclosing £100, a great part of which I shall owe you in a few weeks, and the rest you shall pay me back in reviews whenever you can do so without putting yourself to any uneasiness. If you really want another £100 tell me so plainly, and it shall be heartily at your service" (*Hazlitts*, p. 442).

[2] *Lectures on the English Poets* which had been published shortly after their delivery at the Surrey Institution, beginning in January 1818.

[3] He had written to enquire about giving the Lectures in Edinburgh, and Jeffrey had discouraged it. Cf. Howe, pp. 230-232.

[4] Hazlitt probably wrote the review of Nathan Drake's *Shakespeare and His Time* (1817) in the January 1818 *Edinburgh Magazine,* but no article on Drake's book appeared in the *Edinburgh Review.*

[182]

time to alter the subject if necessary.[5] I remain Dear Sir with repeated thanks for your many kind indulgences, your truly obliged and humble servant,

W. Hazlitt.

P. S. Might I beg once more for my *nervous* article, [6] if it were possible.

---

[5] Perhaps "Self-Love and Benevolence" *(New Monthly Magazine,* October-December, 1828), or an essay that has not been discovered.

[6] This could be any one of several articles written early in this year and submitted to Jeffrey. The strongest possibility is a review by Hazlitt of Thomas Reid's *Inquiry into the Human Mind* which was sent to the Editor but never published. In his letter of 3 May 1818 Jeffrey refers to "your little paper on Dr. Reid's book." Because Hazlitt included Reid among "People with One Idea" *(Works,* VIII, 64), the review was probably very unfavourable and Jeffrey avoided publishing it lest it offend the philosopher's strong following on *The Quarterly Review.* Hazlitt may also have sent Jeffrey the essay "On Thought and Action," which contains a sarcastic remark about the Duke of Wellington's being "obliged to get Mr. Mudford to write the History of his Life." William Mudford, whom Hazlitt had succeeded on the *Morning Chronicle,* published in 1817 *An Historical Account of the Campaign in the Netherlands under the Duke of Wellington and Prince Blücher.*

No. 77

To Archibald Constable

MS. Yale.

Tuesday
July 28, 1818.

Dear Sir,

Could you by any possibility let me have on account the sum of fifty pounds? If you could, I would send you articles to that amount for the Magazine within the next two months on the subjects of which I have given in a list, [1] and which the Editors would then have ready by them for the next year. The occasion of my making this abrupt application is that I am going in the country for the rest of the summer, and I wish to leave all accounts clear behind me.

I am, Dear Sir, your much obliged & very
obedient servant,
W. Hazlitt.

---

[1] Hazlitt's list of articles for Constable's *Edinburgh Magazine* does not survive, though it comprised the four essays referred to as "nonsense" in Letter 78 as well as "Historical Illustrations of Shakespeare," "On Respectable People," and "On the Effects of War and Taxes." The latter was not published until October 1818 because Constable objected to "its general political cast." "Our present course," he wrote on 19 August, "is to avoid political discussions. What change we may make afterwards we do not know. We are much pleased with the art: itself; it is very good indeed" (MS. Letter, Edinburgh).

No. 78

To Macvey Napier

MS. British Library.

Winterslow Hut, near Salisbury.
Aug. 26, 1818

My dear Sir,

I received your favour yesterday, and am sorry to be obliged, from want of health and a number of other engagements, which I am little able to perform, to decline the flattering offer you make me.[1] I have got to write between this and the end of October an octavo volume of a set of Lectures on the Comic Drama of this country for the Surrey Institution, which I am anxious not to slur over, and it will be as much as I can do to get it ready in time.[2] I am also afraid, Sir, that I should not be able to do the article in question or yourself justice, for I am not only without books, but without knowledge of what books are necessary to be consulted on the subject. To get up an article in a review on any subject of general literature is quite as much as I can do without exposing myself. The object of an Encyclopedia is, I take it, to condense and combine all the facts relating to a subject, and all the theories of any consequence already known or advanced. Now where the business of such a work ends, is just where I begin, that is, I might perhaps throw in an idle speculation or two of my own, not contained in former accounts of the subject, and which would have very little pretensions to rank as scientific. I know something about Congreve, but nothing at all of Aristophanes, and yet I conceive the writer of an article on the *Drama* ought to be as well acquainted

---

[1] The article on the Drama for the Encyclopedia Supplement was written by Sir Walter Scott.

[2] *Lectures on the English Comic Writers,* April 1819.

with the one as the other. If you should see Mr. Constable, will you tell [him] I am writing *nonsense* for him as fast as I can.[3]

I remain, Dear Sir, your very respectful and obliged humble servant,

W. Hazlitt.

---

[3] The "nonsense" was "On the Ignorance of the Learned," "On Fashion," "On Nicknames," and "On Taste," all of which appeared in the *Edinburgh Magazine* (1818). The last three essays appear in *Works,* XVII, 44-66. The first title is in *Works,* VIII, 70-77.

No. 79

To Archibald Constable

Times Literary Supplement, 21 March 1936.

[September] 1818
19, York Street,
Westminster

Dear Sir,

I received your obliging communication a day or two after I got
back here. I have asked one or two friends what they thought
about the enclosed paper, [1] and they all think it beneath any kind
of notice. I do not feel tempted to this kind of personal warfare,
and one reason is, if I once entered into it, I should carry the war
into the enemy's quarters in a way that I do not wish to do.[2] I have
hitherto spared them comparatively. If however you think de-
cidedly otherwise, I will see about it.—As to your flattering
invitation to Edin^r., I feel disposed this way; but I must first get my
lectures done, which will not be till after Christmas day. They are
to be on the comic writers of Gt. Britain, etc. I am going to sell
them this time for £200 instead of £100. That is an improvement. I
have forwarded two articles for the Magazine, [3] the last of which I
am afraid was hardly in time. I think you might safely turn the
articles on taxes, [4] at least for the meridian of London. People here
have no objection to their being abused. Do you know anything of

---

[1] "Hazlitt Cross-Questioned," a violent, personal attack probably written by
John Lockhart in *Blackwood's Magazine* for August, 1818.

[2] He did retaliate in *A Reply to Z,* which, however, remained interred in the
Constable archives until it was discovered and printed by Charles Whibley for the
First Edition Club in 1923. Instead of publishing it himself, Hazlitt brought a
successful suit for libel against *Blackwood's* (*Works,* IX, 249).

[3] "On Nicknames" and "On Fashion," *Edinburgh Magazine* (September 1818).

[4] "On the Effects of War and Taxes," *Edinburgh Magazine* (October 1818).

the contents of the next Edinr. Review? I sent a long article for the last, but you know I am expelled from it.[5]

I am dear Sir your much obliged and obedient humble servant,

W. Hazlitt

P. S. In the article on the Ignorance of the Learned there was not one single sentence, or but one, taken from any thing else I had written.[6]

[*In the right-hand bottom corner, written vertically, in Hazlitt's hand:*]

W. Hazlitt. Westminster 1818.

---

[5] "Expelled" refers to a remark in *Blackwood's Magazine*. On 20 September Jeffrey replied: "It is quite false that you have been expelled from the E. R., tho it is not our principle to proclaim or acknowledge any name among our contributors." MS. Letter, Edinburgh. The article forwarded was on philosophy, but it has not been found. Jeffrey answered: "I am distressed with your metaphysics—the article is 5 times too long—you still quote enormously too much." Cf. Letter 76. In its place Hazlitt may have substituted the "Letters of Horace Walpole," which appeared in December, 1818, and has been accepted as by Hazlitt (*Works*, XVI, 138-152; *Wellesley Index*, I, 458.); but argument has been made for J. H. Reynolds as the author (cf. L. M. Jones, "Hazlitt, Reynolds, and the *Edinburgh Review*," *Studies In Bibliography*, XXIV, 342-346).

[6] In "Hazlitt Cross-Questioned," the essay "On the Ignorance of the Learned" is cited as an example of his attempt to "pass off for original communication a quantity of trash already printed in another publication." As Hazlitt points out, the only sentence taken from another work—*The Round Table*—is, "Learning is the knowledge of that which is not generally known."

No. 80

To Archibald Constable

MS. Edinburgh.
Address: Archibald Constable, Esq. Edinburgh.

(PM: SEP 21 1818 BM)

My dear Sir,

I would take it as a favour if you would get the enclosed Letter regularly delivered to Mr. Blackwood *(crossed out:* if you see no *(above:* absolute) reason to the contrary). In making my bargain the other day, the various fabrications in that article [1] were objected to me as lessening the value of my literary e (state). My writings are before the public: *(crossed out:* (person) al) *(above:* my) character I leave to my friends: (but) I conceive the law is the proper defence of my property. The same notice was to have been left with Murray some days ago, but I understand he is down at Edinburgh, arranging the downfall of such as love not the house of Bourbon.

I am, Dear Sir,
Yours respectfully and faithfully
W. Hazlitt

19 Sept.

[A clerical copy of Hazlitt's letter to Blackwood is as follows:]

Sir,

I apply to you as the proprietor of a periodical work entitled "Blackwood's Edinburgh Magazine' to request you will inform me who is the author of an article which appeared in the last number

---

[1] In the August issue of Blackwood's, in the article "Hazlitt Cross-Questioned," Hazlitt was represented as an uneducated ignoramus, one who outraged the purity and decency of simple good people, &c,&c. The same issue also contained contemptuous references to John Keats.

of that work called' Hazlitt Cross-Questioned' in order that I may institute legal proceedings thereon. Should you decline [2] complying with this request I shall immediately institute proceedings against you as the publisher.

I am Sir,
Your &c.

19 York Street
Westminster
19th Sept.
1818

---

[2] Blackwood responded with a curt note refusing to disclose the names of the authors of the offending article. On the 25th, Hazlitt wrote to James Balfour of Edinburgh authorizing him to sue Blackwood for damages.

No. 81

To James Balfour

MS Scottish Record Office.
(Endorsed: MANDATE Mr. Wm Hazlitt to James Balfour
W. S. 25th Sept. 1815)

London, Sept. 25, 1818

Dear Sir,

As Mr. William Blackwood, Bookseller in Edinburgh, the publisher of the periodical work entitled Blackwood's Edinburgh Magazine, has declined to inform me who is the author of an article which appeared in the number of that work for last month (August) called "Hazlitt cross-questioned" as requested in a letter from me to him of the 18th instant, I hereby authorise you to institute and follow out an action of Damages [1] at my instance before the Court of Session against him on account of his having published the above article in the said work.

I am, Sir,
your obedient servant
Wm. Hazlitt

---

[1] Early in October, Blackwood was summoned to appear before the Court of Sessions to defend himself against a suit for £2000 damages. Although Blackwood had refused to give up their names, Wilson and Lockhart had clumsily and inadvertently revealed that they were the authors of the Hazlitt libel. Blackwood, in examining the situation, became increasingly aware of the large and growing hostility felt towards his scurrilous publication. He arranged with Hazlitt to drop the suit in return for payment of £100 to Hazlitt personally and accountability for costs.

No. 82

To the Editor of the *Edinburgh Magazine*

Edinburgh Magazine, January, 1819.

13 November 1818

Mr. Editor,

I dare say you will agree with me in thinking, that whatever throws light on the dramatic productions of Shakespeare, deserves to be made known to the public. I have already, in the volume called *Characters of Shakespear's Plays,* shewn, by a reference to the passages in North's translation of Plutarch, his obligations to the historian in his Coriolanus, [1] and the noble way in which he availed himself of the lights of antiquity in composing that piece. I shall, with your permission, pursue this subject in the present and some future articles. The parallel is even more striking between the celebrated trial-scene in Henry VIII., and the following narrative of that event, as it actually took place, which is to be found in Cavendish's Negociations of Cardinal Wolsey, etc.

[A lengthy quotation follows; the source is the *Harleian Miscellany,* 1744-1746, VII, pp. 254-255; XII, p. 47. Hazlitt then concludes his letter:]

In another article I shall give some remarks on this subject, and the passages in Hollingshed on which Macbeth is, in great measure, founded.[2]

I am, Sir, your humble servant,
W. Hazlitt

---

[1] *Works,* IV, 218-220.

[2] The article on *Macbeth* has not been found, but see Lecture I of *The Age of Elizabeth, Works,* VI, 188. Concerning these historical illustrations of Shakespeare, cf. *Works,* XX, 410ff.

No. 83

To P. G. Patmore

Works, VI, 385.

Wednesday [4 February 1819]
19 York Street
Westminster

Dear Sir,

I conceive the Course of Lectures [1] which I had it in contemplation to propose through you to the Committee for next year on the Age and Literature of Q. Elizabeth would fall nearly into the following divisions.

1. On the effects of the Reformation on intellect and moral energy. Effects of the Translation of the Bible—of the Classics—Progress of letters throughout Europe—Voyages and Travels to the New World—Consequences of the Insular situation of England.

2. On the general state of English manners at this period.

3. Dramatic Writers compared with Shakespear. 1st. Beaumont and Fletcher; and Massinger.

4. The same general subject. Ford, Webster, Marlow, etc., etc. Puritanism of the following age. Otway. Imitations of the French. Decline of English Tragedy.

5. On the comedy before and after this period. Mother Bumby,[2] etc.

6. On the poetry (properly so called) of Queen Elizabeth's reign.

7. On the prose-writers, Sir Philip Sidney, Hooker, etc. Character of Lord Bacon's Works compared as to style with Sir Thos. Brown and Jeremy Taylor.

---

[1] Delivered at the Surrey Institution during November and December 1819 and published as *Lectures on the Dramatic Literature of the Age of Elizabeth.* The topics of the first two lectures were briefly considered in "Lecture I—Introductory." Patmore was Secretary of the Institution.

[2] *Mother Bombie* (1594) by John Lyly.

8 and last. The German Drama and its connection with modern philosophical paradoxes contrasted with the Drama of Shakespear's time.

If the foregoing sketch should be approved of, I shall be happy to set to work upon the Lectures almost immediately. I suppose you have heard of my positive success at Edinburgh,[3] and of my *negative success* in the Quarterly.[4]

I remain, Dear Sir, your much obliged and very
humble servant,
W. Hazlitt

G. P. Patmore, Esq. [sic]
Clapham.

---

[3] The settlement out of court of his libel action against *Blackwood's Magazine.*
[4] The unfair review of *Lectures on the English Poets* had just appeared in the *Quarterly Review.* It led to *A Letter to William Gifford, Esq., Works,* IX, 13-59.

No. 84

To Whitmore and Fenn

MS. Keynes.

February 1819

Mr. Hazlitt would be obliged to Messrs Whitmore and Fenn [1] to let him have the Quarterly Review for August 1817 and that for June last year, and the present one for a few days.[2]

---

[1] Proprietors of a circulating library.

[2] He was borrowing the three issues containing the abusive reviews of *The Round Table* (April, 1817), *Characters of Shakespear's Plays* (January, 1818, but did not appear until June), *Lectures on the English Poets* (July, 1818, which had appeared late in January, 1819) to include extracts from them in his ferocious reply, *A Letter to William Gifford, Esq.* (*Works*, IX, 13-59).

No. 85

To Benjamin Robert Haydon [1]

MS. Willard B. Pope.

[September, 1819] *

Dear Haydon,

Esau sold his birth-right. My copies in the Louvre and the recollections associated with them are all I have left that I care about. You shall have them, if you feel inclined, for a forty pound bill at a twelve-month's date.[2] Would you call tomorrow morning before twelve?

W. H.

---

* Cf. Baker, p. 242; 497, n.41.

[1] Hazlitt met Haydon (1786-1846, the historical painter, at Northcote's studio in 1812 and admired his work, although Haydon was a difficult friend. His most famous painting, "Christ's Entry into Jerusalem," contains a picture of Hazlitt characteristically "looking at Christ as an investigator." At the exhibition of the picture in 1820 Keats and Hazlitt "were up in a corner, really rejoicing," wrote Haydon (*Autobiography*, I, 282).

[2] On his return to London from Winterslow Hut where he had been preparing his last course of "Lectures on the Age of Elizabeth" (delivered at the Surrey Institution in November and December of this year), Hazlitt found a bill amounting to £50 waiting for him. Having written to B. W. Procter for a loan but failing to receive an answer, Hazlitt now wrote to Haydon offering his paintings from his days at the Louvre (Cf. Letters 15-20). A letter from Leigh Hunt of 22 September reveals that Procter had sent the money to Hunt for Hazlitt but had entrusted the letter with a friend "who kept it in his pocket for three or four days." According to Haydon, he "gave him fifty to relieve his wants." Since Hazlitt had now received money from both sources, he probably sent a friend to buy back the copies which he had made sixteen years before and which, as he says, had "recollections associated with them" (Haydon, *Diary*, II, 230, 495-496).

No. 86

To the Editor of the *Edinburgh Magazine*

Edinburgh Magazine,

September, 1819

Mr. Editor,

The following passage in North's translation of Plutarch [1] will be found to have been closely copied in the scene between Brutus and his wife in Julius Caesar.

[*A lengthy quotation follows, after which Hazlitt resumes:*]

Again, the following curious account, extracted from Magellan's Voyage to the South Seas,[2] may throw light on the origin of the Tempest, and the character of Caliban. The mention of the god Setebos seems decisive of the identity of the source from which he borrowed.

[*A lengthy quotation follows.*]

(Unsigned)

---

[1] Temple Classics Edition, IX, 256-258.
[2] Hakluyt Society Edition, 1874, p. 53. Concerning these historical illustrations to Shakespeare, cf. *Works,* XX, 410.

No. 87

To Francis Jeffrey

MS. Yale.
Address: Francis Jeffrey, Esq./Edinburgh.

> Winterslow Hut, near Salisbury,
> Septr. 25. [1819] *

Dear Sir,

I blush when I sit down to write this letter. But you some time ago said if I wanted it and would send to you for *another* 100£. you would let me have it. It would at this present moment interpose between me and almost ruin. I do not know that since that time I have done any thing to deserve your less favourable opinion. I shall receive 150£ for my next Lectures (on the age of Elizabeth) at Christmas, but I shall be prevented from completing them in time to deliver (next month) to the utter discomfiture of all my hopes, if I am not enabled to parry an immediate blow (a bill for 66£) with which I am threatened down here, which I see no means of meeting but through your often experienced liberality. Mr. Thomas Moore interested himself with the Longmans a week or two ago about a literary project [1] in my behalf, but in vain—*tan tum potuit ira* [2] Blackwood. Permit me to add, I have a good 50£ note [3] of hand which has six months to run and which I would transmit you immediately, and my own note of hand for 50£ at 3 months, which I could be certain of honouring, when I receive my money from the Surry [sic] Institution. The 100£ which I am in your debt I hope still to write out in Edinburgh Reviews! Hoping you will excuse the ungraceful importunity of this application, I remain, Dear Sir, you obliged, humble servant,

W. Hazlitt.

---

* Cf. Baker, p. 261.
[1] Perhaps the essays on modern philosophy mentioned in Letter 65 or a collection of "Essays on Character," a projected work which never appeared.
[2] So much can anger do.

No. 88

To Francis Jeffrey

MS. Yale.

Winterslow Hut, near Salisbury,
May 2, 1820

Dear Sir,

I received your last obliging letter in due course, and should have answered it before, but I waited to look out for some work to write an article upon in reference to one or other of the subjects you pointed out, the Fine arts and the Age of Elizabeth, and I have not yet been able to fix upon one. I have had some thoughts of Farington's Memoir of Sir Joshua for the first: "it is the strangest tale that e'er was heard," and a development of its contents would throw some light on the history of the academy and the progress of painting in the country.[1] Some pretty, *piquant* matter might be thrown in incidentally or to supply obvious gaps in Mr. F's narrative. Perhaps the subject is delicate; but it might be treated tenderly, and yet with effect. The text is in bungling openstitch, and presents plenty of loop-holes for *apercus* on the subjects of patronage, public taste, portrait painting, and the grand style of art as pursued in this country by Barry, West, Fuseli, Haydon, etc. But I had better do the thing, and then you will judge. I have nearly exhausted my little stock of knowledge on the Age of Elizabeth, but if anything occurs, I will bear in mind your suggestion.[2] I have been reading the Sketch-Book of Geoffrey Crayon, Gent. [Washington Irving] and think something might be made of it in the way of an extract or two, and of a prefatory

---

[3] As revealed in a letter from Leigh Hunt of 22 September 1819 (Howe, p. 255), Hazlitt had received a loan of £50 from B. W. Procter.

---

[1] "Farington's Life of Sir Joshua Reynolds" appeared in the August 1820 *Edinburgh Review.*

[2] Jeffrey had suggested another book on Elizabethan drama.

sketch of the character of American Literature as here exemplified.[3] Southey's Life of Wesley [4] I am half afraid to ask for. —You ask me about Mr. Procter, and I have to say in answer, that he is young (about 30)—well to do in the world, a solicitor with good connections; a tory, as far as he is anything in politics, and a very good fellow. He has lately made a very good bargain for the copyright of a new poem and of the two former volumes, in accounting for which he does not forget the Edinburgh Review.[5] But I believe he was more pleased with the friendly interest you have shewn about him, than even with your testimony to his literary merits. — In the article on Spence might I beg you to make the following alteration in the last paragraph of the introductory matter? For "still repeat the praises of the most tuneful of its sons"—read "still chide in fond remembrance, of the most tuneful of its sons." [6]

Hoping you will excuse all this trouble, I remain, Dear Sir, your truly obliged and most obedient servant, W. Hazlitt.

P. S. I don't know whether I ought or ought not to remind you (lest you should have forgotten) that Mr. Haydon's bill becomes due about this time, and that it was—what shall I say?—a good one. He told me the other day, it had not been presented.[7]

---

[3] Hazlitt probably did not write the review of *The Sketch Book* in the August number. His long article on "American Literature" did not appear until October 1829. *The Wellesley Index*, I, 927, assigns the *Sketch Book* by Washington Irving to Jeffrey.

[4] Although Southey's *Life of Wesley* was not reviewed in the *Edinburgh Review*, Hazlitt may have selected the "Extracts" from it in *The Edinburgh Magazine* for May 1820.

[5] *A Sicilian Story and other Poems* by B. W. Procter ("Barry Cornwall") was favorably reviewed by Jeffrey in the January 1820 issue.

[6] "Spence's Anecdotes of Pope," May, 1820. *Wellesley Index* (I, 460) attributes authorship ("prob.") to Hazlitt. This tends to confirm Hazlitt as the author, although the phrases referred to do not appear in the *Edinburgh Review*.

[7] Haydon was "deeply in debt" at this time and may have appealed to Jeffrey for a loan.

No. 89

To Benjamin R. Haydon

MS. Professor Willard B. Pope.

Winterslow Hut
Aug. 11, 1820

My dear Haydon,

I have a letter from Jeffrey in these words.

"I shall print your Farington with some corrections—You are too fond of paradoxes."

Can't you upon the strength of this raise the wind for me with some great man? Have you finally settled with Allatt,[1] the little man? I liked your painting *versus* sculpture.[2] Have you seen any more of the historic model,[3] or of a very different person, J. Scott? [4]

I suspect he is at me again.

Yours truly,
W. H.

---

[1] Probably John Allnutt, a collector of pictures and a resident of Clapham.

[2] "On the Relative Encouragement of Sculpture and Painting in England," *London Magazine* (August, 1820).

[3] Unidentified.

[4] John Scott (1783-1821), editor of *The London Magazine*. Hazlitt was drama critic throughout 1820 but failed to submit an article for September; John Hamilton Reynolds provided one in his place.

No. 90

To Robert Baldwin

MS. Berg.
Address: Robert Baldwin, Esq./Paternoster Row/London.

[September, 1820] *

Dear Sir,

I am now down at Winter-slow Hut, where I should take it as a favour if you would transmit the proof of Table-Talk, No. 3.[1] I should be mortified not to have it in the next number of the Magazine. I am busy transcribing Nos. IV, V, VI, VII, and VIII. *On the present state of parliamentary eloquence,—on the pleasure of painting,—on reading old authors,*[2]*—on vulgarity and affectation,—on the look of a gentleman.*[3] If I thought they would be regularly inserted, I would finish the whole 40 nos. out of hand. I am Dear Sir

your truly obliged and very humble servant,

W. Hazlitt.

P. S. I confess I am anxious to contribute my *full* share to determine the question which is the best, Baldwin's or Blackwood's Magazine? W. H.

Mr. Dillon will forward the proof to Winterslow Hut.

---

* Cf. Baker, p. 404n.
[1] *Table-Talk* No. 3, "On the Conversation of Authors," appeared in the September, 1820 *London Magazine* and was later included in *The Plain Speaker.* Baldwin was the publisher of the Magazine.
[2] Changed to "On Reading Old Books."
[3] All of these essays are Table-Talks in *The London Magazine.*

No. 91

To John Scott [1]

MS. Hornby.
Address: John Scott, Esq./4 York Street/Covent Garden/
London.

[January] 1821 *

Dear Sir,

I return the proof which I prefer to the philippic against
Bentham.[2] Do you keep the Past and Future?[3] You see Lamb
argues the same view of the subject.[4] That "young master" will
anticipate all my discoveries, if I don't mind. The last No. was a
very good one—The Living Authors was spirited and fine.[5] Don't
hold out your hand to the Blackwoods yet after having knocked
those blackguards down.[6] My address after you receive this will be
Winterslow Hut near Salisbury. Send me the article on Past and
Future, if you can spare it. Ask Baldwin's,[7] if they would like the
articles on Modern Philosophy 8 in number, at 5 guineas a piece.

W. H.

---

* Cf. Howe, p. 280; Baker, p. 405.

[1] Editor of *The London Magazine* (1820-1821).

[2] The proof of "On Reading Old Books" which appeared in the February
London Magazine; "On People of Sense" containing "the philippic against
Bentham" was *Table-Talk* No. IX in the *Magazine* for April 1821.

[3] "On the Past and Future" was not published until the 1825 *Table-Talk.*

[4] Lamb's essay "New Year's Eve" in the January issue.

[5] Scott's "Byron."

[6] The insulting remarks about Scott and *The London Magazine* led to an
argument between Scott and Lockhart and to Scott's death on 27 February 1821,
the result of a duel with Lockhart's friend J. H. Christie. Cf. Howe, pp. 281-282.

[7] Robert Baldwin, publisher of *The London Magazine.* Hazlitt was now writing
the essays for the first volume of *Table-Talk* which was published in April.
However, the essays on "Modern Philosophy" were not included.

No. 92

To Leigh Hunt

MS. Huntington.

Saturday night [21 April 1821] *

My Dear Hunt,[1]

I have no quarrel with you, nor can I have. You are one of those people that I like, do what they will: there are others that I do not like, do what they may. I have always spoken well of you to friend or foe, *viz.* I have said you were one of the pleasantest and cleverest persons I ever knew; but that you teazed any one you had to deal with out of their lives. I am fond of a theory as you know; but I will give up even that to a friend, if he shews that he has any regard to my personal feelings. You provoke me to think hard things of you, and then you wonder that I hitch them into an Essay, as if that made any difference. I pique myself on doing what I can for others; but I cannot say that I have found any suitable returns for this, and hence perhaps "my outrageousness of stomach." [2] For instance I praised you in the Edinburgh Review [3] and when in a case of life and death I tried to lecture, you refused to go near the place, and gave this as a reason, saying it would seem a collusion if you said any thing in my favour after what I had said of you.

2. I got Reynolds to write in the Edinburgh Review, at a time when I had a great reluctance to ask any favour of Jeffrey, and from that time I never set eyes on him for a year & a half after.[4]

---

* Cf. W. Carew Hazlitt, *Four Generations,* I, 133.

[1] A reply to Hunt's letter of 20 April (Howe, pp. 288-290) In which he reproaches Hazlitt for criticizing Shelley as a "philosophic fanatic . . . sanguine-complexioned, and shrill-voiced" in "On Paradox and Common-place" and for including Hunt among "People with one Idea." *Table-Talk Works,* VIII, 59-69, for the latter title; for the former, *Table-Talk, Works,* VIII, 146-156.

[2] An echo from *I Henry VI,* IV, 1, 139.

[3] His review of "The Story of Rimini" in the *Edinburgh Review,* October 1816.

[4] Hazlitt had also helped Reynolds find a place on *The London Magazine* when he substituted as drama critic for October, 1820.

3. I wrote a book in defence of Godwin some years ago, one half of which he has since stolen without acknowledgment, without once mentioning my name, and yet he comes to me to review this very work and I write to Jeffrey to ask his consent, thinking myself, which you do not, the most magnanimous person in the world in the defence of a cause.[5] 4. I have taken all opportunities of praising Lamb, and I never got a good word from him in return, big or little, till the other day.[6] He seemed struck all of a heap, if I even hinted at the possibility of his giving me a lift at any time. 5. It was but the other day that two friends did all they could to intercept an article [7] about me from appearing in the aforesaid E. R. saying "it would be too late," "that the Editor had been sounded at a distance, and was averse," with twenty other excuses, and at last I was obliged to send it myself, *graciously* and by main force as it were, when it appeared just in time to save me from drowning. Coulson [8] had been backwards and forwards between my house and Bentham's for between 3 and four years, and when the latter philosophically put an execution in my house, the plea was he had never heard of my name, and when I theorised on this the other day as bad policy, and *felo de se* on the part of the radicals, your nephew and that set said "Oh it was an understood thing—the execution, you know!" By God, it is enough to drive one mad. I have not a soul to stand by me, and yet I am to give up my only resource and revenge, a theory. I won't do it, that's flat. Montagu [9] is I fancy cut at my putting him among people with one idea, and yet when the Blackwood's (together with your shirking out of that business) put me nearly underground, he took every opportunity to discourage me, and one evening, when I talked of going there, I was given to understand "that there was a party expected." Yet

---

[5] The book "in defence of Godwin" was the *Reply to Malthus*. Godwin's *Of Population* appeared in 1820, but Hazlitt did not review it.

[6] In praise of Lamb see "On Familiar Style" among many other works. *Table-Talk, Works,* VIII, 242-247.

[7] The review of *Lectures on the Age of Elizabeth* in the *Edinburgh Review* for November 1820.

[8] Walter Coulson, (1794-1860), friend of Lamb and disciple of Bentham. From 1812 to 1819 Hazlitt lived in Bentham's house at No. 19, York Street. In the latter year he was "in want of a certain sum of money" for an extension of the lease, (Howe, p. 257).

[9] Basil Montagu (1770-1851), natural son of the Earl of Sandwich, barrister, and member of the Godwin circle.

after this I am not to look at him a little in *abstracto*. This is what has soured me and made me sick of friendship and acquaintance-ship. When did I speak ill of your brother John? He never played me any tricks. I was in a cursed ill humour with you for two or three things when I wrote the article you find fault with (I grant not without reason)—if I had complained to you, you would only have laughed, you would have played me the same tricks again the very next time; you would not have cared one farthing about annoying me, and yet you complain that I draw a logical conclusion from all this and publish it to the world without your name. As to Shelley, I do not hold myself responsible to him. You say I want imagination. If you mean invention or fancy, I say so too; but if you mean a disposition to sympathise with the claims or merits of others, I deny it. I have been too much disposed to waive my own pretensions in deference to those of others. I am tired with playing at rackets all day, and you will be tired with the epistle. It has little to do with you (for I see no use in raising up a parcel of small grievances) but I think the general ground of defence is good.

W. H.

I have given Hogg's paper [10] to Baldwin, and wish you would write a character of me for the next number.[11] I want to know why every body has such a dislike to me.

---

[10] Thomas Jefferson Hogg (1792-1862), friend and biographer of Shelley. By introducing Hogg to the publisher of the *London Magazine* Hazlitt was in a way making amends for his comments on Shelley.

[11] Hunt did not write a "Character" of Hazlitt for the *London Magazine*. Instead, he replied in a letter of 23 April, part of which follows: "I have often said, I have a sort of irrepressible love for Hazlitt, on account of his sympathy for mankind, his unmercenary disinterestedness, and his suffering; and I should have a still greater and more personal affection for him if he would let one; but I declare to God I never seem to know whether he is pleased or displeased, cordial or uncordial—indeed, his manners are never cordial—and he has a way with him, when first introduced to you, and ever afterwards, as if he said, 'I have no faith in anything, especially your advances; don't you flatter yourself you have any road to my credulity: we have nothing in common between us.' Then you escape into a corner, and your conversation is apt to be as sarcastic and incredulous about all the world as your manner" (Howe, pp. 293-294). The argument was not forgotten, however, for when Hazlitt and Hunt met in Florence in 1824 Hunt gave Hazlitt a paper setting forth his faults. After Hazlitt had read it, he remarked, "By God, Sir, there's a good deal of truth in it" (*Memoirs,* II, 304). But after Hazlitt's death, Hunt wrote about him: "He was essentially a great man—a

No. 93

To Taylor and Hessey

MS. Yale.
Address: Messrs. Taylor and Hessey/93 Fleet Street/London.

9 June 1821

My dear Sir,

I hope the enclosed will do and be in time.[1] In case of necessity, I could get another done instead by the middle of the week. I will send the British Gallery [2] in a day or two. If you will send me a proof of this, I will return it by the next day's coach. I am, my dear Sir, ever yours truly,

W. Hazlitt

Saturday the 9th
Winterslow Hut
near Salisbury

---

master mind; and he had this characteristic of the greatest,—that his regard for human nature, and his power to love truth and loveliness in their humblest shapes, survived his subtlest detections of human pride and folly" (*Tatler*: 28 September 1830).

---

[1] John Taylor and James Hessey, publishers, purchased *The London Magazine* from Robert Baldwin in May 1821. The essay Hazlitt enclosed was probably "Warwick Castle," the lead article for July 1821, which bears many resemblances to Hazlitt's art criticism.

[2] Probably either "Pictures at Windsor Castle" or "Pictures at Hampton Court" included in *The Picture Galleries of England* (1824).

No. 94

To Taylor and Hessey

MS. Yale.
Address: Messrs. Taylor and Hessey/93 Fleet Street/London.

Friday, 22nd.
22 June [1821] *

Dear Sir,

The truth is I have not done the article on the Gallery, and it is too late now. I have been but indifferent since I came here,[1] and after labouring a long article to no purpose, did not feel myself in spirits to begin a new one. I can only say I am sorry it has happened so. Could you return me the Guy Faux;[2] and I will either alter it or try another experiment on some less obnoxious subject?

I am, Dear Sir, yours very truly,
W. Hazlitt

---

* Cf. Baker, page 419n.
[1] Winterslow Hut.
[2] After *Guy Faux* was declined by the *London Magazine,* Hazlitt published it in three parts in the *Examiner* for November, 1821, Cf. *Works,* XX, 96-112. The following letter was attributed to Hazlitt by Professor Edmund Blunden, who printed it in *Keats' Publisher: A Memoir of John Taylor* (1781-1864), 1936, 148-149. Addressed to Taylor, it is dated 1821:

Dear Sir,

I return you very sincere thanks for your handsome present of Clare's Works of which I return the *Poems,* as I already possess them. I cannot, though I feel my own insufficiency, resolve to reject your flattering appointment for this month. I will be ready *at the time!* And if it should not suit,—you are but where you were. To own the truth I have been at the Theatres very little *(personally)* of late; but I have something to say about Mr Young and his rivals which I trust will fill up "pretty middlingly well" at a pinch, and tomorrow I shall *do* the C. G. Pageant; and the *Adelphi Theatre* if necessary. *John Bull* is attacking the poor Minor Houses on the score of rudeness and profligacy on the part of the audience; and recommending the public to give them up for the sake of Morality and the Winter Theatre. Would there be offence in *decently* calling attention to the shameful and most filthy scenes which have lately been acted *before* the curtain at Covent

No. 95

To Francis Jeffrey

MS. Yale.
Address: Francis Jeffrey, Esq./Edinburgh.

Novr. 26, 1821.
Winterslow Hut
near Salisbury

Dear Sir,

I am got down here to try my hand on Lady Morgan.[1] Would you send me word when will be the latest time for forwarding the article if I can succeed in it? I sent you some proof sheets of the new volume of Table-talk.[2] Might I hope (when you have looked at them) for a notice in the next number? [3] The work will I

Garden? I shall advance no charges against individuals nor state anything which 20 witnesses cannot confirm on oath, *myself* among the rest. It shall not be violent though decisive and I shall be sure of the thanks of every decent man and even of the more decorous filles de joi. *One word*—No! or yes! will be an answer sufficient.

Your, Dear Sir, Very Obliged Servt.
(Unsigned)

Since the present location of this MS. is unknown, its handwriting cannot be used as evidence, but it is almost certainly not by Hazlitt, who usually addressed his letters to both partners, Taylor and Hessey. Hazlitt ceased reviewing plays for the *London Magazine* at the end of 1820, and throughout 1821 he was busy writing the *Table-Talk* essays which appeared in that magazine. John Clare is never mentioned in any of his writings. As drama critic on the *Examiner* in 1815 and on various other periodicals until 1817, Hazlitt judged Charles Mayne Young's acting (usually unfavourably), but in no article does he discuss "Mr Young and his rivals," the Covent Garden Pageant, or the activities that went on "before the curtain at Covent Garden." The familiar tone and style of the letter with its many underscored words are other reasons for rejecting it as by Hazlitt.

[1] "Lady Morgan's Life of Salvator" was published in the *Edinburgh Review* in July 1824 (*Works*, XVI, 284-318).

[2] After the failure of John Warren, publisher of the first volume of *Table-Talk,* the second volume was issued by Henry Colburn in June 1822.

[3] A little premature, since the second volume was not completed until the following year, but he was no doubt worried by the unfavourable review of Volume I in the *Quarterly* (October 1821) denouncing him as a "slang whanger." No notice of *Table-Talk* has been found in the *Edinburgh Review*.

understand be transferred to Colburn to publish. I am, Dear Sir, always your truly obliged and obedient servant,

W. Hazlitt.

I had forgot to say what I ought to have acknowldged long ago that I received your kind remittance in due course.

No. 96

To Thomas Noon Talfourd

Howe, *Life,* pp. 304-305.
Address: T. N. Talfourd, Esq./Pump Court/Temple/London.

Winterslow Hut
December 1. [1821] *

My Dear Sir,

I stand exceedingly indebted to you for your kind intentions and exertions in my favour.[1] I am at present driven almost into a corner. What with uneasiness of mind and this failure of Warren's, I hardly know what to do.[2] Could you ask Colburn (with whom I have already communicated) whether he will give me £200 for 20 Essays, advancing one Hundred, that is, the money for the first Ten Essays, which I will engage to complete and deliver in Two months from the present time, and which he may make use of either for the Magazine or in a Volume with what title he pleases—only in the former case I wish to reserve right of copy.[3] I am busy about Lady Morgan, and will do it *con amore* if I can but get out of this present hobble. I have about £50 to pay as soon as I get back to town which the Review of Lady M. alone would do, but I am too unconfortable, I fear, to get through it properly, circumstanced as I am. 50, you will say then, would do. Be it so; but I should work

---

* According to Howe, p.304; cf. Wardle, pp.298-299.

[1] As Lamb's neighbour in Inner Temple Lane where he also met Hazlitt, Talfourd (1795-1854), author and lawyer, became a close friend of both men and the first biographer of Lamb and editor of his letters. His first impression of Hazlitt in 1815 "staggering under the blow of Waterloo" was contributed to the *Literary Remains,* after Talfourd had become famous as the author of *Ion,* journalist in the *New Monthly Magazine,* and Hazlitt's successor as drama critic on the *London Magazine.* In 1837, while M. P. for Reading, Talfourd introduced the Copyright Bill (passed in 1842), and Dickens dedicated *The Pickwick Papers* to him. At his death Talfourd was a Justice of the Court of Common Pleas.

[2] Cf. Letter 95.

[3] The proposal must have been satisfactory, for "On Going a Journey" appeared in the January 1822 *New Monthly Magazine.*

much better for the other. Also, propose to him (if you please) the Picturesque Tour in Italy with an account of the Vatican, at the same price, with one Hundred for my expences. The truth is, I seem to have been hurt in my mind lately, and continual effort to no purpose is too much for any patience, and mine is nearly exhausted. My dear Talfourd, if you have a girl that loves you and that you have regard for, lose no time in marrying, and think yourself happy, whatever else may happen.[4] Excuse this from yours very truly,

W. H.

P. S. A thought has just struck me, that if Colburn chose to buy Warren's volume, he might use the Essays for the Magazine in the first instance (they are all *virgins* but one) [5] and publish the book afterwards, and in the meantime I will write a new series; that is, I will sell him 40 Essays or Table-talks for £400, to do what he pleases with, he advancing me £100 down, and I giving him up half the copy *instanter*. The subjects are not at all blown upon.

---

[4] The first reference to Sarah Walker.

[5] "On a Landscape of Nicolas Poussin," which had appeared in the *London Magazine,* August 1821.

No. 97

To Henry Colburn

Four Generations, I, 193-194.

Saturday evening
[January 1822] *

Dear Sir,

Could you favour me with a proof of the *Fight,*[1] this evening, or on Monday? I wish you would desire the printer to return me the copy. I hope to leave for Scotland next week,[2] and shall begin the new volume of Table-Talk, as soon as I set out.

I am, Dear Sir, Your much obliged
humble servant,
W. Hazlitt

---

* Cf. Howe, p.308.

[1] Appeared in *The New Monthly Magazine* (February 1822).

[2] He left for Edinburgh the following week to obtain a divorce but went first to Stamford, where he began the *Liber Amoris,* then spent a month at the Renton Inn, Berwickshire, where he finished Volume II of *Table-Talk.*

No. 98

To Sarah Walker

MS. Book,[1] *Liber Amoris,* I, Lockwood.

[Renton Inn, Berwickshire
February 1822] *

You will scold me for this, and ask me if this is keeping my promise to mind my work. One half of it was to think of Sarah: and besides, I do not neglect my work either, I assure you. I regularly do ten pages a day, which mounts up to thirty guineas worth a week, so that you see I should grow rich at this rate, if I could keep on so. *And I could keep on so,* if I had you with me to encourage me with your sweet smiles, and share my lot. The Berwick smacks sail twice a week, and the wind sits fair. When I think of the thousand endearing caresses that have passed between us, I do not wonder at the strong attachment that draws me to you; but I am sorry for my own want of power to please. I hear the wind sigh through the lattice, and keep repeating over again to myself two lines of Lord Byron's tragedy—

"So shalt thou find me ever at thy side
Here and hereafter, if the last may be." [2]

applying them to thee, my love, and thinking whether I shall ever see thee again. Perhaps not—for some years at least—till both thou and I are old—and then, when all else have foresaken thee, I will creep to thee, and die in thine arms. You

---

* Cf. Howe, p. 310.

[1] A small octavo notebook containing a rough first draft of the conversations now forming Part I of the *Liber Amoris.* Although this Ms. text is presumably not in Hazlitt's hand, notes (marginal and interlinear) are probably by Hazlitt and have been incorporated in the printed text of the 1823 version *Liber Amoris.*

[2] *Sardanapalus,* IV, i, 166-167.

once made me believe I was not hated by her I loved; and for that sensation, so delicious was it, though but a mockery and a dream, I owe you more than I can ever pay. I thought to have dried up my tears for ever, the day I left you; but as I write this, they stream again. If they did not, I think my heart would burst. I walk out here of an afternoon, and hear the notes of the thrush that come up from a sheltered valley below, welcoming the spring; but they do not melt my heart as they used—it is grown cold and dead. As you say, it will one day be colder. —Forgive what I have written above. I did not intend it: but you were once my little all, and I cannot bear the thought of having lost thee for ever, I fear through my own fault. Has any one called? Do not send any letters that come. I should like you and your mother (if agreeable) to go and see Mr. Kean in Othello, Miss Stephens [3] in Love in a Village, and the Indian Jugglers and the Glass Curtain at the Coburg.[4] If you will, I will write Mr. T[alfourd?] to send you tickets. Has Mr. ——— called? I think I must send to him for the picture to kiss and talk to. Kiss me, my best beloved. Ah! if you can never be mine, still let me be your proud and happy slave.

W. H.

---

[3] For Hazlitt's appreciation of Edmund Kean as Othello see *Characters of Shakespear's Plays, Works*, IV, 300, and *A View of the English Stage, Works*, V, 338-339. Catherine Stephens (1794-1882), later Countess of Essex, "sweetest soprano voice of her time" (D. N. B.), appeared often at Covent Garden from 1813 to 1822. For the popularity of both Miss Stephens and Isaac Bickerstaffe's *Love in a Village*, see Genest, *Some Account of the English Stage* (1832), IX.

[4] See Hazlitt's defence of mere spectacle and show at the Surrey, the Cobourg, and other places in "On Vulgarity and Affectation" in *Table-Talk*. In the same volume the excellent essay. "The Indian Jugglers," indicates how he put to good artistic and intellectual advantage of one of these spectacles.

No. 99

To William Hazlitt, Jr.[1]

Literary Remains (1836), II, 73-109

(Renton Inn, Berwickshire
February or early March 1822)[2]

My dear little Fellow,—

You are now going to settle at school, and may consider this as your first entrance into the world. As my health is so indifferent, and I may not be with you long, I wish to leave you some advice (the best I can) for your conduct in life, both that it may be of use

---

[1] William Carew Hazlitt writes: "In 1822 he was put to school at a Mr. Dawson's, in Hunter Street, London; and it was just before he was going to start for this new scene that my grandfather addressed to him the 'Advice to a Schoolboy,' a letter full of admirable suggestion and counsel. . . . In this letter to a boy of ten, he . . . points obliquely to his own frustrated hopes—" (*Memoirs*, 1867, II, 16-17). In a letter to Patmore of mid-June of 1822, Hazlitt says "Will you call at Mr. Dawson's school, Hunter Street and tell the little boy I'll write to him or see him on Saturday morning." There are further references to the School in the *Journals of Sarah and William Hazlitt: 1822-1831*, pp. 181-182, 237, 239. As for the publication of the letter, Hazlitt writes to his son from Vevey, Switzerland, in the early summer of 1825 to say that the *Table-Talk* and the *Spirit of the Age* have been printed at Paris. He adds *"The Advice to a School-Boy* is in the first." Cf. also Letter 137 to Walter Savage Landor. The first full publication appeared in the *Literary Remains*, the missing portion being added from MS by the son. Presumably Hazlitt's astringently discouraging view of women and love led to partial suppression. The *Remains* restored the portion beginning "Your pain is her triumph . . ." and concluding ". . . The God of Love stands on the shore, and as I stretch out my hands to him in vain, clasps his wings, and mocks me as I pass." That this letter-essay was not published in England in Hazlitt's lifetime is owing perhaps to its personal character.

[2] Hazlitt dates this letter for us in his letter to Sarah Walker, written from Renton Inn, Berwickshire. The letter to Sarah bears the postmark March 9, 1822. Hazlitt writes: "I had a letter from my little boy the other day and I have been writing him a long essay in my book on his conduct in life . . ." This statement indicates that the epistolary essay belongs to February or early March. In the *Memoirs*, II, 68, we learn from a letter to Patmore written in March that the epistolary essay had already been "done magnificently."

to you, and as something to remember me by. I may at least be able to caution you against my own errors, if nothing else.

As we went along to your new place of destination, you often repeated that 'You durst say they were a set of stupid, disagreeable people,' meaning the people at the school. You were to blame in this. It is a good old rule to hope for the best. Always, my dear, believe things to be right, till you find them the contrary; and even then, instead of irritating yourself against them, endeavour to put up with them as well as you can, if you cannot alter them. You said 'You were sure you should not like the school where you were going.' This was wrong. What you meant was that you did not like to leave home. But you could not tell whether you should like the school or not, till you had given it a trial. Otherwise, your saying that you should not like it was determining that you would not like it. Never anticipate evils; or, because you cannot have things exactly as you wish, make them out worse than they are, through mere spite and wilfulness.

You seemed at first to take no notice of your school-fellows, or rather to set yourself against them, because they were strangers to you. They knew as little of you as you did of them; so that this would have been a reason for their keeping aloof from you as well, which you would have felt as a hardship. Learn never to conceive a prejudice against others, because you know nothing of them. It is bad reasoning, and makes enemies of half the world. Do not think ill of them, till they behave ill to you; and then strive to avoid the faults which you see in them. This will disarm their hostility sooner than pique or resentment or complaint.

I thought you were disposed to criticise the dress of some of the boys as not so good as your own. Never despise any one for any thing that he cannot help—least of all, for his poverty. I would wish you to keep up appearances yourself as a defence against the idle sneers of the world, but I would not have you value yourself upon them. I hope you will neither be the dupe nor victim of vulgar prejudices. Instead of saying above—'Never despise any one for any thing that he cannot help'—I might have said, 'Never despise any one at all;' for contempt implies a triumph over and pleasure in the ill of another. It means that you are glad and congratulate yourself on their failings or misfortunes. The sense of inferiority in others, without this indirect appeal to our self-love, is a painful feeling, and not an exulting one.

You complain since, that the boys laugh at you and do not care about you, and that you are not treated as you were at home. My dear, that is one chief reason for your being sent to school, to insure you betimes to the unavoidable rubs and uncertain reception you may meet with in life. You cannot always be with me, and perhaps it is as well that you cannot. But you must not expect others to show the same concern about you as I should. You have hitherto been a spoiled child, and have been used to have your own way a good deal, both in the house and among your play-fellows, with whom you were too fond of being a leader: but you have good-nature and good sense, and will get the better of this in time. You have now got among other boys who are your equals, or bigger and stronger than yourself, and who have something else to attend to besides humouring your whims and fancies, and you feel this as a repulse or piece of injustice. But the first lesson to learn is that there are other people in the world besides yourself. There are a number of boys in the school where you are, whose amusements and pursuits (whatever they may be) are and ought to be of as much consequence to them as yours can be to you, and to which therefore you must give way in your turn. The more airs of childish self-importance you give yourself, you will only expose yourself to be the more thwarted and laughed at. True equality is the only true morality or true wisdom. Remember always that you are but one among others, and you can hardly mistake your place in society. In your father's house, you might do as you pleased: in the world, you will find competitors at every turn. You are not born a king's son to destroy or dictate to millions: you can only expect to share their fate, or settle your differences amicably with them. You already find it so at school; and I wish you to be reconciled to your situation as soon and with as little pain as you can.

It was my misfortune perhaps to be bred up among Dissenters, who look with too jaundiced an eye at others, and set too high a value on their own peculiar pretensions. From being proscribed themselves, they learn to proscribe others; and come in the end to reduce all integrity of principle and soundness of opinion within the pale of their own little communion. Those who were out of it and did not belong to the class of *Rational Dissenters,* I was led erroneously to look upon as hardly deserving the name of rational beings. Being, thus satisfied as to the select few who are 'the salt of the earth,'[3] it is easy to persuade ourselves that we are at the head of them, and to fancy ourselves of more importance in the scale of true desert than all the rest of the world put together, who do not interpret a certain text of Scripture in the manner that we have been taught to do. You will (from the difference of education) be free from this bigotry, and will, I hope, avoid every thing akin to the same exclusive and narrow-minded spirit. Think that the minds of men are various as their faces—that the modes and employments of life are numberless as they are necessary—that there is more than one class of merit—that though others may be wrong in some things, they are not so in all—and that countless races of men have been born, have lived and died without ever hearing of any one of those points in which you take a just pride and pleasure—and you will not err on the side of that spiritual pride or intellectual coxcombry which has been so often the bane of the studious and learned!

I observe you have got a way of speaking of your school-fellows as '*that* Hoare, *that* Harris,' and so on, as if you meant to mark them out for particular reprobation, or did not think them good enough for you. It is a bad habit to speak disrespectfully of others: for it will lead you to think and feel uncharitably towards them. Ill names beget ill blood. Even where there may be some repeated trifling provocations, it is better to be courteous, mild, and forbearing, than captious, impatient, and fretful. The faults of others too often arise out of our own ill-temper; or though they should be real, we shall not mend them, by exasperating ourselves against them. Treat your playmates, as Hamlet advises Polonius to treat the players, 'according to your own dignity, rather than their deserts.' [4] If you fly out at every thing in them that you disapprove or think done on purpose to annoy you, you lie constantly at the mercy of their caprice, rudeness, or ill-nature. You should be more your own master.

Do not begin to quarrel with the world too soon: for, bad as it may be, it is the best we have to live in—here. If railing would have

---

[3] Matthew, v: 13
[4] *Hamlet,* II, ii, 557.

made it better, it would have been reformed long ago: but as this is not to be hoped for at present, the best way is to slide through it as contentedly and innocently as we may. The worst fault it has, is want of charity: and calling *knave* and *fool* at every turn will not cure this failing. Consider (as a matter of vanity) that if there were not so many knaves and fools as we find, the wise and honest would not be those rare and shining characters that they are allowed to be; and (as a matter of philosopy) that if the world be really incorrigible in this respect, it is a reflection to make one sad, not angry. We may laugh or weep at the madness of mankind: we have no right to vilify them, for our own sakes or theirs. Misanthropy is not the disgust of the mind at human nature, but with itself; or it is laying its own exaggerated vices and foul blots at the door of others! Do not, however, mistake what I have here said. I would not have you, when you grow up, adopt the low and sordid fashion of palliating existing abuses or of putting the best face upon the worst things. I only mean that indiscriminate, un-qualified satire can do little good, and that those who indulge in the most revolting speculations on human nature, do not them-selves always set the fairest examples, or strive to prevent its lower degradation. They seem rather willing to reduce it to their theoretical standard. For the rest, the very outcry that is made (if sincere) shews that things cannot be quite so bad as they are represented. The abstract hatred and scorn of vice implies the capacity for virtue: the impatience expressed at the most striking instances of deformity proves the innate idea and love of beauty in the human mind. The best antidote I can recommend to you hereafter against the disheartening effect of such writings as those of Rochefoucault,[5] Mandeville, and others, will be to look at the pictures of Raphael and Correggio. You need not be altogether ashamed, my dear little boy, of belonging to a species which could produce such faces as those; nor despair of doing something worthy of a laudable ambition, when you see what such hands have

---

[5] In 1823, Hazlitt published anonymously a volume entitled: "Characteristics: In the Manner of Rochefoucault's Maxims." In a "Preface," Hazlitt said of Rochefoucault's Maxims and Reflections: "I was so struck with the force and beauty of the style and matter, that I felt an earnest ambition to embody some occasional thoughts of my own in the same form." Cf. Howe *Works,* 9, 167-229.

wrought! You will, perhaps, one day have reason to thank me for this advice.

As to your studies and school-exercises, I wish you to learn Latin, French, and dancing. I would insist upon the last more particularly, both because it is more likely to be neglected, and because it is of the greatest consequence to your success in life. Every thing almost depends upon first impressions; and these depend (besides *person,* which is not in our power) upon two things, *dress* and *address,* which every one may command with proper attention. These are the small coin in the intercourse of life, which are continually in request; and perhaps you will find at the year's end, or towards the close of life, that the daily insults, coldness, or contempt, to which you have been exposed by a neglect of such superficial recommendations, are hardly atoned for by the few proofs of esteem or admiration which your integrity or talents have been able to extort in the course of it. When we habitually disregard those things which we know will ensure the favourable opinion of others, it shews we set that opinion at defiance, or consider ourselves above it, which no one ever did with impunity. An inattention to our own persons implies a disrespect to others, and may often be traced no less to a want of good-nature than of good sense. The old maxim—*Desire to please, and you will infallibly please*—explains the whole matter. If there is a tendency to vanity and affectation on this side of the question, there is an equal alloy of pride and obstinacy on the opposite one. Slovenliness may at any time be cured by an effort of resolution, but a graceful carriage requires an early habit, and in most cases the aid of the dancing-master. I would not have you, from not knowing how to enter a room properly, stumble at the very threshold in the good graces of those on whom it is possible the fate of your future life may depend. Nothing creates a greater prejudice against any one than awkwardness. A person who is confused in manner and gesture seems to have done something wrong, or as if he was conscious of no one qualification to build a confidence in himself upon. On the other hand, openness, freedom, self-possession, set others at ease with you by shewing that you are on good terms with yourself. Grace in women gains the affections sooner, and secures them longer, than any thing else—it is an outward and visible sign of an inward harmony of soul—as the want of it in men, as if the mind and body equally hitched in difficulties and were distracted with doubts, is the greatest impediment in the career of gallantry and road to the female heart. Another thing I would caution you against is not to pore over your books till you are bent almost double—a habit you will never be able to get the better of, and which you will find of serious ill consequence. *A stoop in the shoulders* [6] sinks a man in public and in private estimation. You are at present straight enough, and you walk with boldness and spirit. Do nothing to take away the use of your limbs, or the spring and elasticity of your muscles. As to all worldly advantages, it is to the full of as much importance that your deportment should be erect and manly as your actions.

You will naturally find out all this and fall into it, if your attention is drawn out sufficiently to what is passing around you; and this will be the case, unless you are absorbed too much in books and those sedentary studies,

'Which waste the marrow, and consume the brain.' [7]

You are, I think , too fond of reading as it is. As one means of avoiding excess in this way, I would wish you to make it a rule, never to read at meal-times, nor in company when there is any (even the most trivial) conversation going on, nor ever to let your eagerness to learn encroach upon your play-hours. Books are but one inlet of knowledge; and the pores of the mind, like those of the body, should be left open to all impressions. I applied too close to my studies, soon after I was of your age, and hurt myself irreparably by it. Whatever may be the value of learning, health and good spirits are of more.

I would have you, as I said, make yourself master of French, because you may find it of use in the commerce of life; and I would have you learn Latin, partly because I learnt it myself, and I would not have you without any of the advantages or sources of

---

[6] In his letter to Sarah Walker (Note 2), Hazlitt observes to her of his advice: "I will take care, however, he does not get a stoop in the shoulders by poring over his books or muddle his brain with the contents."

[7] Cf. Spenser concerning Lecherie:

That rots the marrow, and consumes the Braine.

The Faerie Queene, I.iv. 26.

knowledge that I possessed—it would be a bar of separation between us—and secondly, because there is an atmosphere round this sort of classical ground, to which that of actual life is gross and vulgar. Shut out from this garden of early sweetness, we may well exclaim—

> 'How shall we part and wander down
> Into a lower world, to this obscure
> And wild? How shall we breathe in other air
> Less pure, accustom'd to immortal fruits?' [8]

I do not think the Classics so indispensable to the cultivation of your intellect as on another account, which I have seen explained elsewhere,[9] and you will have no objection to turn with me to the passage.

'The study of the Classics is less to be regarded as an exercise of the intellect, than as *a discipline of humanity*. The peculiar advantage of this mode of education consists not so much in strengthening the understand, as in softening and refining the taste. It gives men liberal views; it accustoms the mind to take an interest in things foreign to itself; to love virtue for its own sake; to prefer fame to life, and glory to riches; and to fix our thoughts on the remote and permanent, instead of narrow and fleeting objects. It teaches us to believe that there is something really great and excellent in the world, surviving all the shocks of accident and fluctuations of opinion, and raises us above that low and servile fear, which bows only to present power and upstart authority. Rome and Athens filled a place in the history of mankind, which can never be occupied again. They were two cities set on a hill, which could not be hid; all eyes have seen them, and their light shines like a mighty sea-mark into the abyss of time.

> "Still green with bays each ancient altar stands,
> Above the reach of sacrilegious hands;
> Secure from flames, from envy's fiercer rage,
> Destructive war, and all-involving age.

---

8 Cf. *Paradise Lost*, XI, 282-285.
9 Cf. *The Round Table*, "On Classical Education."

Hail, bards triumphant, born in happier days,
Immortal heirs of universal praise!
Whose honours with increase of ages grow,
As streams roll down, enlarging as they flow!" [10]

It is this feeling more than any thing else which produces a marked difference between the study of the ancient and modern languages, and which, by the weight and importance of the consequences attached to the former, stamps every word with a monumental firmness. By conversing with the *mighty dead,* we imbibe sentiment with knowledge. We become strongly attached to those who can no longer either hurt or serve us, except through the influence which they exert over the mind. We feel the presence of that power which gives immortality to human thoughts and actions, and catch the flame of enthusiasm from all nations and ages.'

Because however, you have learnt Latin and Greek, and can speak a different language, do not fancy yourself of a different order of beings from those you ordinarily converse with. They perhaps know and can do more *things* than you, though you have learnt a greater variety of *names* to express the same thing by. The great object indeed of these studies is to be 'a cure for a narrow and selfish spirit,' and to carry the mind out of its petty and local prejudices to the idea of a more general humanity. Do not fancy, because you are intimate with Homer and Virgil, that your neighbours who can never attain the same posthumous fame are to be despised, like those impudent valets who live in noble families and look down upon every one else. Though you are master of Cicero's 'Orations,' think it possible for a cobbler at a stall to be more eloquent than you. 'But you are a scholar, and he is not.' Well, then, you have that advantage over him, but it does not follow that you are to have every other. Look at the heads of the celebrated poets and philosophers of antiquity in the collection at Wilton,[11] and you will say they answer to their works: but you will find others in the same collection whose names have hardly come down to us, that are equally fine, and cast in the same classic mould. Do you imagine that all the thoughts, genius, and capacity

---

[10] Cf. Pope's *Essay On Criticism,* Part I, a conflation of lines 181-184 and 189-192.
[11] Cf. *Sketches of the Picture Galleries.*

of those old and mighty nations are contained in a few odd volumes, to be thumbed by school-boys? This reflection is not meant to lessen your admiration of the great names to which you will be accustomed to look up, but to direct it to that solid mass of intellect and power, of which they were the most shining ornaments. I would wish you to excel in this sort of learning and to take a pleasure in it, because it is the path that has been chosen for you: but do not suppose that others do not excel equally in their line of study or exercise of skill, or that there is but one mode of excellence in art or nature. You have got on vastly beyond the point at which you set out; but others have been getting on as well as you in the same or other ways, and have kept pace with you. What then, you may ask, is the use of all the pains you have taken, if it gives you no superiority over mankind in general? It is this—You have reaped all the benefit of improvement and knowledge yourself; and farther, if you had not moved forwards, you would by this time have been left behind. Envy no one, disparage no one, think yourself above no one. Their demerits will not piece out your deficiences; nor is it a waste of time and labour for you to cultivate your own talents, because you cannot bespeak a monopoly of all advantages. You are more learned than many of your acquaintance who may be more active, healthy, witty, successful in business or expert in some elegant or useful art than you; but you have no reason to complain, if you have attained the object of your ambition. Or if you should not be able to compass this from want of genius or parts, yet learn, my child, to be contented with a mediocrity of acquirements. You may still be respectable in your conduct, and enjoy a tranquil obscurity, with more friends and fewer enemies than you might otherwise have had.

There is one almost certain drawback on a course of scholastic study, that it unfits men for active life. The *ideal* is always at variance with the *practical*. The habit of fixing the attention on the imaginary and abstracted deprives the mind equally of energy and fortitude. By indulging our imaginations on fictions and chimeras, where we have it all our own way and are led on only by the pleasure of the prospect, we grow fastidious, effeminate, lapped in idle luxury, impatient of contradiction, and unable to sustain the shock of real adversity, when it comes; as by being taken up with abstract reasoning or remote events in which we are merely passive spectators, we have no resources to provide against it, no readiness, or expedients for the occasion, or spirit to use them, even if they occur. We must think again before we determine, and thus the opportunity for action is lost. While we are considering the very best possible mode of gaining an object, we find that it has slipped through our fingers, or that others have laid rude, fearless hands upon it. The youthful tyro reluctantly discovers that the ways of the world are not his ways, nor their thoughts his thoughts. Perhaps the old monastic institutions were not in this respect unwise, which carried on to the end of life the secluded habits and romantic associations with which it began, and which created a privileged world for the inhabitants, distinct from the common world of men and women. You will bring with you from your books and solitary reveries a wrong measure of men and things, unless you correct it by careful experience and mixed observation. You will raise your standard of character as much too high at first as from disappointed expectation it will sink too low afterwards. The best qualifier of this theoretical *mania* and of the dreams of poets and moralists (who both treat of things as *they ought to be* and not *as they are*) is in one sense to be found in some of our own popular writers, such as our Novelists and periodical Essayists. But you had, after all, better wait and see what things are than try to anticipate the results. You know more of a road by having travelled it than by all the conjectures and descriptions in the world. You will find the business of life conducted on a much more varied and individual scale than you would expect. People will be concerned about a thousand things that you have no idea of, and will be utterly indifferent to what you feel the greatest interest in. You will find good and evil, folly and discretion more mingled, and the shades of character running more into each other than they do in the ethical charts. No one is equally wise or guarded at all points, and it is seldom that any one is quite a fool. Do not be surprised, when you go out into the world, to find men talk exceedingly well on different subjects, who do not derive their information immediately from books. In the first place, the light of books is diffused very much abroad in the world in conversation and at second-hand; and besides, common sense is not a monopoly, and experience and observation are sources of information open to the man of the world as well as to the retired student. If you know more of the outline and principles, he knows more of the details and 'pratique part of life.' [12] A man may discuss the adventures of a campaign in which he was engaged very agreeably without having read the *Retreat of the Ten Thousand*,[13] or give a singular account of the method of drying teas in China without being a profound chemist. It is the vice of scholars to suppose that there is no knowledge in the world but that of books. Do you avoid it, I conjure you; and thereby save yourself the pain and mortification that must otherwise ensue from finding out your mistake continually!

Gravity is one great ingredient in the conduct of life, and perhaps a certain share of it is hardly to be dispensed with. Few people can afford to be quite unaffected. At any rate, do not put your worst qualities foremost. Do not seek to distinguish yourself by being ridiculous; nor entertain that miserable ambition to be the sport and butt of the company. By aiming at a certain standard of behaviour or intellect, you will at least show your taste and value for what is excellent. There are those who *blurt* out their good things with so little heed of what they are about that no one thinks any thing of them; as others by keeping their folly to themselves gain the reputation of wisdom. Do not, however, affect to speak only in oracles, or to deal in *bon-mots:* condescend to the level of the company, and be free and accessible to all persons. Express whatever occurs to you, that cannot offend others or hurt yourself. Keep some opinions to yourself. Say what you please of others, but never repeat what you hear said of them to themselves. If you have nothing to offer yourself, laugh with the witty, assent to the wise; they will not think the worse of you for it. Listen to information on subjects you are unacquainted with, instead of always striving to lead the conversation to some favourite one of your own. By the last method you will shine, but will not improve. I am ashamed myself ever to open my lips on any question I have ever written upon. It is much more difficult to be able to converse on an equality with a number of persons in turn, than to soar above their heads, and excite the stupid gaze of all companies by bestriding some senseless topic of your own and confounding the

---

[12] Cf. *Henry V*, I, i, 51.
[13] Xenophon's *Anabasis*.

understandings of those who are ignorant of it. Be not too fond of argument. Indeed, by going much into company (which I do not, however, wish you to do) you will be weaned from this practice, if you set out with it. Rather suggest what remarks may have occurred to you on a subject than aim at dictating your opinions to others or at defending yourself at all points. You will learn more by agreeing in the main with others and entering into their trains of thinking, than by contradicting and urging them to extremities. Avoid singularity of opinion as well as of everything else. Sound conclusions come with practical knowledge, rather than with speculative refinements: in what we really understand, we reason but little. Long-winded disputes fill up the place of common sense and candid inquiry. Do not imagine that you will make people friends by showing your superiority over them: it is what they will neither admit nor forgive, unless you have a high and acknowledged reputation beforehand, which renders this sort of petty vanity more inexcusable. Seek to gain the good-will of others, rather than to extort their applause; and to this end, be neither too tenacious of your own claims, nor inclined to press too hard on their weaknesses.

Do not affect the society of your inferiors in rank, nor court that of the great. There can be no real sympathy in either case. The first will consider you as a restraint upon them, and the last as an intruder or *upon sufferance.* It is not a desirable distinction to be admitted into company as a man of talents. You are a mark for invidious observation. If you say nothing or merely behave with common propriety and simplicity, you seem to have no business there. If you make a studied display of yourself, it is arrogating a consequence you have no right to. If you are contented to pass as an indifferent person, they despise you; if you distinguish yourself, and show more knowledge, wit, or taste than they do, they hate you for it. You have no alternative. I would rather be asked out to sing than to talk. Every one does not pretend to a fine voice, but every one fancies he has as much understanding as another. Indeed, the secret of this sort of intercourse has been pretty well found out. Literary men are seldom invited to the tables of the great; they send for players and musicians, as they keep monkeys and parrots!

I would not, however, have you run away with a notion that the rich are knaves or that lords are fools. They are for what I know as honest and as wise as other people. But it is a trick of our self-love, supposing that another has the decided advantage of us in one way, to strike a balance by taking it for granted (as a moral antithesis) that he must be as much beneath us in those qualities on which we plume ourselves, and which we would appropriate almost entirely to our own use. It is hard indeed if others are raised above us not only by the gifts of fortune, but of understanding too. It is not to be credited. People have an unwillingness to admit that the House of Lords can be equal in talent to the House of Commons. So in the other sex, if a woman is handsome, she is an idiot or no better than she should be: in ours, if a man is worth a million of money, he is a miser, a fellow that cannot spell his own name, or a poor creature in some way, to bring him to our level. This is malice, and not truth. Believe all the good you can of every one. Do not measure others by yourself. If they have advantages which you have not, let your liberality keep pace with their good fortune. Envy no one, and you need envy no one. If you have but the magnanimity to allow merit wherever you see it—understanding in a lord or wit in a cobbler—this temper of mind will stand you instead of many accomplishments. Think no man too happy. Raphael died young. Milton had the misfortune to be blind. If any one is vain or proud, it is from folly or ignorance. Those who pique themselves excessively on some one thing, have but that one thing to pique themselves upon, as languages, mechanics, &c. I do not say that this is not an enviable delusion where it is not liable to be disturbed; but at present knowledge is too much diffused and pretensions come too much into collision for this to be long the case; and it is better not to form such a prejudice at first than to have it to undo all the rest of one's life. If you learn any two things, though they may put you out of conceit one with the other, they will effectually cure you of any conceit you might have of yourself, by shewing the variety and scope there is in the human mind beyond the limits you had set to it.

You were convinced the first day that you could not learn Latin, which now you find easy. Be taught from this, not to think other obstacles insurmountable that you may meet with in the course of your life, though they seem so at first sight.

Attend above all things to your health; or rather, do nothing wilfully to impair it. Use exercise, abstinence, and regular hours. Drink water when you are alone, and wine or very little spirits in company. It is the last that are ruinous by leading to unlimited excess. There is not the same headlong *impetus* in wine. But one glass of brandy and water makes you want another, that other makes you want a third, and so on, in an increased proportion. Therefore no one can stop midway who does not possess the resolution to abstain altogether; for the inclination is sharpened with its indulgence. Never gamble. Or if you play for any thing, never do so for what will give you uneasiness the next day. Be not precise in these matters: but do not pass certain limits, which it is difficult to recover. Do nothing in the irritation of the moment, but take time to reflect. Because you have done one foolish thing, do not do another; nor throw away your health or reputation or comfort, to thwart impertinent advice. Avoid a spirit of contradiction, both in words and actions. Do not aim at what is beyond your reach, but at what is within it. Indulge in calm and pleasing pursuits, rather than violent excitements; and learn to conquer your own will, instead of striving to obtain the mastery of that of others.

With respect to your friends, I would wish you to choose them neither from caprice nor accident, and to adhere to them as long as you can. Do not make a surfeit of friendship through over-sanguine enthusiasm, nor expect it to last for ever. Always speak well of those with whom you have once been intimate, or take some part of the censure you bestow on them to yourself. Never quarrel with tried friends, or those whom you wish to continue such. Wounds of this kind are sure to open again. When once the prejudice is removed that sheathes defects, familiarity only causes jealousy and distrust. Do not keep on with a mockery of friendship after the substance is gone—but part, while you can part friends. Bury the carcase of friendship: it is not worth embalming.

As to the books you will have to read by choice or for amusement, the best are the commonest. The names of many of them are already familiar to you. Read them as you grow up with all the satisfaction in your power, and make much of them. It is perhaps the greatest pleasure you will have in life, the one you will think of longest, and repent of less. If my life had been more full of calamity than it has been (much more than I hope yours will be) I would live it over again, my poor little boy, to have read the books I did in my youth.

In politics I wish you to be an honest man, but no brawler. Hate injustice and falsehood for your own sake. Be neither a martyr, nor a sycophant. Wish well to the world without expecting to see it much better than it is; and do not gratify the enemies of liberty by putting yourself at their mercy, if it can be avoided with honour.

If you ever marry, I would wish you to marry the woman you like. Do not be guided by the recommendations of friends. Nothing will atone for or overcome an original distaste. It will only increase from intimacy; and if you are to live separate, it is better not to come together. There is no use in dragging a chain through life, unless it binds one to the object we love. Choose a mistress from among your equals. You will be able to understand her character better, and she will be more likely to understand yours. Those in an inferior station to yourself will doubt your good intentions, and misapprehend your plainest expressions. All that you swear is to them a riddle or downright nonsense. You cannot by possibility translate your thoughts into their dialect. They will be ignorant of the meaning of half you say, and laugh at the rest. As mistresses, they will have no sympathy with you; and as wives, you can have none with them. But they will do all they can to thwart you, and to retrieve themselves in their own opinion by trick and low cunning. No woman ever married into a family above herself that did not try to make all the mischief she could in it. Be not in haste to marry, nor to engage your affections, where there is no probability of a return. Do not fancy every woman you see the heroine of a romance, a Sophia Western, a Clarissa, or a Julia; and yourself the potential hero or it, Tom Jones, Lovelace, or St. Preux. Avoid this error as you would shrink back from a precipice. All your fine sentiments and romantic notions will (of themselves) make no more impression on one of these delicate creatures, than on a piece of marble. Their soft bosoms are steel to your amorous refinements, if you have no other pretensions. It is not what you think of them that determines their choice, but what they think of you. Endeavour, if you would escape lingering torments and the gnawing of the worm that dies not, to find out this, and to abide by the issue. We trifle with, make sport of, and despise those who are attached to us, and follow those that fly from us. 'We hunt the wind, we worship a statue, cry aloud to the desert.' [14] Do you, my dear boy, stop short in this career, if you find yourself setting out in it, and make up your mind to this, that if a woman does not like you of her own accord, that is, from involuntary impressions, nothing you can say or do or suffer for her sake will make her, but will set her the more against you. So the song goes—

> 'Quit, quit for shame; this will not move:
> If of herself she will not love,
> Nothing will make her, the devil take her!' [15]

Your pain is her triumph; the more she feels you in her power, the worse she will treat you: the more you make it appear you deserve her regard, the more will she resent it as an imputation on her first judgment. Study first impressions above all things; for every thing depends on them, in love especially. Women are armed by nature and education with a power of resisting the importunity of men, and they use this power according to their discretion. They enforce it to the utmost rigour of the law against those whom they do not like, and relax their extreme severity proportionably in favour of those that they do like and who in general care as little about them. Hence we see so many desponding lovers and forlorn damsels. Love in women (at least) is either vanity, or interest, or fancy. It is a merely selfish feeling. It has nothing to do (I am sorry to say) with friendship, or esteem, or even pity. I once asked a girl, the pattern of her sex in shape and mind and attractions, whether she did not think Mr. Coleridge had done wrong in making the heroine of his beautiful ballad story of Geneviève take compassion on her hapless lover—

> 'When on the yellow forest-leaves
> A dying man he lay—' [16]

---

[14] Cf. *Don Quixote:* Part I, Book II, Chapter XIII. The imagery of worshipping a statue suggests the "New Pygmalion" of the *Liber Amoris,* being composed near to the date of this letter.

[15] Cf. Sir John Suckling's song: "Why So Pale and Wan." Hazlitt in quoting the final stanza has omitted a line and made the last two lines into a single line.

[16] Cf. Stanza No. 16 of Coleridge's "Love."

And whether she believed that any woman ever fell in love through a sense of compassion; and she made answer—'Not if it was against her inclination!' I would take the lady's word *for a thousand pound,* on this point. Pain holds antipathy to pleasure; pity is not akin to love; a dying man has more need of a nurse than of a mistress. There is no forcing liking. It is as little to be fostered by reason and good-nature, as it can be controlled by prudence or propriety. It is a mere blind, headstrong impulse. Least of all flatter yourself that talents or virtue will recommend you to the favour of the sex, in lieu of exterior advantages. Oh! no. Women care nothing about poets, or philosophers, or politicians. They go by a man's looks and manner. Richardson calls them 'an eye-judging sex;' and I am sure he knew more about them than I can pretend to do. If you run away with a pedantic notion that they care a pin's-point about your head or your heart, you will repent it too late. Some blue-stocking may have her vanity flattered by your reputation or be edified by the solution of a metaphysical problem or a critical remark or a dissertation on the state of the nation, and fancy that she has a taste for intellect and is an epicure in sentiment. No true woman ever regarded any thing but her lover's person and address. Gravity will here answer all the same purpose without understanding, gaiety without wit, folly without good-nature, and impudence without any other pretension. The natural and instinctive passion of love is excited by qualities not peculiar to artists, authors, and men of letters. It is not the jest but the laugh that follows, not the sentiment but the glance that accompanies it, that *tells*—in a word, the sense of actual enjoyment that imparts itself to others, and excites mutual understanding and inclination. Authors, on the other hand, feel nothing spontaneously. The common incidents and circumstances of life with which others are taken up, make no alteration in them, nor provoke any of the common expressions of surprise, joy, admiration, anger, or merriment. Nothing stirs their blood or accelerates their juices or tickles their veins. Instead of yielding to the first natural and lively impulses of things, in which they would find sympathy, they screw themselves up to some far-fetched view of the subject in order to be unintelligible. Realities are not good enough for them, till they undergo the process of imagination and reflection. If you offer them your hand to shake, they will hardly take it; for this does not amount to a proposition. If you enter their room suddenly, they testify neither surprise nor satisfaction: no new idea is elicited by it. Yet if you suppose this to be a repulse, you are mistaken. They will enter into your affairs or combat your ideas with all the warmth and vehemence imaginable, as soon as they have a subject started. But their faculty for thinking must be set in motion, before you can put any soul into them. They are intellectual dram-drinkers; and without their necessary stimulus, are torpid, dead, insensible to every thing. They have great life of mind, but none of body. They do not drift with the stream of company or of passing occurrences, but are straining at some hyperbole or striking out a bye-path of their own. Follow them who list. Their minds are a sort of Herculaneum, full of old, petrified images;—are set in stereotype, and little fitted to the ordinary occasions of life.

What chance, then, can they have with women, who deal only in the pantomime of discourse, in gesticulation and the flippant bye-play of the senses, 'nods and winks and wreathed smiles;' [17] and to whom to offer a remark is an impertinence, or a reason an affront? The only way in which I ever knew mental qualities or distinction tell was in the clerical character; and women do certainly incline to this with some sort of favourable regard. Whether it is that the sanctity of pretension piques curiosity, or that the habitual submission of their understandings to their spiritual guides subdues the will, a popular preacher generally has the choice among the *élite* of his female flock. According to Mrs. Inchbald (see her 'Simple Story') there is another reason why religious courtship is not without its charms! But as I do not intend you for the church, do not, in thinking to study yourself into the good graces of the fair, study yourself out of them, millions of miles. Do not place thought as a barrier between you and love: do not abstract yourself into the regions of truth, far from the smile of earthly beauty. Let not the cloud sit upon your brow: let not the canker sink into your heart. Look up, laugh loud, talk big, keep the colour in your cheek and the fire in your eye, adorn your person, maintain your health, your beauty, and your animal spirits, and you will pass for a fine

---

[17] Cf. Milton's *L'Allegro,* line 128, which reads: "Nods, and Becks, and wreathèd Smiles."

man. But should you let your blood stagnate in some deep metaphysical question, or refine too much in your ideas of the sex, forgetting yourself in a dream of exalted perfection, you will want an eye to cheer you, a hand to guide you, a bosom to lean on, and will stagger into your grave, old before your time, unloved and unlovely. If you feel that you have not the necessary advantages of person, confidence, and manner, and that it is *up-hill* work with you to gain the ear of beauty, quit the pursuit at once, and seek for other satisfactions and consolations.

A spider, my dear, the meanest creature that crawls or lives, had its mate or fellow: but a scholar has no mate or fellow. For myself, I had courted thought, I had felt pain; and Love turned away his face from me. I have gazed along the silent air for that smile which had lured me to my doom. I no more heard those accents which would have burst upon me, like a voice from heaven. I loathed the light that shone on my disgrace. Hours, days, years, passed away; and only turned false hope to fixed despair. And as my frail bark sails down the stream of time, the God of Love stands on the shore, and as I stretch out my hands to him in vain, claps his wings, and mocks me as I pass!

There is but one other point on which I meant to speak to you, and that is the choice of a profession. This, probably, had better be left to time or accident or your own inclination. You have a very fine ear, but I have somehow a prejudice against men-singers, and indeed against the stage altogether. It is an uncertain and ungrateful soil. All professions are bad that depend on reputation, which is 'as often got without merit as lost without deserving.' Yet I cannot easily reconcile myself to your being a slave to business, and I shall hardly be able to leave you an independence. A situation in a public office is secure, but laborious and mechanical, and without the two great springs of life, Hope and Fear. Perhaps, however, it might ensure you a competence, and leave you leisure for some other favourite amusement or pursuit. I have said all reputation is hazardous, hard to win, harder to keep. Many never attain a glimpse of what they have all their lives been looking for, and others survive a passing shadow of it. Yet if I were to name one pursuit rather than another, I should wish you to be a good painter, if such a thing could be hoped. I have failed in this myself, and should wish you to be able to do what I have not—to paint like

Claude or Rembrandt or Guido or Vandyke, if it were possible. Artists, I think, who have succeeded in their chief object, live to be old, and are agreeable old men. Their minds keep alive to the last. Cosway's spirits never flagged till after ninety, and Nollekins, though nearly blind, passed all his mornings in giving directions about some group or bust in his workshop. You have seen Mr. Northcote,[18] that delightful specimen of the last age. With what avidity he takes up his pencil, or lays it down again to talk of numberless things! His eye has not lost its lustre, nor 'paled its ineffectual fire.' [19] His body is a shadow: he himself is a pure spirit. There is a kind of immortality about this sort of ideal and visionary existence that dallies with Fate and baffles the grim monster, Death. If I thought you could make as clever an artist and arrive at such an agreeable old age as Mr. Northcote, I should declare at once for your devoting yourself to this enchanting profession; and in that reliance, should feel less regret at some of my own disappointments, and little anxiety on your account!

[18] In his *Table-Talk* VIII, "On the Old Age of Artists," Hazlitt portrayed vividly and warmly the three artists last mentioned: Richard Cosway (1740-1821), Joseph Nollekins (1737-1823), and James Northcote (1746-1831), all prosperous and noted members of the Royal Academy. Hazlitt was particularly fascinated by the sharp, stinging flavor of Northcote's personality. The latter's studio was one of Hazlitt's favorite stopping places, where he so often rejoiced in conversation which he insisted had the force and brilliancy of "one of Titian's faces speaking." Hazlitt published in periodicals variations on these conversations entitled "Boswell Redivivus." Cf. Letter 164 to Northcote and the accompanying note on the publication of *Conversations of James Northcote,* published in 1830.
[19] Cf. *Hamlet,* I, v, 90: "And 'gins to pale his uneffectual fire:"

No. 100

To P. G. Patmore

Memoirs, II, 68.

[Renton Inn, Berwickshire,
Early March 1822]*

[My dear friend]

You may tell Colburn, [1] when you see him, that his work [2] is done magnificently, to wit:

in all 340 pp.

To do by Saturday night:

390 pp.

---

* Cf. Howe, p. 309; also Patmore: *My Friends and Acquaintance,* Volume 3, 1854, p. 13.

[1] William Carew Hazlitt *(Memoirs,* II, 68) indicated that this record of Hazlitt's extraordinary productiveness comes at the *end* of a letter to Patmore. The original MS of it has not been found.

[2] The second volume of *Table-Talk.*

[3] Baker (p. 412) reminds us that "On Individuality" never appeared in print.

No. 101

To Henry Colburn

Works, IX, 216.

Renton-Inn, Berwickshire, Scotland.
Sunday, March 3 [1822]

My Dear Sir,

By the time you receive this, the New Volume [1] will be done, and ready, if you desire it, to go to press with, or to send up in lumps of 50 pages at a time for the Magazine. It contains, I hope, better things than any I have done. I thank God for my escape, [2] and have now done with essay-writing for ever.[3] I do wish you would send me 30£ by return of post, or I shall be obliged to write to Jeffrey for money to get away from here, which I wish to do immediately after my task is done.[4] I have worked at it, I assure you, without ceasing and like a tyger. I am on the whole better in health, and hope to take a trip into the Highlands [5] before I return. Has Mr. Patmore called on you in my behalf? I remain, Dear Sir,

Your obliged and very humble servant,
W.Hazlitt

---

[1] *Table-Talk,* Volume II.

[2] He was qualifying for residence under Scottish law in order to obtain the divorce.

[3] Several of his finest essays, including "My First Acquaintance with Poets" and "On the Feeling of Immortality in Youth," were written after this date.

[4] He arrived in Edinburgh on March 30th.

[5] In May, while awaiting the final oath for the divorce, Hazlitt delivered two lectures on poetry at Glasgow and went on a walking tour to Ben Lomond with his friend, the dramatist James Sheridan Knowles. Cf. Letters 126-128.

No. 102

To P. G. Patmore

Liber Amoris, Letter II.

Renton Inn (PM: March 9, 1822) *

Dear P[atmore],

Here, without loss of time, in order that I may have your opinion upon it, is little YES and NO's answer to my last.

'Sir,

I should not have disregarded your injunction not to send you any more letters that might come to you, had I not promised the Gentleman who left the enclosed to forward it the earliest opportunity, as he said it was *of consequence.* Mr. P— called the day after you left town. My mother and myself are much obliged by your kind offer of tickets to the play, but must decline accepting it. My family send their best respects, in which they are joined by

Your's, truly,
S.L.[1]

The deuce a bit more is there of it. If you can make anything out of it (or any body else) I'll be hanged. You are to understand, this comes in a frank, [2] the second I have received from her, with a name I can't make out, and she won't tell me, though I asked her, where she got franks, as also whether the lodgings were let, to neither of which a word of answer.—is the name on the frank: see if you can decypher it by a Red-book.[3] I suspect her grievously of

---

* Cf. Howe, *Works, IX,* p.264.

[1] Sarah Walker.

[2] Superscribed signature (commonly of a member of Parliament) entitling the letter to go post free.

[3] A popular name for *The Royal Kalendar, or Complete Annual Register* (published from 1767 to 1893), *an Alphabetical List of the Nobility and Gentry.*

being an arrant jilt, to say no more—yet I love her dearly. Do you know I'm going to write to that sweet rogue presently, having a whole evening to myself in advance of my work? Now mark, before you set about your exposition of the new Apocalypse of the New Calypso, [4] the only thing to be endured in the above letter is the date. It was written the very day after she received mine. By this she seems willing to lose no time in receiving these letters 'of such sweet breath composed.' [5] If I thought so—but I wait for your reply. After all, what is there in her but a pretty figure, and that you can't get a word out of her? Her's is the Fabian method [6] of making love and conquests. What do you suppose she said the night before I left her?

'H. Could you not come and live with me as a friend?

S. I don't know: and yet it would be of no use if I did, you would always be hankering after what could never be!'

I asked her if she would do so at once—the very next day? And what do you guess was her answer—'Do you think it would be prudent?' As I didn't proceed to extremities on the spot, she began to look grave, and declare off. 'Would she live with me in her own house—to be with me all day as dear friends, if nothing more, to sit and read and talk with me?'—'She would make no promises, but I should find her the same.' 'Would she go to the play with me sometimes, and let it be understood that I was paying my addresses to her?'—'She could not, as a habit—her father was rather strict, and would object.'—Now what am I to think of all this? Am I mad or a fool? Answer me to that, Master Brook! [7] You are a philosopher.

---

[4] Calypso, one of the daughters of Atlas, offered Ulysses immortality if he would remain with her. The "New Calypso" is a parallel to his ironic image for the *Liber Amoris: the New Pygmalion.* In both instances "New" means in reverse.

[5] *Hamlet,* III, i, 98.

[6] Extreme caution, indecisiveness, avoidance of major clashes. (The successful military practice of Quintus Fabius Maximus against Hannibal).

[7] Cf. *Merry Wives of Windsor,* III, v, 124.

No. 103

To Sarah Walker [1]

John Bull, June 22, 1823.

[Renton Inn, Berwickshire]
(PM Dunbar, March 9, 1822)

My dear Sarah,

I have got an evening to spare, and shall employ in it writing to you, the only pleasure I have here, except receiving your answers, and seeing your hand-writing, for it is little more, they are so short; and then scarce one kind word in them, *in the way of friendship.* You are such a girl for business. Shall I scold thee, my love—'my beautiful, my own, my only love'? [2] Not for the world would I send

---

[1] Three successive issues of the London weekly, *John Bull,* in June of 1823 contained matter attacking Hazlitt by way of the Sarah Walker affair. On June 8 *John Bull* charged (p. 180) that a favorable review of *Liber Amoris; or, the New Pygmalion* in the *Times* was a puff written by "Billy Hazlitt" himself, "the Cockney lecturer" on Shakespeare who "is not able to write English." On June 15 *John Bull* (pp. 188-189) devoted more than one of its tall columns to a play-book burlesque of two passages from *Liber Amoris* complete with gratuitous stage directions, cast of characters, intentional misquotations, and sneering asides, ending *"(To be continued.)"*. On June 22 *John Bull* (pp. 197-198) proposed to drop "the foolery of our last" and to "set Mr. Hazlitt down in a manner he little expects." Proceeding to inform readers that Hazlitt's letter "To the same" in *Liber Amoris* was but an extract, *John Bull* laid before its readers *"the whole of his letter* of that date (Dunbar, March 9, 1822)." Thereupon both the extract and the whole original letter were printed, purporting to justify the effrontery as answering "the *ends of justice* moral and literary."

The circumstances surrounding this attack *ad hominem* are illuminating. The tone of righteous indignation at a "disappointed dotard" and "impotent sensualist," who was said to write a book of love in order to "SPITE" a "very pretty and innocent girl," is a lively sample of Tory rancor in the game of politics in 1823. Some of Hazlitt's blows against *John Bull* and other representatives of the "Ministerial" press appear in "My First Acquaintance with Poets," "The Periodical Press," and "On the Spirit of Partisanship." *(Works,* XVI, 106; 236-239, XVII: 41ff., and 307.) P.P. Howe knew of the existence of this letter and refers to it in *Works,* IX, 262; Professor Stanley Jones of the University of Glasgow republished it in 1966.

[2] Not identified.

thee an unkind word—so far away. I may be rash and hasty when I am with thee, but deliberately can I never say or do aught to cast the slightest blame upon thee. You are my little idol—the dear image in my heart, as 'that little image' [3] on the mantle-piece (or *somebody like it*) is in thine. Little did I think, thou glorious and lovely girl, when I once gave it thee to kiss, what I was doing. Keep it, cherish it in thy breast, as I would cherish thee for ever, and bless thee with my latest breath. It is *for your steadfast attachment there* that I esteem you; you ought to show some regard to me for *his* sake? Yet it is not what you think of me—it is what you think and feel towards another—it is your own little heart, that seat and throne of fond affection, to which mine is wedded. Do I offend thee, my dear, by talking so? I hope not; I do not mean it; but you know how I love THEE, and I try to express it as well as I can. If my letters pain THEE tell me so, and I will write differently, as long as you will give me leave.

The house-maid, in the absence of the waiter, (you can't think what an ugly fellow the waiter is) has been up to know what I will have for supper, for the cook wishes to get her things done out of the way. 'Why, what's the matter?' 'Oh! nothing, only it's our cook's *court-night.*' 'Court-night! what's that?' 'Why, her sweetheart's coming to see her.' 'And is not he come yet then?' 'No; nor won't go away till morning light.' 'And when are they to be married?' 'Oh, as soon as they can get money to buy some bedding.' And away she goes laughing ready to split her sides, that I should not know what *court-night* means in Scotch. The wind raves like ten demons at the window, has broken a pane in one of them, blown out the candles, and I think will blow the cook's lover away if he does not make haste. I am better in my health than I was. I have lived regular, and have had two letters from Sarah. Do you know I *have done my work,* [4] or shall by Saturday? It *will take another month to finish,* but all the labour and anxiety is over. I am glad I have got through it so well, for I was afraid I should lose reputation by it, (which I can little afford to lose) and besides, my dear, I now have another motive, I like thee to hear me spoken well

---

[3] The small bronze figure of Bonaparte that Sarah had said somewhat resembled a former lover of hers.

[4] The second volume of *Table-Talk.*

of, if at all. I walk out between dinner and tea along the valley [5] that winds before the house, and hear the birds sing as I told thee; and think, if I had thee hanging on my arm, *and for life,* how happy I should be—happier than I ever hope to be, or had even a conception of till I knew THEE. 'But that can never be'—I hear you answer in a soft, low murmur. Well, let me dream of it sometimes, I am not blest too often, except when that favourite note, the harbinger of spring, recalling the hopes of my youth, whispers thy name and peace together in my ear. I was writing something to-day about Mr. Macready, [6] and that put me in mind of that delicious night I saw Romeo and Juliet with YOU and your mother. Can I ever forget it for a moment—your sweet modest looks, your infinite propriety of behavior, all your sweet ways—your hesitating about taking my arm as we came out till your mother did—your laughing about losing your cloak—your stepping into the coach without my being able to make an inch of discovery—and oh! my sitting down beside you, you whom I loved so well, so long, and your assuring me I had not lessened your pleasure at the play by being with you, and giving me that dear hand to press in mine— I seemed to be in Heaven—that slight, exquisitely turned form contained my all of heaven upon earth—I sat beside the adorable creature by her own permission—and as I followed [folded] [7] you, yes, you, my best Sarah, to my heart, there was, as you say, 'a tie between us,' you did seem to be mine for a few short moments, in all truth and honour, and sacredness! Oh! could we but be always so—do not mock me, for I am indeed a very child in love. I ought to beg your pardon for my behaviour afterwards, but I hope *the little image* made it up between us.[8] Kiss it for its own sake first, and then for mine if you can in earnest.—I shall leave this next Sunday or Monday for Edinburgh. I shall then have been in Scotland five weeks and expect to be joined there soon. I had a letter from my

---

[5] Valley of the Eye Water.

[6] Hazlitt edited this in *Liber Amoris* to "reading something" about Macready. He refers to that "delicious night" in "Whether Actors Should Sit in the Boxes" (*Table-Talk,* VIII, 277).

[7] In *Liber Amoris* Hazlitt altered this to "folded," as indeed the sense requires.

[8] It may have been at this moment, but Hazlitt, having returned to London in May, quarreled with Sarah and trampled on the "little image," shattering it (*Works,* IX, 145).

little boy the other day, and I have been writing him a long essay [9] in my book on his conduct in life, shewing him how to avoid his father's errors, and particularly pointing out to him the dangers of love, you may well laugh at this. I will take care, however, he does not get a stoop in the shoulders by poring over his books or muddle his brain with the contents. There is a picture [10] of me when a little boy which my brother who painted it is to let me have. Should I— might I desire it to be left with you to *keep for me,* or forward it to me? You would hardly believe it was once like me. It was, however; nay more, *you* could make it like me again, even now. My face, I fear, belies my heart; or expresses the bad passions more strongly than my good feelings. Does not this show that the bad ones preponderate? I ask you, because I think you will not judge me harshly. Tell me what you think, and whether you have been able to get to the end of this scrawl.

Is the lodgings let to any one I know? I love you and die for you.

Please to direct to me, Mr. Hazlitt, Post-Office, Edinburgh. You did not answer a good many things in my last. Never do, if I ask impertinent questions.

W.H.

P.S. I desired Mr. P.[11] to call and request you not to give my address, as I expected a dunning letter; but it does not signify now. He says he saw you, and that you looked charmingly, but that your mother was unwell. I hope she is better. Give my remembrances to all at home, and to your aunt. I was mopish when I wrote to P. and he says he was going to tell you I was in a dying way, but didn't.

---

[9] "On the Conduct of Life; or, Advice to A Schoolboy." *Works,* XVIII, 86-100. Commonly shortened to "Advice to A Schoolboy."

[10] Reproduced by Moyne in *The Journal of Margaret Hazlitt* (Lawrence, Kansas: University of Kansas Press, 1967), p. 17, with comment (pp. 20-21); and by Howe as the frontispiece in Volume VIII of *Works.*

[11] P.G. Patmore.

No. 104

To P. G. Patmore

Liber Amoris, Letter I.

[Renton Inn, Berwickshire
middle of March 1822]

My Good Friend,

Here I am in Scotland (and shall have been here three weeks, next Monday) as I may say, *on my probation.* This is a lone inn, but on a great scale, thirty miles from Edinburgh. It is situated on a rising ground (a mark for all the winds, which blow here incessantly)—there is a woody hill opposite, with a winding valley below, and the London road stretches out on either side. You may guess which way I oftenest walk. I have written two letters to S.L.[1] and got one cold, prudish answer, beginning *Sir,* and ending *From your's truly,* with *Best respects from herself and relations.* I was going to give in, but have returned an answer, which I think is a touch-stone. I send it you on the other side to keep as a curiosity, in case she kills me by her exquisite rejoinder. I am convinced from the profound contemplations I have had on the subject here and coming along, that I am on a wrong scent. We had a famous parting-scene, a complete quarrel and then a reconciliation, in which she did beguile me of my tears, but the deuce a one did she shed. What do you think? She cajoled me out of my little Bonaparte as cleverly as possible, in manner and form following. She was shy the Saturday and Sunday (the day of my departure) so I got in dudgeon, and began to rip up grievances. I asked her how she came to admit me to such extreme familiarities, the first week I entered the house. "If she had no particular regard for me, she must do so (or more) with everyone: if she had a liking to me from the first, why refuse me with scorn and wilfulness?" If you had seen how she flounced, and looked, and went to the door, saying "She was obliged to me for letting her know the opinion I

---

1 Sarah Walker.

had always entertained of her"—then I said, "Sarah!"—and she came back and took my hand, and fixed her eyes on the mantle-piece—(she must have been invoking her idol then—if I thought so, I could devour her, the darling—but I doubt her)—So I said "There is one thing that has occurred to me sometimes as possible, to account for your conduct to me at first—there wasn't a likeness, was there, to your old friend?" She answered "No, none—but there was a likeness." I asked, to what? She said, "to that little image!" I said, "Do you mean Buonaparte?" She said, "Yes, all but the nose." "And the figure?" "He was taller."—I could not stand this. So I got up and took it, and gave it her, and after some reluctance, she consented to "keep it for me." [2] What will you bet that it wasn't all a trick? I'll tell you why I suspect it, besides being fairly out of my wits about her. I had told her mother half an hour before, that I should take this image and leave it at Mrs. B's, [3] for that I didn't wish to leave anything behind me that must bring me back again. Then up she comes and starts a likeness to her lover: she knew I should give it her on the spot—"No, she would keep it for me!" So I must come back for it. Whether art or nature, it is sublime. I told her I should write and tell you so, and that I parted from her, confiding, adoring!—She is beyond me, that's certain. Do go and see her, and desire her not to give my present address to a single soul, and learn if the lodging is let, and to whom. My letter to her is as follows. If she shews the least remorse at it, I'll be hanged, though it might move a stone, I modestly think.

[*His letter beginning, "You will scold me for this"* [4] *undoubtedly followed here. Hazlitt deleted it in order to place it at the end of Part I of* Liber Amoris.]

N.B.—I have begun a book of our conversations (I mean mine and the statue's), which I call *Liber Amoris.* I was detained at Stamford and found myself dull, and could hit upon no other way of employing my time so agreeably.

---

[2] This dialogue figures as the climax of "The Reconciliation," which ends Part I of *Liber Amoris.* Repetitions and similarities in phrases and dialogue indicate that Hazlitt was working back and forth from letter to book, or book to letter. See also his remark at the very end of this letter. Hazlitt trampled the talisman to pieces a few weeks later. Cf. Letter 126.
[3] Probably a screen for a friend.

No. 105

To P. G. Patmore

MS. Lockwood.
Address: P. G. Patmore, Esq./12 Greek Street/Soho/London.

[30 March 1822] *

[My Dear Friend, [1]]

I ought to have written to you before, but since I received your letter, I have been in a sort of Hell, and what is worse, I see no prospect of getting out of it. I would put an end to my torments at once, but I am as great a coward as I am a fool. Do you know I have not had a word of answer from her since? What can be the reason? Is she offended at my letting you know she wrote to me or is it some new amour. I wrote to her in the tenderest, most respectful manner, poured my soul at her feet, and this is the way she serves me! Can you account for it except on the admission of my worst suspicion, that she has. . . . Oh! my God! can I bear to think of her so, or that I am scorned and made a sport of by the creature to whom I had given my very heart? I feel like one of the damned. To be hated, loathed as I have been all my life, and to feel the utter impossibility of its ever being otherwise while I live— take what pains I may! If you *do* know anything, good or bad, tell me, I intreat you. I can bear any thing but this horrid [suspense. If I knew] she was a mere abandoned creature, I should try to forget her: but till I do know this, nothing can tear me from her, I have sucked in poison from her lips too long—Alas! mine do not poison again. I sit and cry my eyes out, my weakness grows upon me and I have no hope left unless I could lose my senses quite. I think I should like this—to forget, ah! to forget—there would be something

---

[4] Cf. Letter 98.

---

* Cf. Howe, p. 310; Wardle, p. 313.
[1] The salutation is cut out of the MS. The restored words are those conventionally used at this time to address Patmore.

in that—to be an ideot for some few years and then to wake up a poor wretched old man, to recollect my misery as past, and die. Yet oh! with her, only a little while ago, I had different hopes, forfeited for nothing that I know of—[two lines crossed out] It is well I had finished Colburn's work [2] before all this came upon me. It is one comfort I have done that . . . . If you can give me any consolation on the subject of my tormentor, pray do. The grievous pain I suffer wears me out by inches. I write this on the supposition that Mrs. H.[3] may still come here and that I may be kept in suspense a week or two longer. But for God's sake, don't go near the place, *on my account*. Direct to me at the Post-Office, and if I return to town directly as I fear, I will leave word for them to forward the letter to me in London—not in S.B.[4] Can I breathe away from her? Her hatred of me must be great, [since] my love of her could not overcome it. I have finished the book of my conversations with her, which I call *Liber Amoris:* it is very nice reading. Yours truly, W.H. Edinburgh, March 30.

I have seen the great little man, [5] and he is very gracious to me—*Et sa femme aussi!* I tell him I am dull and out of spirits. He says he cannot perceive it. He is a person of an infinite vivacity. My Sardanapalus [6] is to be in.

[*Written across the last page.*]
In my judgment Myrrha [7] is just like S.W., only I am not like Sardanapalus!

---

[2] Essays for the second volume of *Table-Talk.* Cf. *Memoirs*, II, 68.
[3] Mrs. Hazlitt.
[4] Southampton Buildings.
[5] Francis Jeffrey, editor of the *Edinburgh Review.*
[6] A review of Byron's tragedy. The authorship, however, is clouded. Apparently Jeffrey freely revised and rewrote much of it, as was frequently his editorial practice. In the *Review* for February 1822 (Volume 36, pp. 413-452) Hazlitt's work was combined with *The Two Foscari* and *Cain* in a longer, comprehensive treatment of "Lord Byron's Tragedies," as the running title has it. P. P. Howe saw in it "something of Hazlitt and a good deal of Jeffrey" (*Life,* 399), though he knew that Jeffrey claimed it as his own. The *Wellesley Index* (I, 462) assigns it to Jeffrey.
[7] The high-minded Greek slave girl in *Sardanapalus.*

No. 106

To P. G. Patmore

MS. Lockwood.
Address: P. G. Patmore/12 Greek Street/Soho/London.

(PM: 7 April 1822)

My dear friend,

I received your letter this morning with gratitude. I have felt somewhat easier since. It shewed your interest in my vexations, and also that you knew nothing worse than I did. I cannot describe the weakness of mind to which she has reduced me. I am come back to Edinburgh about this cursed business, and Mrs H[azlitt] is coming down next week. How it will end, I can't say, and don't care except with reference to the other affair. I should like to have it in my power to make her the offer direct and unequivocal, to see how she'd take it. It would be worth something at any rate to see her superfine airs upon it; and if she should take it into her head to turn round her sweet neck, drop her eyelids and say—"Yes, I will be yours"—treason domestic, foreign levy, nothing could touch me further. By Heaven, I doat on her. The truth is, I never had any pleasure, like love, with any one but her. Then how can I bear to part with her? Do you know I like to think of her best in her morning gown, in her dirt and her mob-cap; it is so she has oftenest sat [on my knee with her arms round my neck—Damn her, I could devour her, it is *herself* that I love.]¹ [two lines obliterated]² and though it's what I hate, I adored her the more for it. When I but touch her hand, I enjoy perfect happiness and contentment of soul. Yet I think I am in the wrong box. What security can I have that she does not flirt or worse with every one that comes in her way

---

¹ The square brackets here are Hazlitt's, probably indicating matter to be omitted in *Liber Amoris*. Actually Hazlitt rephrased this sentence and omitted the remainder of the letter, though supplying a small amount of new matter.

² But written in another hand: "I went with a girl that was what they call—and fancied she was 15."

when I recollect how she took my first advances? How can I think she has any regard for me when she knows the tortures she puts me to by her silence? And what can I think of a girl who grants a man she has no particle of regard for the freedoms she has done to me? My idea is that in refusing to marry she has made up her mind to a sporting-life (keeping safe as well as she can) between disappointment and wantonness and a love of intrigue. I think she would sooner come and live with me than marry me. So that I have her in my arms and *for life,* I care not how; I never could tire of her sweetness, I feel as if I could grow to her, body and soul!—A thought has struck me. Her father has a bill of mine for ten pounds unhonoured, about which I tipped her a cavalier epistle ten days ago, saying I should be in town this week and "would *call* and take it up," but nothing reproachful. Now if you could get Colburn who has a deposit of 220 pp. of the new Vol.[3] to come down with 10£ you might call and take up the aforesaid bill, saying that I am prevented from coming to town as I expected by the business I came about, and if you saw fit, that a line from her, mentioning the receipt of the same and stating that no great harm had been done by the delay, would be a favour conferred upon me here at Edinburgh—*greater than an angel's visit!* You might add (supposing her to seem gracious) that you believe I have been hurt, thinking I had *offended her.* Yet I doubt about all this; only I am afraid of being kept some time longer in the dark—yet that is better than the Hell of detecting her in an independent intrigue with some other fellow. I don't see how I should stand it. I must say Farewel, for the thought drives me mad.

W.H.

P. S. Could you fill up two blanks for me in an Essay on Burleigh-House[4] in Colburn's hands, one Lamb's description of the sports in the Forest, see John Woodvil.[5]

"To see the sun to bed and to arise," etc. the other Northcote's account of Claude Lorraine in his Vision of a Painter at the end of

---

[3] *Table-Talk,* II.

[4] Appeared in the *London Magazine,* April 1822.

[5] Lamb's verse tragedy written in 1799 but not acted. "To see the sun to bed and see him rise."

his life of Sir Joshua? [6] [Several words obliterated]. I feared as much all along; and yet he used to lecture me as a henpecked lover. I hope to God he'll get the better of it; yet he's just in my situation—glued to a bitch, a little damned incubus—sucking in her soul and her breath about twice as [several words obliterated] It's dreadful work, I will say—.

[*Inserted in the middle of the P.S.:*]

Give me all the advice you can. I shall be thankful for it. I will get the MS.

[*Written across the top of the first page:*]

FINAL. Don't go at all. I believe her to be a common lodging-house drab, and that any attempt to move only hardens her.

[*One line crossed out, but the meaning has been written in above in another hand, as follows:*]

"All she wants is to be tickled and go all lengths but the last—to be thrown on the floor and felt and all" and still resist and keep up the game. To think that I should feel as I have done for such a monster.

[*Written across page 3:*]

It won't do at all. The way would be (if you got the stuff) to call and ask for Mr. W [7] and treat it as a mere matter of business and if they ask how I am, say "not very well." And if she comes poking out, to say I desired my love or my best respects to her, or something of that grave easy sort. But ask her for nothing, for whatever you do, she'll refuse—except kisses! But use your own discretion about it.

---

[6] James Northcote, R.A. (1746-1831), *Memoirs of Sir Joshua Reynolds, Knt.*, 1813. Hazlitt did not begin to publish his famous series of conversations with Northcote until 1826. Cf. Letter 164.

[7] Mr. Walker, Sarah's father.

No. 107

To Taylor and Hessey

London Mercury, March, 1923.
Address: Mssrs. Taylor and Hessey/Fleet Street/London.

April 10. [1822]

My Dear Sir,

I beg pardon but send the enclosed.[1] I propose to send you some account in two or three days of Williams's Views in Greece [2] exhibiting here, which will make up the sheet and I hope nearly balance our account. I am going to Lanark to give a description of it *tandem.* Will you have it for next month? If so, and you could send me 10£ upon it by return of post, it would be an especial favour in addition to so many others granted to Dear Sir,

your obliged friend and servant,
W. Hazlitt.

Mr. Hazlitt,
at Mrs. Dow's,
10, George Street,
Edinburgh.

---

[1] The second half of his article "On the Elgin Marbles."

[2] Hugh Williams (1773-1829), painter, known as "Grecian Williams." The exhibition was in the Calton Convening Room, Edinburgh. Hazlitt's article on Williams's water colours appeared in the *London Magazine* (May 1822).

No. 108

To Taylor and Hessey

MS. Morgan.
Address: Messrs. Taylor and Hessey/Fleet Street/London/By
the Edinburgh Mail.

Edinburgh
April 16, 1822

Dear Sir,

I have just received your kind letter with the contents for which I
am much obliged to you.

I send the enclosed, but fear it is hardly worth the while. Yet it
may oblige a meritorious artist here and keep my word unbroken.[1]

W. H.

I expect to be in town soon and will do the Leonardo, unless W.[2]
likes.

---

[1] An article on Hugh Williams's "Views in Greece," *London Magazine* (May
1822).

[2] Thomas Griffiths Wainewright (1794-1852) (Janus Weathercock), who sometimes reviewed art exhibitions in the *London Magazine*.

No. 109

To P. G. Patmore

MS. Lockwood.
Address: P. G. Patmore/12 Greek Street/Soho/London.

(PM: 21 April 1822)

My dear Patmore,

I got your letter this morning, and I kiss the rod not only with submission but gratitude. Your rebukes of me and your defences of her are the only things that save my soul from Hell. She is my soul's idol, and believe me those words of yours applied to the dear creature, "To lip a chaste one and suppose her wanton," [1] were balm and rapture to me. I have *lipped her,* God knows, thought I, and Oh! is it even possible that she is a chaste one and that she has bestowed her loved "endearments" on me (her own sweet word) out of true regard? That thought, out of the lowest depths of despair, would at any time make me strike my head against the stars. [2] Be it known to you that while I write this I am drinking ale at the Black Bull, celebrated in Blackwood. It is owing to your letter. Could I think her [3] *love* "honest," I am proof against

---

[1] *Othello,* IV, i, 73:

> "To lip a wanton in a secure couch,
> And to suppose her chaste."

[2] Horace, *Odes,* I, i, 35-36:

> Quod si me lyricis vatibus inseris
> Sublimi feriam sidera vertice.

> But if you include me among the lyric poets
> I shall hit the stars with my exalted head.

[3] "The" written below.

Edinburgh ale. She by her silence makes my "dark hour," [4] and you dissipate it—for four and twenty hours. Another thing has brought me to life. [Mrs. H[azlitt] is actually on her way here. I was going to set off home and to throw myself at *her* feet once more, when coming up Leith Walk I met an old friend come down here to settle, who said, "I saw your wife at the wharf. She had just paid her passage by the Superb."] [5] Here's a change. This *Bell* [6] whom I met is the very man to negotiate the business between us. Should the business succeed, and I should be free, do you think S.W.[7] will be Mrs.[Hazlitt]? If she *will*, she *shall;* and to call her so to you, or to hear her called so by others, will be music to my ears, such as they never heard. Do you think if she knew how I love her, my depressions and my altitudes, my wanderings and my pertinacity, it would not melt her? She knows it all, and if she is not a bitch, she loves me or regards me with a feeling next to love. I don't believe that any human being was ever courted more passionately than she has been by me. As Rousseau said [8] of Madame d'Houdetot (forgive the allusion) my soul has found a language in speaking to her, and I have talked to her the divine language of love. Yet she says she is insensible to it. Am I to believe her or you? You, for I wish it, and wish it to madness, now that I am like to be free and to have it in my power to say to her without a possibility of suspicion, "Sarah, will you be mine?" When I sometimes think of the time I first saw the sweet apparition, August 16, 1820, and that perhaps, *possibly* she may be my wife before that day two years, it makes me mad with incredible joy and love of her. I hear [a few words obliterated but above in another hand: "the bitch"] Anne Sk.[9] is going to marry one of the nastiest scrubs in the city of London. If I knew Procter's address, I'd tip him an epistle. I am glad you go on

---

[4] *Macbeth,* III, i, 138.

[5] The square brackets are Hazlitt's.

[6] Adam Bell, who officiously assisted the Hazlitts. See Bonner, *passim (The Journals of Sarah and William Hazlitt, 1822-1831.* Edited by Willard Hallam Bonner, University of Buffalo Studies, v. 24, no. 3, 1959)

[7] Sarah Walker.

[8] *Confessions,* ed. Garnier, Liv. IX, p. 393.

[9] Anne Skepper, stepdaughter of Basil Montagu. A friend of Mary Lamb, she may have sympathised with Mrs. Hazlitt. She married B. W. Procter in October, 1824.

so swimmingly with the N.M.M.[10] I shall be back in a week or a month. I won't write to her.

[*Written across the top of MS p. 1.:*]

[I wish Colburn would send me word what he is about. Tell him what I am about, if you think it wise to do so][11]

---

[10] *New Monthly Magazine.*
[11] The square brackets are Hazlitt's.

No. 110

To P. G. Patmore

MS. Lockwood.

[May 1822]*

My only friend,

I should like you to fetch the MSS.[1] and try to ascertain for me whether I had better return there or not, as soon as this affair is over. I cannot give her up without an absolute certainty. Only however sound the matter [2] by saying for instance that you are desired to get me a lodging, and that you believe I should prefer being there to any where else. You may say that the affair of the divorce is over and that I am gone a tour in the Highlands. Ascertain if that wretched rival [3] is there still. I am almost satisfied she is a wretched creature herself, but my only hope of happiness rests on the alternative. Ours was the sweetest friendship—oh! might the delusion be renewed that I might die in it! If there is any insolence—TRY HER through (anyone) someone, [4] E. for example, [5] who will satisfy my soul I have lost only a lovely frail one that I was not like to gain by true love. Oh! that I was once back to London. I am going to see Knowles to get him to go with me to the Highlands, [6] and talk about *her*. I shall be back Thursday week, to

---

* Cf. Le Gallienne's *Liber Amoris* (1894) p. 219; cf. Wardle, pp. 329-330.

[1] "Things" crossed out and "MSS" written above. Hazlitt left many books and manuscripts at 9 Southampton Buildings.

[2] "whether I" crossed out and "the matter" written above.

[3] Griffiths, a fellow lodger.

[4] Both words appear in the MS.

[5] Written in above. Hazlitt makes many such references to "E" in this relation. However, when the actual attempt was made in 1823, he used the initial "F," possibly for William Farren, an actor and close friend. For Hazlitt's notes of the occasion, see *Appendix A*.

[6] He went with Knowles on May 14. This dates the letter in the first half of May, not June as has been hitherto assumed.

appear in court *pro formâ* the next day, and then for Heaven or for Hell. Send me a line about my little boy.

W.H.

10 George Street
Edinburgh.

No. 111

To James Hessey

MS. Rylands.
Address: Messers. Taylor and Hessey/93 Fleet Street/London.

[Middle of May 1822]

My dear Sir,

Will you oblige me by letting me [have] the following, prettily bound: viz. Vicar of Wakefield, Man of Feeling, and Nature and Art.[1] I am here [2] for a day or two but am going down to Salisbury. I have been to New Lanark.[3]

Yours ever truly,
W. Hazlitt.

I wish you would send a small gilt memorandum book, green with gold edges.

---

[1] Intended as gifts for Sarah Walker, but she refused them. Cf. Letter 125.

[2] At his rooms in London, 9 Southampton Buildings.

[3] Hazlitt was there on Tuesday, 30 April. He returned to London on 17 May, where he remained until the 28th. Apparently he did not go to Salisbury at this time.

No. 112

To P. G. Patmore

Liber Amoris, Letter VI.[1]

[30 or 31 May 1822] *

Dear Patmore,

What have I suffered since I parted with you! [2] A raging fire is in my heart and in my brain, that never quits me. The steamboat (which I foolishly ventured on board) seems a prison-house, a sort of spectre-ship, moving on through an infernal lake, without wind or tide, by some necromantic power—the splashing of the waves the noise of the engine gives me no rest, night or day—no tree, no natural object varies the scene—but the abyss is before me, and all my peace lies weltering in it! I feel the eternity of punishment in this life; for I see no end of my woes. The people about me are ill, uncomfortable, wretched enough, many of them—but tomorrow or next day, they reach the place of their destination, and all will be new and delightful. To me it will be the same. I can neither escape from her, nor from myself. All is endurable where there is a limit: but I have nothing but the blackness and the fiendishness of scorn around me—mocked by her (the false one) in whom I placed my hope, and who hardens herself against me!—I believe you thought me quite gay, vain, insolent, half mad, the night I left the house—no tongue can tell the heaviness of heart I felt at that moment. No footsteps ever fell more slow, more sad than mine; for every step bore me farther from her, with whom my soul and every thought

---

* Cf. Wardle, p. 326n.

[1] Two somewhat modified excerpts from the original of this letter were printed by Patmore (III, 176) and reprinted in Appendix II of Le Gallienne's *Liber Amoris* (1894), p. 362, validating "Letter VI" of *Liber Amoris.* Another instance of Hazlitt's impulse to use his own emotionally charged letters for literary purposes is to be seen in the first version of "The Fight." Cf. *Hazlitt in the Workshop: The Manuscript of "The Fight"* (p. 18) by Stewart C. Wilcox (Baltimore, 1943).

[2] Hazlitt left London on the 28th to return to Edinburgh.

lingered. I had parted with her in anger, and each had spoken words of high disdain, not soon to be forgiven. Should I ever behold her again? Where go to live and die far from her? In her sight there was Elysium; her smile was heaven; her voice was enchantment; the air of love waved round her, breathing balm into my heart: for a little while I had sat with the Gods at their golden tables, I had tasted of all earth's bliss, "both living and loving!" [3] But now Paradise barred its doors against me; I was driven from her presence, where rosy blushes and delicious sighs and all soft wishes dwelt, the outcast of nature and the scoff of love! I thought of the time when I was a little happy careless child, of my father's house, of my early lessons, of my brother's picture of me when a boy, of all that had since happened to me, and of the waste of years to come—I stopped, faultered, and was going to turn back once more to make a longer truce with wretchedness and patch up a hollow league with love, when the recollection of her words—"I always told you I had no affection for you"—steeled my resolution, and I determined to proceed. You see by this she always hated me, and only played with my credulity till she could find some one to supply the place of her unalterable attachment to *the little image.* I am a little, a very little better to-day. Would it were quietly over; and that this misshapen form (made to be mocked) were hid out of the sight of cold, sullen eyes! The people about me even take notice of my dumb despair, and pity me. What is to be done? I cannot forget *her;* and I can find no other like what *she seemed.* I should wish you to call, if you can make an excuse, and see whether or no she is quite marble—whether I may go back again at my return, and whether she will see me and talk to me sometimes as an old friend. Suppose you were to call on M—[4] from me, and ask him what his impression is that I ought to do. But do as you think best. Pardon. Pardon.

P.S. I send this from Scarborough, where the vessel stops for a few minutes. I scarcely know what I should have done, but for this relief to my feelings.

---

[3] Conclusion of Thekla's song in Lamb's play, *John Woodvil.*
[4] Robert Roscoe, the young barrister who married Sarah Walker's older sister.

No. 113

To William Hazlitt, Jr.

MS. Keynes.

[c. 30 or 31 May 1822]

My dear little baby, [1]

The only comfort or tie poor Father has left! I send thee a pound to spend. Be happy as thou canst, my love, and I will come back to thee soon, that is, before the holidays, and we will go to Winterslow Hut together, and seek for peace. I have got a hundred pound since I came, and hope before that is spent, to recover spirits to work and support thy little life. Call on Mr. Patmore, my dear, and tell him to write what he knows to poor Father and to intreat Mr. Colburn without loss of time to send the new volume of Table Talk to Mr. Jeffrey, if he has not sent it to me already, or we shall miss another Review. I got the 100£ from Mr. Jeffrey, and it has perhaps saved us both from ruin. I was so ill in the Steam-Boat, [2] but am a little better. I will write to you again soon to tell you when I shall be up. Farewel, my blessed child. Thy mother is to take the oath [3] next Tuesday, the only thing that can save me from madness. Once more, farewel. I have got a present of a knife for thee. Every one pities poor father, but the monster who has destroyed him. Your ever

affectionate parent,
W. H.

---

[1] William Hazlitt, the Younger, born in September of 1811 was eleven years of age.

[2] Hazlitt had just returned to Edinburgh from London, having left London on 28 May 1822.

[3] The Oath of Calumny required by law in the divorce proceedings. Mrs. Hazlitt took the Oath on Friday, 14 June 1822.

No. 114

To P. G. Patmore

MS. Lockwood.
Address: P. G. Patmore, Esq./12 Greek Street/Soho/London.

(PM: 31 May 1822)

My dear friend,

I wrote yesterday by Scarborough to say that the iron had entered my soul—forever. I have since thought more profoundly about it than ever before, and am convinced beyond a doubt that she is a regular lodging-house decoy, who leads a sporting life with every one who comes in succession, and goes different lengths according as she is urged or inclined. This is why she will not marry, because she hankers after this sort of thing. She has an itch for being slabbered and felt, and this she is determined to gratify upon system, and has a pride in making fools of the different men she indulges herself with and at the same time can stop short from the habit of running the gauntlet with so many. The impudent whore to taunt me, that "she had always told me she had no affection for me," as a salve for her new lewdness—and how did she tell me this, sitting in my lap, twining herself round me,

[*About a line inked out, but above, in another hand:*]

["letting me enjoy her through her petticoats"] [1] looking as if she would faint with tenderness and modesty, admitting all sorts of indecent liberties and declaring "however she might agree to her own ruin, she would never consent to bring disgrace upon her family," as if this last circumstance only prevented her, and all this without any affection—is it not to write whore, hardened, impudent, heartless whore after her name? Her look is exactly this. It is that of suppressed lewdness and conscious and refined hypocrisy,

---

[1] A possible reading is "patchwork."

instead of innocence or timidity or real feeling. She never looks at you, nor has a single involuntary emotion. For any one to suffer what she has done from me, without feeling it, is unnatural and monstrous. A common whore would take a liking to a man who had shewn the same love of her and to whom she had granted the same incessant intimate favours. But her heart is seared, as her eyes gloat, with habitual hypocrisy and *lech* for the mere act of physical contact with the other sex. "Do you let any one else do so," I said to her when I was kissing her. "No, not now," was her answer, that is, because there was nobody in the house to do it with her. While the coast was clear, I had it all my own way: but the instant Tomkins came, she made a dead set at him, ran breathless upstairs before him, blushed when his foot was heard, watched for him in the passage, and he going away either tired of her or without taking the hint, she has taken up in my absence with this quack-doctor, a tall, stiff-backed able bodied half blackguard that she can make use of and get rid of when she pleases. The bitch wants a *stallion*, and hates a lover, that is, any one who talks of affection and is prevented by fondness or regard for her from going or attempting to go all lengths. I at present think she liked me to a certain extent as a friend but still I was not good enough for her. She wanted to be courted not as a bride, but as a common wench. "Why, could we not go on as we were, and never mind about the word, *forever?*" She would not agree to "a tie," because she would leave herself open to any new pretender that answered her purpose better, and *bitch* me without ceremony or mercy, and then say— "She had always told me she had no regard for me"—as a rea[son for] transferring her obscenities (for such they were without [doubt) from] me to her next favourite. Her addicting herself to Tomkins was endurable, because he was a gentlemanly sort of man, but her putting up with this prick of a fellow, merely for bore and measurement and gross manners, sets me low indeed. The monster of lust and duplicity! I that have spared her so often because I hoped better things of her and to make her my future wife, and to be refused in order that she may be the trull of an itinerant apothecary, a fellow that she made a jest of and despised, till she had nobody else in the way to pamper her body and supply her morning's meal of studied wantonness. "That way madness lies." [2] I do not feel as if I can ever get the better of it: I have sucked in the poison of her seeming modesty and tenderness too long. I thought she was dreaming of her only love and worshipped her equivocal face, when she wanted only a codpiece and I ought to have pulled up her petticoats and felt her. But I could not insult the adored of my heart, and find out her real character; and you see what has become of me. I was wrong at first in fancy[ing] a wench at a lodging house to be a Vestal, merely for her demure looks. The only chance I had was the first day: after that my hands were tied and I became the fool of love. Do you know the only thing that soothes or melts me is the idea of taking my little boy whom I can no longer support and wandering through the country as beggars, not through the wide world, for I cannot leave the country where she is. Oh God! Oh God! The slimy, varnished, marble fiend to bring me to this when three kind words would have saved me! Yet if I only knew she was a whore, *flagrante delicto,* it would wean me from her, and burst my chain. Could you ascertain this fact for me, by any means or through any person [3] (E. for example) who might try her as a lodger? I should not like her to be seduced by elaborate means, but if she gave up as a matter of course, I should then be no longer the wretch I am or the God I might have been, but what I was before.[4] . . . . plain,

W. H.

---

[2] *King Lear,* III, iv, 21.

[3] Cf. Letter 110.

[4] A word obliterated: "poor" (?). W. Carew Hazlitt prints "poor plain W.H.," *Memoirs,* II, p. 45.

No. 115

To P. G. Patmore

MS. Lockwood.
Address: P. G. Patmore, Esq./12 Greek Street/Soho/London.

(PM: 9 June 1822) [1]

My dear Patmore,

Your letter raised me for a moment from the depths of despair; but not hearing from you yesterday or today (as I hoped) I am gone back again. You say I want to get rid of her. I hope you are more right in your conjectures about her than in this about me—Oh! no! believe it, I love her as I do my own soul, my heart is wedded to her, be she what she may, and I would not hesitate a moment between her and an angel from Heaven. I grant all you say about my self-tormenting madness; but has it been without cause? Has she not refused me again and again with scorn and abhorrence, after going all lengths with a man for whom she disclaims all affection, and what security can I have for her continence with others, who will not be restrained by feelings of delicacy towards her, and whom she must have preferred to me for their very grossness? "She can make no more confidences!"—These words ring forever in my ears and will be my death-watch. My poor fond heart, that brooded over her and the remains of her affections as my only hope of comfort upon earth, cannot brook or survive this vulgar degradation. Who is there so low as me? Who is there besides, after the homage I have paid her and the caresses she has lavished on me, so vile, so filthy, so abhorrent to love, to whom such an indignity could have happened? When I think of this (and

---

[1] Le Gallienne (1894), pp. 220-23, dates the letter from "Renton Inn, Berwickshire." This phrase is indeed written in the upper right-hand corner of the first page in another hand. The letter was written, however, before Hazlitt had returned to Renton, as his remarks near the end indicate.

I think of it forever, except when I read your letters) the air I breathe stifles me. I am pent up in burning, impotent desires which can find no vent or object. I am hated, repulsed, bemocked by all I love. I cannot stay in any place, and find no rest or intermission from the thought of her contempt and her ingratitude. I can do nothing. What is the use of all I have done? Is it not that my thinking beyond my strength, my feeling more than I ought about so many things, that has withered me up and made me a thing for Love to shrink from and wonder at? Who could ever feel that peace from the touch of her dear hand that I have done, and is it not torn forever from me? My state is that I feel I shall never lie down again at night nor rise up of a morning in peace, nor ever behold my little boy's face with pleasure while I live—unless I am restored to her favour. Instead of that delicious feeling I had when she was heavenly-kind to me and my heart softened and melted in its own tenderness and her sweetness, I am now inclosed in a dungeon of despair. The sky is marble like my thoughts, nature is dead without me as hope is within me, no object can give me one gleam of satisfaction now or the prospect of it in time to come. I wander or rather crawl by the sea-side, and the eternal ocean and lasting despair and her face are before me. Hated, slighted, mocked by her on whom my heart by its last fibre hung. I wake with her by my side, not as my sweet bedfellow but as the corpse of my love, without a heart in her, cold, insensible or struggling from me; and the worm gnaws me and the sting of unrequited love and the canker of a hopeless, endless sorrow. I have lost the taste of my food by feverish anxiety and my tea which used to refresh me when I got up has no moisture in it. Oh cold, solitary, sepulchral breakfasts, compared to those which I made when she had been standing an hour by my side, my Eve, my guardian-angel, my wife, my sister, my sweet friend, my all, and had blest a wretch with her cherub—say rather her seraph—kisses. Ah! what I suffer only shews what I have felt before.—But "The girl is a good girl, if there is goodness in human." I thank you for those words, and I will fall down and worship you if you can prove them true: and I would not do much less to him that proves her a demon. Do let me know if any thing has passed: suspense is my greatest torture. Jeffrey (to whom I did a tale unfold) came down with a 100£ to give me time to recover, and I am going to Renton-Inn to see if I can work a little in the three weeks before it will be over, if all goes well. Tell Colburn to send the Table talk to him, 92 George Street, Edinburgh, unless he is mad and wants to ruin me and the book. Write on the receipt of this, and believe me your unspeakably obliged.

W.H.

No. 116

To P. G. Patmore

MS. Lockwood.
Address: P. G.Patmore, Esq./12 Greek Street/Soho/London.

(PM: 18 June 1822)

My dear friend,

Here I am at Renton amid the hills and groves which I greeted in their barrenness in winter, but which have now put on their full green attire that shews lovely in this northern twilight, but speaks a tale of sadness to this heart widowed of its last, its dearest, its only hope! [1] For a man who writes such nonsense, I write a good hand. Musing over my only subject (Othello's occupation, alas! is gone) seeking for rest and finding none, I have at last hit upon a truth, that if true explains all and satisfies me, I hope forever. This is it. You will by this time probably know something from having called and seen how the land lies that will make you a judge how far I am stepped into madness in my conjectures. If you think me right, all engines set at work at once that punish ungrateful woman. Oh! lovely Renton-Inn, here I wrote a volume of Essays, here I wrote my enamoured follies to her, thinking her human and that "below was not all the fiend's" [2] here I got two answers from the little witch, and here I was cuckolded and I was damned. I am only a fool, would I were mad! By this time you probably know enough to know whether this following solution is *in rerum natura* at No. 9 S.B. Mark. The conversation that passed in the kitchen that evening that ruined me was this.

---

[1] This first sentence and the seventh ("Oh lovely Renton Inn . . .") are the only ones from this long letter to appear in *Liber Amoris*, Letter X.

[2] *King Lear*, IV, vi, 128-129:

> But to the girdle do the gods inherit,
> Beneath is all the fiends'.

Betsey. "Oh! if those trowsers were to come down, what a sight there would be." *(A general loud laugh)*

Mother. "Yes! he's a proper one: Mr. Follett is nothing to him."

Mr. Cajah. (aged 17) "Then, I suppose he must be seven inches."

Mother W. "He's quite a monster. He nearly tumbled over Mr. Hazlitt one night."

Sarah. (At that once, that still as ever dear name, ah! why do I grow pale, why do I weep and forgive) said something inaudible, but in connection.

Cajah. (Laughing) "Sarah says . . ."

Sarah. "I say, Mr. Follett wears straps"—

————— [I ask you candidly whether on hearing this I ought not to have walked quietly out of the house and never have thought of it again.] [3]

She also said to me the other evening when I told her (I don't know what) that "she had heard enough of that sort of conversation." No wonder, when she had heard for years this kind of kitchen-stuff. Who do you think this hero, this Hercules, this plenipotentiary was? Why, I recollect the person who once tumbled over me half drunk was this very Griffiths who keeps possession of his ten-shillings Garrett, in spite of an offer of marriage from *me,* and a hundred guineas a year for his apartment. Can there be a doubt, when the mother dilates in this way on codpieces and the son replies in measured terms, that the girl runs mad for size? Miss is small, and exaggerates dimensions by contrast. Misjudging fair! Yet it is she whom [I have] spared a hundred times from witnessing this consummation devoutly wished by the whole kitchen in chorus, after she has been rubbing against me, hard at it for an hour together, thinking to myself, "The girl is a good [girl] etc. and means no harm—it is only [her fondness] for me, not her lech after a man ["] she taunted me the other night, "She a[ssured] me she had no affection for me [yet she] owned she had been guilty of [making confidences to] me, *viz.* one for whom she had—[4] which were not to be repeated in future, they having been transferred to one whom her mother has singled out for her daughter's endear-

---

[3] The square brackets here are Hazlitt's.

[4] The edges of the last two pages are torn away.

ments. "A strappan youth, he taks the mother's eye!" [5] If you know nothing to contradict this theory, ask somebody to verify it [or do] it yourself, if you like as [hastily] as possible in proving some things. But did I not overhear the conversation? [I will] stake my existence on it. Whenever I poked her up she liked me best; and I stupidly declined the *ultimate* outcome "Which I had treasured" [6]— ——alone. *Hinc illae lachrymae!* [7] [Death, death, death. But then] When I said I should ————she sighed, as if she then felt she must————— fascination. This view of the thing ———— forgave it for her in demure looks————.[8] [If I don't hear something good from you tomorrow, I shall send this letter post-paid.] [9]
I hesitated [10] about sending this letter. But let it go. I believed it to be true. I thank you for your Thursday's letter and for the Postscript. Oh! that it were wellfounded! But did she not tell me "she had heard enough of my conversations," and has she not, instead of the man she used to "make confidences to," the man she wants to make confidences about? She thinks that a better thing, I assure you. You say I accuse her of grossness inconsistent with her character. It is she who accuses herself of it; for did she not tell me "she never had any affection for me," and do I not know what she has done with me a hundred times? Will she not do so much or more with her *fancy-man,* in spite of her hypocritical looks and pretty speeches? Did she not say to me once, in the height of our caresses, and struggling from me—"However I might agree to my own ruin, I never will consent to bring disgrace upon my family!"—This speech she addressed to one she never could like— What will she *do* with one she does like, and is just as mad after? You seem inclined at present to give up "her real regard and affection for me," and yet without this, having done what she has, is she not all that I say of her, a whore or a consummate hypocrite,

---

[5] *The Cotter's Saturday Night,* 1.65.

[6] Not identified.

[7] Terence *(Andria,* I, i, 99), imitated by Horace *(Epistles,* I, xix, 41). "Hence those tears" (i.e., "that was the cause of the trouble").

[8] Edge of page torn away. Two lines at bottom heavily inked out.

[9] The square brackets are Hazlitt's. The line appears at the top of the outside page, top fold, as if added after the first stage of writing.

[10] Hazlitt apparently wrote the letter and held it a day hoping to get word from Patmore. A letter did come, and thereupon Hazlitt added the matter overwritten the long way on pages one and two.

a little monster of lust or avarice or treachery? I don't suppose she goes with every one, but that she must have a man to wheedle and fondle her, and that she took up with me for no other reason. What else can it be by her own repeated declaration? She says she'll never marry and that it was not love, so that it could be nothing but either a hoax or to gratify her soft itch without a particle of affection. I call this unnatural, but not impossible. If it had been friendship or esteem, she would not have treated me as she has. The instant I slackened in my lascivious approaches and wanted to fix her forever, she was off—first flinging herself at Tomkins [11] and he failing, taking up with her present groom, but still "she has no tie" and would I daresay sacrifice him to a more gentlemanly pretender. As to her looking like a whore, look in her eyes, if you can catch them, and then tell me. Besides, I do not say she is a whore, I only say she is a bitch, and I believe her object is to go all lengths but the last, which her changing about and want of natural affection enables her to do. She hates me only because I did not try to "ruin her." I believe the whole family to be bad, and *you* have no proof but her appearance that she is different from the rest, and her looks, I know, are not a clue to her conduct with me.—Do you know that last night I had given up all thoughts of her. I thought the [fury?] was over and my burning love turned to indifference and even disgust. Your letter had this effect, I mean the contrast between the picture you drew of her, *viz.* of the creature I loved, and what I felt to be her true character. This morning my fit is on again, that is, I think she would make the most delicious whore alive, but by God, I do not stomach her as a wife in my present humour—you will say, circumstances. Oh no! The very thought that she may have in spite of all appearances, a true and tender regard for me, *namely,* that she would have me and therefore doesn't hate me, makes my heart gush with its old tenderness and melt in heavenly sweetness towards the little [darling *del.*] cherub. Don't go to Roscoe, [12] nor let me have any more formal refusals, till I am quite free at any rate and then if she gives herself airs, she must be *tried.* But I think you might go and take away the MSS and if you see her, say "You think it a pity we should part otherwise than friends, for that you know I had the truest regard

---

[11] A fellow-lodger at Southampton Buildings, and a rival.
[12] Robert Roscoe, who married Sarah's older sister.

for her, and that I should never think of any other lodging but that I feared she had a dislike to seeing me there" in consequence of my past misconduct. [I have hit it.] *Say that I shall want it very little the next year, as I shall be abroad for some months, but that I wish to keep it on to have a place to come to when I am in London and not to seem to have parted in anger, where I feel nothing but friendship and esteem.*[13] If you get a civil answer to this, take it for me and send me word. Otherwise, get E.[14] or anybody to see what flesh she is made of, and send her to hell if possible. She may then, you know, take compassion on me, as Killigrew's cousin [15] said.—I have half a mind to come up in the Steam-Boat to watch the operation. Learn first whether the great man of Penman-Mawr [16] is still there. You may do this by asking after my hamper of books which was in the back parlour and you will see his great coat, a drab (not the only drab he has) lying about. Hint that I am free, and that I have had a severe illness. W.H.

[*Written at the top of page 1:*]
I would give a thousand worlds to believe her anything but what I suppose. *I love her, Heaven knows.* W.H.
You say I am to try her after she agrees to have me: No: but I hate her for this, that she refuses me, when she could go to—[several words obliterated] aye, and with a grave air,—I'm mad! So much for sentiment.
The oath is to be taken (God willing) tomorrow. Oh! let me be free that I may *not* make her an offer—The hideous little hypocritical anomaly!
[*Three short lines along the edge of page 3 are obliterated. Then:*]

Alas, alas for me! Keep these letters. And in all use your own discretion. Treat me as a child,—i.e. a Child Harold!

---

13 The square brackets and underscoring are Hazlitt's.
14 Cf. Letter 110.
15 Cf. "On Coffee-House Politicians," *Works,* VIII, 189-204:

We took our favourite passages [from Grammont's *Memoirs*] one preferring that of Killigrew's country-cousin, who having been resolutely refused by Miss Warminster ... when he found she had been unexpectedly brought to bed, fell on his knees and thanked God that now she might take compassion on him.

16 Griffiths, who came from Pennmaenmawr.

No. 117

To P. G. Patmore

MS. Lockwood.
Address: P. G. Patmore, Esq./12 Greek Street/Soho/London.

(PM: 20 June 1822)

My dear friend,

The deed is done, and I am virtually a free man. Mrs. H. took the oath on Friday (they say *manfully*)—and nothing remains but to wait a week or two longer for the sentence of divorce. What had I better do in these circumstances? I dare not write to her, I dare not write to her father, or else I would. She has shot me through with poisoned arrows, and I think another "winged wound" would finish me. It is a pleasant sort of balm she has left in my heart. One thing I agree with you in, it will remain there forever, but yet not very long. It festers and consumes me. If it were not for my little boy, whose face I see struck blank at the news, and looking through the world for pity and meeting with contempt, I should settle the question by my death. That is the only thought that brings my wandering reason to an anchor, that excites the least interest, or gives me fortitude to bear up against what I am doomed to feel for the *ungrateful.* Otherwise, I am dead to all but the agony of what I have lost. She was my life—it is gone from me, and I am grown spectral. If it is a place I know, it reminds me of her, of the way my fond heart brooded over her. If it is a strange place, it is desolate, hateful, barren of all interest, for nothing touches me but what has a reference to her. There is only she in the world, "the false, the fair, the inexpressive she." [1] If the clock strikes, the sound jars me, for a million of hours will never bring peace to my breast. The light startles me, the darkness terrifies me: I seem falling into a pit without a hand to help me. She came (I knew not how) and sat by

---

[1] *As You Like It,* III, ii, 10. "The fair, the chaste, the unexpressive she."

my side and was folded in my arms, a vision of love and as if she had dropped from the Heavens to help me by some especial dispensation of a favouring Providence to make me amends for all, and now without any fault of mine but too much love, she has vanished from me and I am left to wither. My heart is torn out of me, and every feeling for which I wished to live. It is like a dream, an enchantment; it torments me and it makes me mad. I lie down with it, I rise up with it, and I see no chance of repose, I grasp at a shadow, I try to undo the past, or to make that mockery real, and I weep with rage and pity over my own weakness and misery. I spared her again and again (idiot, fop, pedant that I was) thinking what she suffered was love, friendship, sweetness, not wantonness. How could I, looking at her face, and hearing her soft words, like sighs breathed from the gentlest of all bosoms? The she-goat! Damn her! I had hopes, I had prospects to come, the flattery of something like fame, a pleasure in writing, health even would have come back with her smile—she has blighted all, turned all to poison and tears. Yet the barbed arrow is in my heart. I can neither endure it nor draw it out, for with it flows my life's-blood. I had dwelt too long upon truth to trust myself with the immortal thoughts of love—*that S.W. might have been mine, and now never can*— these are the two sole propositions that forever stare me in the face, and look ghastly in at my poor brain. I am in some sense proud that I can feel this dreadful passion—it makes me a kind of peer in the kingdom of love, but I could have wished it had been for an object that at least could have understood its value and pitied its excess. Do you know I think G.[2] (the fellow in the back parlour) is the very man her mother was commending to her daughter's lecherous thoughts (if she has any)

[Parts of two lines heavily inked out, but restored above in another hand is:]

"that night on the seven inch conversation"] for I recollect he tumbled over me one night half drunk which was one of the circumstances related as proof of his huge prowess. Do you think this might not sink into the nun's mind in my absence, considering

---

[2] Griffiths.

the [*over five lines obliterated*] [3] The gates of paradise, the gates of paradise once were open to me, and I blushed to enter but with the golden keys of love! I would die, but her lover, my love of her, ought not to die. When I am dead, who will love her as I have done? If she should be in misfortune, who will comfort her? When she is old, who will look in her face and bless her? Would there be any harm in speaking to [*name inked out*] *confidentially* to know if he thinks it [would be worth] while to make her an offer the instant I am free, or suppose you try the 100£ a year whenever the 3 apartment [is vacant]

[*Written at the top of page 1:*]

Will you call at Mr. Dawson's school, Hunter Street and tell the little boy [4] I'll write to him or see him on Saturday morning. Poor little fellow!
Oh answer me and save me if possible, *for* her and *from* myself.
W.H.
See Colburn for me about the book.[5] The letter, I take it was from him.

---

[3] Some of the words of these heavily inked out lines are written in above in another hand (seemingly suggested by lines in *Liber Amoris*, Letter VII) as follows: "That is the reason she doesn't want me there, lest I should discover a new affair— wretch that I am! Another has possession of her, oh Hell! I'm satisfied of it from her manner, which had a wanton insolence in it. Well might I run wild when I received no letters from her. I foresaw, I felt my fate."

[4] His son William.

[5] *Table-Talk,* II.

No. 118

To Sarah Walker

Liber Amoris, To S.L., pp. 102-103.

[Edinburgh, between 20 and 28 June, 1822]
My dear Miss L [1] ———

Evil to them that evil think, is an old saying; and I have found it a true one. I have ruined myself by my unjust suspicions of you. Your sweet friendship was the balm of my life; and I have lost it, I fear forever, by one fault and folly after another. What would I give to be restored to the place in your esteem, which, you assured me, I held only a few months ago! Yet I was not contented, but did all I could to torment myself and harass you by endless doubts and jealousy. Can you not forget and forgive the past, and judge of me by my conduct in future? Can you not take all my follies in the lump, and say, like a good, generous girl, "Well, I'll think no more of them?" In a word, may I come back, and try to behave better? A line to say so would be an additional favour to so many already received by

Your obliged friend,
And sincere well-wisher.

---

[1] The same disguise for Sarah Walker used in Letter 102.

No. 119

To P. G. Patmore

MS. Lockwood.
Address: P. G. Patmore/12 Greek Street/Soho/London.

(PM: 28 June 1822)

My dear and good friend,

I am afraid I trouble you with my querulous epistles, but this is probably the last. Tomorrow decides my fate with respect to *her;* and the next day I expect to be a free man. ["In vain! There has been a delay *(pro forma)* of ten days".[1]] Was it not for her and to lay my freedom at her feet that I took this step that has cost me infinite wretchedness, and now to be discarded with contumely and abhorrence! And for the first blackguard [2] that fell in her way! If so, I do not think I can survive it. You who have been a favourite with women do not know what it is to be deprived of one's only hope, and to have it turned to a mockery and a scorn. There is nothing in the world left that can give me one drop of comfort— *that* I feel more and more. Every thing is to me a mockery of pleasure like her love. The breeze does not cool me, the blue sky does not allure my eye. I gaze only on her face (like a marble image) averted from me—ah! the only face that ever was turned fondly to me! And why? Because I wanted her to be mine forever in love or friendship, and did not push my gross familiarities with her as far as I should with a common wench. "Why can you not go on as we have done, and say nothing about the word *forever?*" Did not this shew that she even then meditated an escape from me to some less sentimental lover? I was v[ery] well as a stop-gap, but I was to be nothing more. The instant Tomkins came, she flung herself at his head in the most barefaced way, and used to run

---

[1] Written in apparently later in the cramped style of the postscripts to this letter. Letters XI and XII of the *Liber Amoris* derive from this letter.
[2] Tomkins, a fellow lodger.

blushing and breathless to meet him. God knows she was always cool enough with me, even in our closest intimacies and endearments. I thought her warmth was reserved for the *little image*,[3] till I saw her always running upstairs with this fellow and then watching for him when he went down again and in close confab. in the passage. It was then my mad proceedings commenced. Had I not reason to be jealous of every appearance of familiarity with others, knowing how familiar she had been with me at first, and that she only grew shy, when I did not take further liberties? What has her character to rest upon but her attachment to me, which she now denies not modestly, but impudently? Will you yourself say that if she had all along no regard for me, she will not do as much or more with other more likely men? [She] has had, she says, enough of my [conversa]tion, so it was not that! Ah! [ ] the truth is, it was not likely I sh[ould ever meet] even with the outward demonstration [4] of love [from] any woman but a common lodging-house decoy—I have tasted the sweets, and now feel the bitterness of knowing what a bliss I am deprived of and must ever be deprived of! Intolerable conviction! Yet I might, I believe, have had her in the *sporting-line;* but some demon held my hand. How could I when I worshipped her, and even now pay her divine honours in my inmost heart, abused and brutalised as I have been by that Circean cup of kisses, of enchantments, of which I have drunk! I am choked, withered, dried up with chagrin, remorse, despair, from which I have not a moment's respite, day or night. I have always some horrid dream about her, and wake wondering what is the matter that "she is no longer the same to me as ever." I thought at least we should always be dear friends (did she not talk of coming to live with me? only the day before I left London) but she's gone and my revenge must be—to love her—damn her, the little sorceress, the cruel, heartless destroyer! I see nothing for it but madness, unless Friday brings a change, or unless she lets me go back. You must know I wrote to her to that purpose, but it was a very quiet, rational letter,* begging pardon and promising reform for the future and all that. What effect it will have, I shall know

---

* Cf. Letter 118, the dating of which derives from this statement.
[3] Cf. Letter 104.
[4] "Profession" crossed out; "outward demonstration" written above.

tomorrow, and you probably know already. I was forced to get out of the way of her answer till Friday. [Yours, W.H.]

P.S. I shall I hope be in town next Friday at furthest—Not till Friday week. Write for God's sake to let me know the worst.

[Across the top of page 1:]
P.S. I have no answer from her. I *wish* you to call on Roscoe in confidence to say that I intend to make her an offer of marriage and that I will write to her father to that purpose the instant I am free (next Friday week) and to ask him whether he thinks it will be to any purpose and what he would advise me to do.

[Written across page 1:]

If Roscoe's answer is positive and final, it is plain she hates me because I neglected certain opportunities, and has got some one to supply my inattentions. In that case, I entreat you to get some one to work to ascertain for me, without loss of time, whether she is a common sporter, or not? Nothing else but the knowledge of her being common can reconcile me to myself, after what has passed.— It has occurred to me that as Roscoe was thought by the family to be like the bust of Buonaparte, it might be a brother of his: and that in these circumstances the affair has been received. If that were the case, I should be happy even to lose her for her heart's love: but to any one else (except by way of learning what she is) I will not part with her, to that I have made up my mind. ——— You don't know what I suffer or you would not be so severe upon me. My death will I hope satisfy every one before long.

No. 120

To P. G. Patmore

MS. Lockwood.
Address: P. G. Patmore, Esq./12 Greek Street/Soho/London.

Friday, 5
Wednesday, 3 July [1] [1822]

My dear Patmore,

You have been very kind to me in this business, but I fear even your indulgence for my infirmities is failing. To what state am I reduced, and for what? For fancying a little lodging-house decoy to be an angel and a saint, because she affected to look like one to hide her rank thoughts and deadly purposes. Has she not murdered me under the mask of the tenderest friendship? And why? Because I have loved her with unutterable love, and sought to make her my wife. You say it is my own "outrageous conduct". I ask you first in candour whether the ambiguity of her situation with respect to me, kissing, fondling a married man as if he were her husband and then declaring she had no love for him and professing never to marry, was not enough to excite my suspicions, which the different *exposés* from the conversations in the kitchen must blow into a flame with any one? I ask you what you yourself would have felt or done, if loving her as I did, you had heard what I did, time after time? Did not her mother own to one of the grossest charges, "the habit of pulling up her petticoats" [2] and is this action to be reconciled with her pretended character (that character with which I fell in love, and to which I *made* love) without supposing her to be the greatest hypocrite in the world?

---

[1] Both dates, both in Hazlitt's hand, appear in the MS. As this letter is also crowded with postscripts, it seems likely that Hazlitt began it on 3 July and held it for a day. It is postmarked 4 July.

[2] Some words obliterated; these words within quotation marks are written in another hand.

My conduct instead of being outrageous has been "too gentle:" ["I did not pull up her petticoats . . . in good earnest as she did her [3] . . ."] that has been my unpardonable offence. "This was looked for at my hands and this was baulked." After exciting her loose desires by the fondest embraces and the purest kisses, as if she had been made "my wedded wife yestreen," [4] or was to become so tomorrow, I did not gratify them or follow up my advantage by any action which should say, "I think you a whore," or will lay aside the feeling of love and adoration I cherish for you to see whether you are not a Miss Wills.[5] Yet any one but a fond fool like me would have made the experiment, with whatever violence to himself, as a matter of life and death, for I had every reason to distrust appearances. Her conduct has been of a piece from the beginning: for in the midst of her closest and falsest endearments, she has always (with one or two exceptions) disclaimed the natural inference to be drawn from them, and made a verbal reservation by which she might lead me on in a Fool's Paradise and make me the tool of her lust, her avarice, and her love of intrigue as long as she liked, and dismiss me whenever it suited her. This, you see, she has done, because my intentions grew serious, and if complied with, would put an end to her *sporting life*. Offer marriage to this "tradesman's daughter, who has as nice a sense of honour as any one can have," and like Lady Bellaston in Tom Jones, she cuts you immediately in a fit of abhorrence and alarm. She was not by any means so horrified when in our first intimacy I asked to go to bed to her, and she only answered in her pretty, mincing way, "It would be of no use if you did, for Betsey sleeps with me!" That I should have spared the traitress when I had her melting in my arms, after expressions like this and when I must know that if I did not, she would get somebody else that would, astonishes me when I look back to it. Wretched being that I am, lost, undone forever! I have thrown away my heart and soul upon an unfeeling jilt, and my life (that might have been so happy, had she been what I thought her) will soon follow, either voluntarily, or by the force of grief, remorse, and madness at my cruel disappointment. I can

---

[3] A line and a half inked out; these words written in another hand above.
[4] Burns, *Lament for James, Earl of Glencairn*, Stanza 10.
[5] Not identified.

never get rid of the reflection, I have only that one subject of contemplation in time to come, and the thought stifles me. I cannot even seek relief from its pressure. The bond grows tighter, instead of being lightened. Ah! what a heart she has lost! All the love and affection of my whole life was centered in her, who, I thought, alone of all women had found out my true character and knew how to value my tenderness. Alas! alas! that this, the only hope, joy, or comfort I ever had, should turn to a mockery, and blast the remainder of my days. Miss Wills. I was at Roslin Castle yesterday, and the exquisite beauty of the scene, with the thought of what I should feel should I ever be restored to her and have to lead her through such places as my adored, my angel-wife, almost drove me beside myself. For this picture, this extatic vision, what have I instead as the image of the reality? Demoniacal possessions. I see the young witch seated in another's lap, twining her serpent arms round him, her eyes glancing and her cheeks on fire—Damn the unnatural hag. Oh! Oh! why does not the hideous thought choke me? It is so and she can make no confidences. The gentleman [6] who lodges in the old room is a fat, red-faced, pot-bellied, powdered gentleman of sixty—a pleasant successor! For what am I reserved? The bitch likes the nasty, the wilful, the *antipathetic.* That was why she pitched upon me, because I was out of the ordinary calculation of love. I'll say no more about that, however. You will say if I have only lost a Miss Wills, a girl that will be a bawd to elderly gentlemen and that with her own person, enjoying the incongruity of the combination, what have I lost? If I had known it from the first, nothing—but as it is, I have lost her, myself, Heaven and am doomed to Hell. Where is E—? Why tarry the wheels of his chariot? When, how shall I be released from these horrors? Do go and ask Roscoe what it all means? And send me one *fact* in her favour. I wish to God you could come down in the steamboat next Wednesday and return with me the Wednesday after, when all will be [over]

[*Written across Page 2:*]
  To be sure, the mother let me the lodgings entire, which did not look like keeping them for another person; but then Miss took care

---

6 See below in this letter.

to send me away with a flea in my ear; for she knew very well what would be the effect of her oration that I was to be treated like a common lodger. Again, the gentleman's not coming for five weeks and only staying three does not look like very hot love and she does not like the lukewarm. Oh! if this newcomer should turn out to be her first love, how would I lift up my hands in thankfulness to be so discarded, how would I fall down and worship him and her! I hope you will think this last sentiment worthy of me, and so I conclude. Do come next Wednesday, if you can, for the fun of the thing; and to see Auld Reekie.[7] I am to be made a free man next Monday week, please the lawyers. —W. H. Looking in the glass to see why I am so hated, I think I see FREEDOM written on my brow, and then for Miss ———!

[*Interlinear lines at top of last page:*]
The mother also said that while I was away, Sarah thought it best not to encourage a passion that perhaps might never be fulfilled. But she did not give over encouraging till the end of the five weeks. Q.E.D. If it is the same old fellow that was there before, I shall go mad. Besides, she kept repeating that she "despised looks," and objected to Tomkins as a new lodger, so that it takes time to insinuate the feeling of obscenity into her veins. Life is hideous to me and death horrible. What shall I do? Oh! that I knew she was a strumpet, and that she knew I did.

[*Written across top of Page 1:*]
P.S. Get some one to try her, or I am destroyed forever. To go and see E [four or five letters obliterated] there after [he had taken her] for the asking, would lift my soul from Hell. It would be sweet and full revenge. *You* may try her, if you like. Pity me, Pity [. . .] W. H. A pot belly and a slender waist match by contrast. Do they not? I shall soon be in town and see. By the tone of your last letter, I perceive you think it is all going against me. Write to me once more before I leave this. You will perhaps excuse all this as a picture of a divided mind.

Coincidences. 1. Five weeks after I go away, she desists from writing. 2. The lodging was taken the day I left, (singular) but the

---

[7] Edinburgh.

gentleman, Mrs. W.[8] told me, did not come till five weeks after. 3. When I return, there is a total alteration in Miss's behaviour, and on my asking if there is any one else, she tells me, "she can make no more confidences." [9]

---

[8] Sarah's mother.

[9] Le Gallienne (1894), pp. 232-236, omitted these itemized Coincidences. Some passages were added to this letter in the *Liber Amoris,* Letter IX.

No. 121

To P. G. Patmore

MS. Lockwood.
Address: P. G. Patmore, Esq./12 Greek Street/Soho/London.

(PM: 8 July 1822)

My dear Patmore,

I can only say you have saved my life.[1] If I make enemies with her now, I deserve to be hanged, drawn, and quartered. She is an angel from heaven, and you cannot say I ever said to the contrary! The little devil must have liked me from the first, or she never could have stood all these hurricanes without slipping her cable. What could she find in me? "I have mistook my person all this while," etc.[2] Do you know I mean to be the very *ideal* of a lodger when I get back, and if ever I am married, if I don't make her the best bedfellow in the world, call me *cut*.[3] I saw a picture of her naked figure [4] the other day at Dalkeith Palace before this blessed news came, and it drove [me] mad. Roscoe is just the man I wish for a brother-in-law. Tell him I feel my obligations to him, and send the enclosed letter if you think it a proper one. You have the face to doubt my making her a good husband: you might as well

---

[1] Two things in Patmore's letter to Hazlitt of 4 July had sent Hazlitt's spirits soaring: "She is still to be won by wise and prudent conduct on your part"; and Roscoe's comment that Sarah was "a *good girl*, and *likely to make any man an excellent wife*" (*Liber Amoris*, letter captioned "From C.P. Esq.," preceding Letter XIII).

[2] *Richard III*, I, ii, 253.

[3] A base fellow.

[4] The figure in "Hope Finding Fortune in the Sea," one of the Duke of Buccleugh's pictures he viewed at Dalkeith House on 6 July. While there, he encountered Mrs Hazlitt, who recorded in her *Journal* two later conversations they had about the picture. In the first conversation he allowed that the "female figure floating on the water" was tolerable. In the second, he thought "the picture at Dalkeith house ... was like her [Sarah Walker]" (Bonner, 239, 242, 247 and *Journals of Sarah and William Hazlitt, 1822-1831*, University of Buffalo Studies, v. 24, no. 3, 1959.)

doubt it if I was married to one of the Houris of Paradise. She is a saint, an angel, a love. I now worship her and fall down on my knees in thankfulness to God and Nature—for this reprieve at least. If she deceives me again, she kills me. But I will have such a kiss when I go back as shall last me twenty years. Bless her, may God bless her for not utterly disowning and destroying me! What a sublime little thing it is, and how she holds out to the last in her system of consistent contradictions! I have been thinking of her little face these two last days looking like a marble statue,[5] as cold, as fixed and graceful as ever statue did.[6] No, I think I'll never believe again that she will not be mine, for I think she was made on purpose for me. I had half begun a new amour,[7] but it's all off, God bless you! I'll never think of another woman, while she even thinks it worth her while to *refuse to have me.* You see I am not hard to please, after all. Did Roscoe know the intimacies that had passed between us? Or did you hint at it? I think it would be a *clencher,* if he did. How ought I to behave when I go back? I think not romantic but mild and somewhat melancholy. Eh? Advise a fool, who had nearly lost a Goddess by his folly. The thing is, I could not think it probable she could ever like *me.* Her taste is singular, but not the worse for that. I'd rather have her love, or liking (call it what you will) than empires. Don't you think she's a maid? She'll have enough of my conversation and of something else before she has done with me, I suspect. I deserve to call her mine, for nothing else *can*[8] atone for what I've gone through for her.[9] I hope your next letter won't reverse all,[10] and then I shall be happy till I see her—one of the blest when I do see her, if she looks like my beautiful love. I may perhaps write again when I come to

---

[5] Hazlitt was fascinated by the image of cold marble, especially statuary. He uses the term "marble" over and over. His original description of *Liber Amoris* was: "a book of our conversations (I mean mine and the statue's)." And of course the subtitle was "The New Pygmalion." Cf. Letter 104.

[6] Written above in another hand: "and I could not believe the lies I told of her."

[7] There are only conjectures about who this lady was. Mrs Hazlitt observed Hazlitt's assignation with a specific woman of the town but this could scarcely be called an amour.

[8] "but that" crossed out.

[9] "suffered," alternate word, not used.

[10] "be a crucifier," alternate phrase, not used.

my right wits—Farewel at present and thank you a thousand times for what you have done for your poor friend.[11]

P.S.[12] I like what Roscoe said about her sister [13] much, much. There are good people in the world: I begin to see it and believe it.[14]

---

[11] "W. H." crossed out.

[12] "I have written formally to bespeak the lodging," alternate sentence, not used.

[13] "his wife" crossed out. The revisions on the past page of this letter (noted above) are all made toward their use in the *Liber Amoris*. They conform there to the language of Letter XIII. The deletions have been carefully, however awkwardly, noted because they are what Hazlitt wrote and mailed to Patmore.

[14] Three or four illegible words in lower right-hand corner.

No. 122

To P. G. Patmore

Liber Amoris, Letter the Last, pp. 122-124.

Edinburgh. (PM: July 17, 1822)*

Dear Patmore,

To-morrow is the decisive day [1] that makes me or mars me. I will let you know the result by a line added to this. Yet what signifies it, since either way I have little hope there, "whence alone my hope cometh!" [2] You must know I am strangely in the dumps at this present writing. My reception with her is doubtful, and my fate is then certain. The hearing of your happiness [3] has, I own, made me thoughtful. It is just what I proposed her to do—to have crossed the Alps with me,[4] to sail on sunny seas, to bask in Italian skies, to have visited Vevai and the rocks of Meillerie, and to have repeated to her on the spot the story of Julia and St. Preux, and to have shewn her all that my heart had stored up for her—but on my forehead alone is written—REJECTED! Yet I too could have adored as fervently, and loved as tenderly as others, had I been permitted. You are going abroad, you say, happy in making happy. Where shall I be? In the grave, I hope, or else in her arms. To me, alas! there is no sweetness out of her sight, and that sweetness has turned to bitterness, I fear; that gentleness to sullen scorn! Still I hope for the best. If she will but *have* me, I'll make her *love* me: and I think her not giving a positive answer looks like it, and also shews that there is no one else. Her holding out to the last

---

* Cf. Howe, *Works,* IX, p. 266.

[1] The divorce was granted on 17 July. Hence 16 July, the probable date of the letter.

[2] Psalm CXXI. "I will lift up mine eyes unto the hills, from whence cometh my help."

[3] Patmore married Eliza Robertson in 1822, a Scottish lady who had been companion to his mother.

[4] The plan was to write a series of essays on the great galleries of France and Italy. He did go in 1824, but with his second wife. Cf. Letter 137.

also, I think, proves that she was never to have been gained but with honour. She's a strange, almost an inscrutable girl: but if I once win her consent, I shall kill her with kindness.—Will you let me have a sight of *somebody* [5] before you go? I should be most proud. I was in hopes to have got away by the Steam-boat to-morrow, but owing to the business not coming on till then, I cannot; and may not be in town for another week, unless I come by the Mail, which I am strongly tempted to do. In the latter case I shall be *there,* and visible on Saturday evening. Will you look in and see, about eight o'clock? I wish much to see you and her and J[ohn] H[unt] and my little boy once more; and then, if she is not what she once was to me, I care not if I die that instant.[6] I will conclude here till to-morrow, as I am getting into my old melancholy.—

It is all over, and I am my own man, and your's ever—

---

[5] Patmore's bride.

[6] The four sentences lying between "I was in hopes" and "die that instant" were printed with one omission by Patmore (III, 187) and later by Le Gallienne (1894), pp. 362-363. Patmore's brief extract helps to authenticate this lost letter.

No. 123

To Francis Jeffrey

MS. Yale.
Address: Francis Jeffrey, Esq./Edinburgh.

(PM 24 August 1822)

Dear Sir,

Would you let me have Napoleon in Exile to do for the next No. if it is not already in the present one? [1] Do you think Sir Marmaduke Maxwell would make an article? [2] I have since I returned found out the person I told you of to be a regular lodging-house decoy.[3] I hope the state of distraction I was in about that affair will plead my excuse for any offenses I might be guilty of while in Edinburgh. I am better a good deal, but feel much like a man who has been thrown from the top of a house. I wish you would give my best respects to Mrs. Jeffrey, and believe me your obliged friend and servant,

W. Hazlitt.

I am still at No. 9 Southampton Buildings Holborn

---

[1] A review of Barry E. O'Meara's *Napoleon in Exile, or a Voice from St. Helena* did appear in "the present one" of June 1822. Authorship is uncertain, but the *Wellesley Index* (I, 463) attributes it to Brougham. Hazlitt may have selected the "Extracts" from O'Meara which were printed in *The London Magazine* (July 1822).

[2] No article on Allan Cunningham's *Sir Marmaduke Maxwell, a Dramatic Poem* appeared in the *Edinburgh Review,* but Hazlitt probably wrote the review in *The London Magazine* (November 1822).

[3] Sarah Walker.

No. 124

To James Sheridan Knowles

Liber Amoris, Part III.
ADDRESSED TO J. S. K [1]-----

[Late Spring and Summer of 1822?] *

My dear K—,

It is all over, and I know my fate. I told you I would send you word, if any thing decisive happened; but an impenetrable mystery hung over the affair till lately. It is at last (by the merest accident in the world) dissipated; and I keep my promise, both for your satisfaction, and for the ease of my own mind.

You remember the morning [2] when I said "I will go and repose my sorrows at the foot of Ben Lomond"—and when from Dumbarton-bridge its giant-shadow, clad in air and sunshine, appeared in view. We had a pleasant day's walk. We passed Smollet's monument [3] on the road (somehow these poets touch one in reflection more than most military heroes)—talked of old times; you repeated Logan's [4] beautiful verses to the cuckoo,[5] which I wanted to compare with Wordsworth's, but my courage failed me; you then told me some passages of an early attachment which was suddenly broken off; we considered together which was the most to be pitied, a disappointment in love where the attachment was mutual or one where there has been no return, and we both agreed, I think that the former was best to be endured, and that to have

---

* [*Undated themselves, this and the two following letters give a terminal account of the events of the summer of 1822.*]

[1] This is Hazlitt's heading.

[2] 14 May 1822.

[3] According to Howe (*Works,* IX, 266), erected by the novelist's cousin, James Smollett. Johnson and Boswell visited it, and Boswell records that the Latin inscription was partly the work of Johnson, which Johnson then sat down to revise and improve (*Life,* Hill-Powell ed., V, 366-368).

[4] John Logan (1748-1788), "To the Cuckoo" in *Poems on Several Occasions by Michael Bruce,* 1770. There is some doubt as to the actual author, as Michael Bruce was a fellow student of Logan's.

[292]

the consciousness of it a companion for life was the least evil of the two, as there was a secret sweetness that took off the bitterness and the sting of regret, and "the memory of what once had been" atoned, in some measure, and at intervals, for what "never more could be." [6] In the other case, there was nothing to look back to with tender satisfaction, no redeeming trait, not even a possibility of turning it to good. It left behind it not cherished sighs, but stifled pangs. The galling sense of it did not bring moisture into the eyes, but dried up the heart ever after. One had been my fate, the other had been yours!—

You startled me every now and then from my reverie by the robust voice, in which you asked the country people (by no means prodigal of their answers)—"If there was any trout-fishing in those streams?"—and our dinner at Luss set us up for the rest of our day's march. The sky now became overcast; but this, I think, added to the effect of the scene. The road to Tarbet is superb. It is on the very verge of the lake—hard, level, rocky, with low stone bridges constantly flung across it, and fringed with birch trees, just then budding into spring, behind which, as through a slight veil, you saw the huge shadowy form of Ben Lomond. It lifts its enormous but graceful bulk direct from the edge of the water without any projecting lowlands, and has in this respect much the advantage of

---

[5] In a performance quite uncharacteristic of him, Hazlitt at this point provides a supplemental footnote, as follows:

> Sweet bird, thy bower is ever greer,
> Thy sky is ever clear;
> Thou hast no sorrow in thy song,
> No winter in thy year.

So they begin. It was the month of May; the cuckoo sang shrouded in some woody copse; the showers fell between whiles; my friend repeated the lines with native enthusiasm in a clear, manly voice, still resonant of youth and hope. Mr. Wordsworth will excuse me, if in these circumstances I declined entering the field with his profounder metaphysical strain, and kept my preference to myself.

Howe reminds us, however, that Logan's "To the Cuckoo" actually begins quite differently, and that Hazlitt is quoting the sixth stanza (*Works*, IX, 266).

[6] From the last two lines of Wordsworth's fourth "Lucy" poem, "Three Years She Grew in Sun and Shower."

Skiddaw. Loch Lomond comes upon you by degrees as you advance, unfolding and then withdrawing its conscious beauties like an accomplished coquet. You are struck with the point of a rock, the arch of a bridge, the Highland huts (like the first rude habitations of men) dug out of the soil, built of turf, and covered with brown heather, a sheep-cote, some straggling cattle feeding half-way down a precipice; but as you advance farther on, the view expands into the perfection of lake scenery. It is nothing (or your eye is caught by nothing) but water, earth, and sky. Ben Lomond waves to the right, in its simple majesty, cloud-capt or bare, and descending to a point at the head of the lake, shews the Trossacs beyond, tumbling about their blue ridges like woods waving; to the left is the Cobler, whose top is like a castle shattered in pieces and nodding to its ruin; and at your side rise the shapes of round pastoral hills, green, fleeced with herds, and retiring into mountainous bays and upland valleys, where solitude and peace might make their lasting home, if peace were to be found in solitude! That it was not always so, I was a sufficient proof; for there was one image that alone haunted me in the midst of all this sublimity and beauty, and turned it to a mockery and a dream!

The snow on the mountain would not let us ascend; and being weary of waiting and of being visited by the guide every two hours to let us know that the weather would not do, we returned, you homewards, and I to London—

"Italiam, Italiam!" [7]

You know the anxious expectations with which I set out:—now hear the result.—

As the vessel sailed up the Thames, the air thickened with the consciousness of being near her, and I "heaved her name pantingly forth." [8] As I approached the house, I could not help thinking of the lines—

"How near am I to a happiness,
That earth exceeds not! Not another like it.
The treasures of the deep are not so precious

---

[7] Virgil, *Aeneid*, III, 522-523 *(Works*, IX, 266). There was also Byron's virtual translation *(Childe Harold*, IV, 42) of the then-popular sonnet Vincenzo da Filicaja (1642-1707), "Italia, Italia! O tu cui feo la sorte."

[8] *King Lear*, IV, iii, 25-26 (loosely quoted).

As are the concealed comforts of a man
Lock'd up in woman's love. I scent the air
Of blessings when I come but near the house.
What a delicious breath true love sends forth!
The violet-beds not sweeter. Now for a welcome
Able to draw men's envies upon man:
A kiss now' that will hang upon my lip,
As sweet as morning dew upon a rose,
And full as long!" [9]

I saw her, but I saw at the first glance that there was something amiss. It was with much difficulty and after several pressing intreaties that she was prevailed on to come up into the room; and when she did, she stood at the door, cold, distant, averse; and when at length she was persuaded by my repeated remonstrances to come and take my hand, and I offered to touch her lips, she turned her head and shrunk from my embraces, as if quite alienated or mortally offended. I asked what it could mean? What had I done in her absence to have incurred her displeasure? Why had she not written to me? I could get only short, sullen, disconnected answers, as if there was something labouring in her mind which she either could not or would not impart. I hardly knew how to bear this first reception after so long an absence, and so different from the one my sentiments towards her merited; but I thought it possible it might be prudery (as I had returned without having actually accomplished what I went about) or that she had taken offence at something in my letters. She saw how much I was hurt. I asked her, "If she was altered since I went away?"—"No." "If there was any one else who had been so fortunate as to gain her favourable opinion?"—"No, there was no one else." "What was it then? Was it anything in my letters? Or had I displeased her by letting Mr. P [10] know she wrote to me?"—"No, not at all; but she did not apprehend my last letter required any answer, or she would have replied to it." All this appeared to me very unsatisfactory and evasive; but I could get no more from her, and was obliged to let

9 From Middleton's *Women Beware Women*, III, i, 83-106, with the omission of thirteen lines and the substitution of "true love" for "marriage."
10 Patmore.

her go with a heavy, foreboding heart. I however found that C [11] was gone, and no one else had been there, of whom I had cause to be jealous.— "Should I see her on the morrow?"—"She believed so, but she could not promise." The next morning she did not appear with the breakfast as usual. At this I grew somewhat uneasy. The little Buonaparte, however, was placed in its old position on the mantel-piece, which I considered as a sort of recognition of old times. I saw her once or twice casually; nothing particular happened till the next day, which was Sunday. I took occasion to go into the parlour for the newspaper, which she gave me with a gracious smile, and seemed tolerably frank and cordial. This of course acted as a spell upon me. I walked out with my little boy, intending to go and dine out at one or two places, but I found that I still contrived to bend my steps towards her, and I went back to take tea at home. While we were out, I talked to William about Sarah, saying that she too was unhappy, and asking him to make it up with her. He said, if she was unhappy, he would not bear her malice any more. When she came up with the tea-things, I said to her, "William has something to say to you—I believe he wants to be friends." On which he said in his abrupt, hearty manner, "Sarah, I'm sorry if I've ever said anything to vex you"—so they shook hands, and she said, smiling affably—"*Then* I'll think no more of it!" I added—"I see you've brought me back my little Buonaparte" [12]—She answered with tremulous softness—"I told you I'd keep it safe for you!"—as if her pride and pleasure in doing so had been equal, and she had, as it were, thought of nothing during my absence but how to greet me with this proof of her fidelity on my return. I cannot describe her manner. Her words are few and simple; but you can have no idea of the exquisite, unstudied, irresistible graces with which she accompanies them, unless you can suppose a Greek statue to smile, move, and speak. Those lines in Tibullus seem to have been written on purpose for her—

> Quicquid agit, quoquo vestigià vertit,
> Componuit furtim, subsequiturque decor. [13]

---

[11] Tomkins, a fellow lodger at Southampton Bldgs.
[12] Cf. Letter 94, and "The Reconciliation" scene in *Liber Amoris*.
[13] Tibullus (?). From the first of the Sulpicia poems in the *Elegies*, Book IV.

Or what do you think of those in a modern play, which might actually have been composed with an eye to this little trifler (though that's a secret)—

—"See with what a waving air she goes
Along the corridor. How like a fawn!
Yet statelier. No sound (however soft)
Nor gentlest echo telleth when she treads,
But every motion of her shape doth seem
Hallowed by silence. So did Hebe grow
Among the Gods a paragon! Away, I'm grown
The very fool of Love!" [14]

The truth is, I never saw anything like her, nor I never shall again. How then do I console myself for the loss of her? Shall I tell you, but you will not mention it again? I am foolish enough to believe that she and I, in spite of everything, shall be sitting together over a sea-coal fire, a comfortable good old couple, twenty years hence! But to my narrative.—

I was delighted with the alteration in her manner, and said, referring to the bust—"You know it is not mine, but your's; I gave it you; nay, I have given you all—my heart, and whatever I possess, is your's!" She seemed good-humouredly to decline this *carte blanche* offer, and waved, like a thing of enchantment, out of the room. False calm!—Deceitful smiles!—Short interval of peace, followed by lasting woe! I sought an interview with her that same evening. I could not get her to come any farther than the door. "She was busy—she could hear what I had to say there." "Why do you seem to avoid me as you do? Not one five minutes' conversation, for the sake of old acquaintance? Well, then, for the sake of *the little image!*" The appeal seemed to have lost its efficacy; the charm was broken; she remained immoveable. "Well, then, I must come to you, if you will not run away." I went and sat down in a chair near the door and took her hand, and talked to her for three quarters of an hour; and she listened patiently, thoughtfully, and seemed a good deal affected by what I said. I told her how much I had felt, how much I had suffered for her in my absence, and how much I

---

[14] B. W. Procter's *Mirandola*, I, iii.

had been hurt by her sudden silence, for which I knew not how to account. I could have done nothing to offend her while I was away; and my letters were, I hoped, tender and respectful. I had had but one thought ever present with me; her image never quitted my side, alone or in company, to delight or distract me. Without her I could have no peace, nor ever should again, unless she would behave to me as she had done formerly. There was no abatement of my regard to her; why was she so changed? I said to her, "Ah! Sarah, when I think that it is only a year ago that you were everything to me I could wish, and that now you seem lost to me for ever, the month of May (the name of which ought to be a signal for joy and hope) strikes chill to my heart.—How different is this meeting from that delicious parting, when you seemed never weary of repeating the proofs of your regard and tenderness, and it was with difficulty we tore ourselves asunder at last! I am ten thousand times fonder of you than I was then, and ten thousand times more unhappy." "You have no reason to be so; my feelings towards you are the same as they ever were." I told her "She was my all of hope or comfort: my passion for her grew stronger every time I saw her." She answered, "She was sorry for it; for *that* she never could return." I said something about looking ill: she said in her pretty, mincing, emphatic way, "I despise looks!" So, thought I, it is not that; and she says there's no one else: it must be some strange air she gives herself, in consequence of the approaching change in my circumstances. She has been probably advised not to give up till all is fairly over, and then she will be my own sweet girl again. All this time she was standing just outside the door, my hand in hers (would that they could have grown together!) she was dressed in a loose morning-gown, her hair curled beautifully; she stood with her profile to me, and looked down the whole time. No expression was ever more soft or perfect. Her whole attitude, her whole form, was dignity and bewitching grace. I said to her, "You look like a queen, my love, adorned with your own graces!" I grew idolatrous, and would have kneeled to her. She made a movement, as if she was displeased. I tried to draw her towards me. She wouldn't. I then got up, and offered to kiss her at parting. I found she obstinately refused. This stung me to the quick. It was the first time in her life she had ever done so. There must be some new bar between us to produce these continued denials; and she had not even esteem enough left to tell me so. I followed her half-way down-stairs, but to no purpose, and returned into my room, confirmed in my most dreadful surmises. I could bear it no longer. I gave way to all the fury of disappointed hope and jealous passion. I was made the dupe of trick and cunning, killed with cold, sullen scorn; and, after all the agony I had suffered, could obtain no explanation why I was subjected to it. I was still to be tantalized, tortured, made the cruel sport of one, for whom I would have sacrificed all. I tore the locket which contained her hair (and which I used to wear continually in my bosom, as the precious token of her dear regard) from my neck, and trampled it in pieces. I then dashed the little Buonaparte on the ground, and stamped upon it, as one of her instruments of mockery. I could not stay in the room; I could not leave it; my rage, my despair were uncontroulable. I shrieked curses on her name, and on her false love; and the scream I uttered (so pitiful and so piercing was it, that the sound of it terrified me) instantly brought the whole house, father, mother, lodgers and all, into the room. They thought I was destroying her and myself. I had gone into the bed-room, merely to hide away from myself, and as I came out of it, raging-mad with the new sense of present shame and lasting misery, Mrs. F [15] said, "She's in there! He has got her in there!" thinking the cries had proceeded from her, and that I had been offering her violence. "Oh! no," I said, "she's in no danger from me; I am not the person;" and tried to burst from this scene of degradation. The mother endeavoured to stop me, and said, "For God's sake, don't go out, Mr.—! for God's sake, don't!" Her father, who was not, I believe, in the secret, and was therefore justly scandalised at such outrageous conduct, said angrily, "Let him go! Why should he stay?" I however sprang down stairs, and as they called out to me, "What is it?—What has she done to you?" I answered, "She has murdered me!—She has destroyed me for ever!—She has doomed my soul to perdition!" I rushed out of the house, thinking to quit it forever; but I was no sooner in the street, than the desolation and the darkness became greater, more intolerable; and the eddying violence of my passion drove me back to the source, from whence it sprung. This unexpected explosion, with the conjectures to which it would give rise, could not be very

[15] Mrs. Walker, Sarah's mother.

agreeable to the *precieuse* or her family; and when I went back, the father was waiting at the door, as if anticipating this sudden turn of my feelings, with no friendly aspect. I said, "I have to beg pardon, Sir; but my mad fit is over, and I wish to say a few words to you in private." He seemed to hesitate, but some uneasy forebodings on his own account, probably, prevailed over his resentment; or, perhaps (as philosophers have a desire to know the cause of thunder) it was a natural curiosity to know what circumstances of provocation had given rise to such an extraordinary scene of confusion. When we reached my room, I requested him to be seated. I said, "It is true, Sir, I have lost my peace of mind forever, but at present I am quite calm and collected, and I wish to explain to you why I have behaved in so extravagant a way, and to ask for your advice and intercession." He appeared satisfied, and I went on. I had no chance either of exculpating myself, or of probing the question to the bottom, but by stating the naked truth, and therefore I said at once, "Sarah told me, Sir (and I never shall forget the way in which she told me, fixing her dove's eyes upon me, and looking a thousand tender reproaches for the loss of that good opinion, which she held dearer than all the world) she told me, Sir, that as you one day passed the door, which stood a-jar, you saw her in an attitude which a good deal startled you; I mean sitting in my lap, with her arms round my neck, and mine twined round her in the fondest manner. What I wished to ask was, whether this was actually the case, or whether it was a mere invention of her own, to enhance the sense of my obligations to her; for I begin to doubt everything?"—"Indeed, it was so; and very much surprised and hurt I was to see it." "Well, then, Sir, I can only say, that as you saw her sitting then, so she had been sitting for the last year and a half, almost every day of her life, by the hour together; and you may judge yourself, knowing what a nice modest-looking girl she is, whether, after having been admitted to such intimacy with so sweet a creature, and for so long a time, it is not enough to make anyone frantic to be received by her as I have been since my return, without any provocation given or cause assigned for it." The old man answered very seriously, and, as I think, sincerely, "What you now tell me, Sir, mortifies and shocks me, as much as it can do yourself. I had no idea such a thing was possible. I was much pained at what I saw; but I thought it an accident, and that it would never happen again."—"It was a constant habit; it has happened a hundred times since, and a thousand before. I lived on her caresses as my daily food, nor can I live without them." So I told him the whole story, "what conjurations, and what mighty magic I won his daughter with," [16] to be anything but *mine for life*. Nothing could well exceed his astonishment and apparent mortification. "What I had said," he owned, "had left a weight upon his mind that he should not easily get rid of." I told him "For myself, I never could recover the blow I had received. I thought, however, for her own sake, she ought to alter her present behaviour. Her marked neglect and dislike, so far from justifying, left her former intimacies without excuse; for nothing could reconcile them to propriety, or even a pretence to common decency, but either love, or friendship so strong and pure that it could put on the guise of love. She was certainly a singular girl. Did she think it right and becoming to be free with strangers, and strange to old friends?" I frankly declared, "I did not see how it was in human nature for any one who was not rendered callous to such familiarities by bestowing them indiscriminately on every one, to grant the extreme and continued indulgences she had done. to me, without either liking the man at first, or coming to like him in the end, in spite of herself. When my addresses had nothing, and could have nothing honourable in them, she gave them every encouragement; when I wished to make them honourable, she treated them with the utmost contempt. The terms we had been all along on were such as if she had been to be my bride next day. It was only when I wished her actually to become so, to ensure her own character and my happiness, that she shrunk back with precipitation and panic-fear. There seemed to me something wrong in all this; a want both of common propriety, and I might say, of natural feeling; yet, with all her faults, I loved her, and ever should, beyond any other human being. I had drank in the poison of her sweetness too long ever to be cured of it; and though I might find it to be poison in the end, it was still in my veins. My only ambition was to be permitted to live with her, and to die in her arms. Be she what she would, treat me how she would, I felt that my soul was wedded to hers; and were she a mere lost creature, I

---

16 *Othello*, I, iii, 103-105.

would try to snatch her from perdition, and marry her to-morrow if she would have me. That was the question—Would she have me, or would she not?" He said he could not tell; but should not attempt to put any constraint upon her inclinations, one way or other. I acquiesced, and added, that "I had brought all this up-on myself, by acting contrary to the suggestions of my friend, Mr.---,[17] who had desired me to take no notice whether she came near me or kept away, whether she smiled or frowned, was kind or contemptuous—all you have to do, is to wait patiently for a month till you are your own man, as you will be in all probability; then make her an offer of your hand, and if she refuses, there's an end of the matter." Mr. L.[18] said, "Well, Sir, and I don't think you can follow a better advice!" I took this as at least a sort of negative encouragement, and so we parted.

---

[17] Patmore.
[18] Mr. Walker, Sarah's father.

No. 125

To James Sheridan Knowles

Liber Amoris.

TO THE SAME
(In continuation)

My dear friend,

The next day I felt almost as sailors must do after a violent storm over-night, that has subsided towards day-break. The morning was a dull and stupid calm, and I found she was unwell, in consequence of what had happened. In the evening I grew more uneasy, and determined on going into the country for a week or two. I gathered up the fragments of the locket of her hair, and the little bronze statue, which were strewed about the floor, kissed them, folded them up in a sheet of paper, and sent them to her, with these lines written in pencil on the outside—*"Pieces of a broken heart, to be kept in remembrance of the unhappy. Farewell."* No notice was taken; nor did I expect any. The following morning I requested Betsey [1] to pack up my box for me, as I should go out of town the next day, and at the same time wrote a note to her sister to say, I should take it as a favour if she would please to accept of the enclosed copies of the *Vicar of Wakefield, The Man of Feeling,* and *Nature and Art,* in lieu of three volumes of my own writings, which I had given her on different occasions, in the course of our acquaintance. I was piqued, in fact, that she should have these to shew as proof of my weakness, and as if I thought the way to win her was by plaguing her with my own performances. She sent me word back that the books I had sent were of no use to her, and that I should have those I wished for in the afternoon; but that she could not before, as she had lent them to her sister, Mrs. M. [2] I said, "Very well;" but observed (laughing) to Betsey, "It's a bad rule to

---

[1] Betsey Walker, Sarah's younger sister.
[2] Mrs. Roscoe, Sarah's older sister.

give and take; so, if Sarah won't have these books, you must; they are very pretty ones, I assure you." She curtsied and took them, according to the family custom. In the afternoon, when I came back to tea, I found the little girl on her knees, busy in packing up my things, and a large paper-parcel on the table, which I could not at first tell what to make of. On opening it, however, I soon found what it was. It contained a number of volumes which I had given her at different times (among others, a little Prayer-Book, bound in crimson velvet, with green silk linings; she kissed it twenty times when she received it, and said it was the prettiest present in the world, and that she would shew it to her aunt, who would be proud of it)—and all these she had returned together. Her name in the title-page was cut out of them all. I doubted at the instant whether she had done this before or after I had sent for them back, and I have doubted of it since; but there is no occasion to suppose her *ugly all over with hypocrisy.* Poor little thing! She has enough to answer for, as it is. I asked Betsey if she could carry a message for me, and she said *"Yes."* "Will you tell your sister, then, that I did not want all these books; and give my love to her, and say that I shall be obliged if she will still keep these that I have sent back, and tell her that it is only those of my own writing that I think unworthy of her." What do you think the little imp made answer? She raised herself on the other side of the table where she stood, as if inspired by the genius of the place, and said—"AND THOSE ARE THE ONES THAT SHE PRIZES THE MOST!" If there were ever words spoken that could revive the dead, those were the words. Let me kiss them, and forget that my ears have heard aught else! I said, "Are you sure of that?" and she said, "Yes, quite sure." I told her, "If I could be, I should be very different from what I was." And I became so that instant, for these casual words carried assurance to my heart of her esteem—that once implied, I had proofs enough of her fondness. Oh! how I felt at that moment! Restored to love, hope, and joy, by a breath which I had caught by the merest accident, and which I might have pined in absence and mute despair for want of hearing! I did not know how to contain myself; I was childish, wanton, drunk with pleasure. I gave Betsey a twenty-shilling note which I happened to have in my hand, and on her asking "What's this for, Sir?" I said, "It's for you. Don't you think it worth that to be made happy? You once made me very wretched by some words I heard you drop, and now you have made me as happy; and all I wish you is, when you grow up, that you may find some one to love you as well as I do your sister, and that you may love better than she does me!" I continued in this state of delirium or dotage all that day and the next, talked incessantly, laughed at everything, and was so extravagant, nobody could tell what was the matter with me. I murmured her name; I blest her; I folded her to my heart in delicious fondness; I called her by my own name; I worshipped her; I was mad for her. I told P——³ I should laugh in her face, if ever she pretended not to like me again. Her mother came in and said, she hoped I should excuse Sarah's coming up. "Oh! Ma'am," I said, "I have no wish to see her; I feel her at my heart; she does not hate me after all, and I wish for nothing. Let her come when she will, she is to me welcomer than light, than life; but let it be in her own sweet time, and at her own dear pleasure." Betsey also told me she was "so glad to get the books back." I, however, sobered and wavered (by degrees) from seeing nothing of her, day after day; and in less than a week I was devoted to the Infernal Gods. I could hold out no longer than the Monday evening following. I sent a message to her; she returned an ambiguous answer; but she came up. Pity me, my friend, for the shame of this recital. Pity me for the pain of having ever had to make it! If the spirits of mortal creatures, purified by faith and hope, can (according to the highest assurances) ever, during thousands of years of smooth-rolling eternity and balmy, sainted repose, forget the pain, the toil, the anguish, the helplessness, and the despair they have suffered here, in this frail being, then may I forget that withering hour, and her, that fair, pale form that entered, my inhuman betrayer, and my only earthly love! She said, "Did you wish to speak to me, Sir?" I said, "Yes, may I not speak to you? I wanted to see you and be friends." I rose up, offered her an armchair which stood facing, bowed on it, and knelt to her adoring. She said (going) "If that's all, I have nothing to say." I replied, "Why do you treat me thus? What have I done to become thus hateful to you?" *Answer,* "I always told you I had no affection for you." You may suppose this was a blow, after the imaginary honeymoon in which I had passed the preceding week. I was

---

³ Patmore.

stunned by it; my heart sunk within me. I contrived to say, "Nay, my dear girl, not always neither; for did you not once (if I might presume to look back to those happy, happy times) when you were sitting on my knee as usual, embracing and embraced, and I asked if you could not love me at last, did you not make answer, in the softest tones that ever man heard, *'I could easily say so, whether I did or not: you should judge by my actions!'* Was I to blame in taking you at your word, when every hope I had depended on your sincerity? And did you not say since I came back, *'Your feelings to me were the same as ever?'* Why then is your behaviour so different? S. "Is it nothing, your exposing me to the whole house in the way you did the other evening?" H. "Nay, that was the consequence of your cruel reception of me, not the cause of it. I had better have gone away last year, as I proposed to do, unless you would give some pledge of your fidelity; but it was your own offer that I should remain. 'Why should I go?' you said. 'Why could we not go on the same as we had done, and say nothing about the word *forever?'* " S. "And how did you behave when you returned?" H. That was all forgiven when we last parted, and your last words were, "I should find you the same as ever" when I came back? Did you not that very day enchant and madden me over again by the purest kisses and embraces, and did I not go from you (as I said) adoring, confiding, with every assurance of mutual esteem and friendship?" S. "Yes, and in your absence I found that you had told my aunt what had passed between us." H. "It was to induce her to extort your real sentiments from you, that you might no longer make a secret of your true regard for me, which your actions (but not your words) confessed." S. "I own I have been guilty of improprieties, which you have gone and repeated, not only in the house, but out of it; so that it has come to my ears from various quarters, as if I was a light character. And I am determined in future to be guided by the advice of my relations, and particularly of my aunt, whom I consider as my best friend, and keep every lodger at a proper distance." You will find hereafter that her favourite lodger, whom she visits daily, had left the house; so that she might easily make and keep this vow of extraordinary self-denial. Precious little dissembler! Yet her aunt, her best friend, says, "No, Sir, no; Sarah's no hypocrite!" which I was fool enough to believe; and yet my great and unpardonable offence is to have entertained passing

[306]

doubts on this delicate point. I said, Whatever errors I had committed, arose from my anxiety to have everything explained to her honour: my conduct shewed that I had that at heart, and that I built on the purity of her character as on a rock. My esteem for her amounted to adoration. "She did not want adoration." It was only when any thing happened to imply that I had been mistaken, that I committed any extravagance, because I could not bear to think her short of perfection. "She was far from perfection," she replied, with an air and manner (oh, my God!) as near it as possible. "How could she accuse me of a want of regard to her? It was but the other day, Sarah," I said to her, "when that little circumstance of the books happened, and I fancied the expressions your sister dropped proved the sincerity of all your kindness to me—you don't know how my heart melted within me at the thought, that after all, I might be dear to you. New hopes sprung up in my heart, and I felt as Adam must have done when his Eve was created for him!" "She had heard enough of that sort of conversation," (moving towards the door). This, I own, was the unkindest cut of all. I had, in that case, no hopes whatever. I felt that I had expended words in vain, and that the conversation below stairs [4] (which I told you of when I saw you) had spoiled her taste for mine. If the allusion had been classical I should have been to blame; but it was scriptural, it was a sort of religious courtship, and Miss L.[5] is religious!

> At once he took his Muse and dipt her
> Right in the middle of the Scripture.[6]

It would not do—the lady could make neither head nor tail of it. This is a poor attempt at levity. Alas! I am sad enough. "Would she go and leave me so? If it was only my own behaviour, I still did not doubt of success. I knew the sincerity of my love, and she would be convinced of it in time. If that was all, I did not care: but

---

[4] Cf. Letter 116.
[5] Sarah Walker.
[6] John Gay, "Verses to be placed under the Picture of Sir Richard Blackmore."

> Then he took his Muse at once and dipt her
> Full in the middle of the Scripture.

tell me true, is there not a new attachment that is the real cause of your estrangement? Tell me, my sweet friend, and before you tell me, give me your hand (nay, both hands) that I may have something to support me under the dreadful conviction." She let me take her hands in mine, saying, "She supposed there could be no objection to that,"—as if she acted on the suggestions of others, instead of following her own will—but still avoided giving me any answer. I conjured her to tell me the worst, and kill me on the spot. Anything was better than my present state. I said, "Is it Mr. C——?" [7] She smiled, and said with gay indifference, "Mr. C——— was here a very short time." "Well, then, was it Mr. ———?" [8] She hesitated, and then replied faintly, "No." This was a mere trick to mislead; one of the profoundnesses of Satan, in which she is an adept. "But," she added hastily, "she could make no more confidences." "Then," said I, "you have something to communicate." "No; but she had once mentioned a thing of the sort, which I had hinted to her mother, though it signified little." All this while I was in tortures. Every word, every half-denial, stabbed me. "Had she any tie?" "No, I have no tie." "You are not going to be married soon?" "I don't intend ever to marry at all!" "Can't you be friends with me as of old?" "She could give no promises." "Would she make her own terms?" "She would make none."—"I was sadly afraid the *little image* was dethroned from her heart, as I had dashed it to the ground the other night."—"She was neither desperate nor violent." I did not answer—"But deliberate and deadly,"—though I might; and so she vanished in this running fight of question and answer, in spite of my vain efforts to detain her. The cockatrice, I said, mocks me: so she has always done. The thought was a dagger to me. My head reeled, my heart recoiled within me. I was stung with scorpions; my flesh crawled; I was choked with rage; her scorn scorched me like flames; her air (her heavenly air) withdrawn from me, stifled me, and left me gasping for breath and being. It was a fable. She started up in her own likeness, a serpent in place of a woman. She had fascinated, she had stung me, and had returned to her proper shape, gliding from me after inflicting the mortal wound, and instilling deadly poison

---

[7] Tomkins.

[8] Perhaps Sarah's former lover who had broken off with her.

into every pore; but her form lost none of its original brightness by the change of character, but was all glittering, beauteous, voluptuous grace. Seed of the serpent or of the woman, she was divine! I felt that she was a witch, and had bewitched me. Fate had enclosed me round about. *I* was transformed too, no longer human (any more than she, to whom I had knit myself) my feelings were marble; my blood was of molten lead; my thoughts on fire. I was taken out of myself, wrapt into another sphere, far from the light of day, of hope, of love. I had no natural affection left; she had slain me, but no other thing had power over me. Her arms embraced another; but her mock-embrace, the phantom of her love, still bound me, and I had not a wish to escape. So I felt then, and so perhaps shall feel till I grow old and die, nor have any desire that my years should last longer than they are linked in the chain of those amorous folds, or than her enchantments steep my soul in oblivion of all other things! I started to find myself alone—for ever alone, without a creature to love me. I looked round the room for help; I saw the tables, the chairs, the places where she stood or sat, empty, deserted, dead. I could not stay where I was; I had no one to go to but to the parent-mischief, the preternatural hag, that had "drugged this posset" [9] of her daughter's charms and falsehood for me, and I went down and (such was my weakness and helplessness) sat with her for an hour, and talked with her of her daughter, and the sweet days we had passed together, and said I thought her a good girl, and believed that if there was no rival, she still had a regard for me at the bottom of her heart; and how I liked her all the better for her coy, maiden airs: and I received the assurance over and over that there was no one else; and that Sarah (they all knew) never staid five minutes with any other lodger, while with me she would stay by the hour together, in spite of all her father could say to her (what were her motives, was best known to herself!) and while we were talking of her, she came bounding into the room, smiling with smothered delight at the consummation of my folly and her own art; and I asked her mother whether she thought she looked as if she hated me, and I took her wrinkled, withered, cadaverous, clammy hand at parting, and kissed it. Faugh!—

---

[9] *Macbeth,* II, ii, 6. "Drugg'd their possets."

I will make an end of this story; there is something in it discordant to honest ears. I left the house the next day, and returned to Scotland in a state so near to phrenzy, that I take it the shades sometimes ran into one another. R———[10] met me the day after I arrived, and will tell you the way I was in. I was like a person in a high fever; only mine was in the mind instead of the body. It had the same irritating, uncomfortable effect on the bye-standers. I was incapable of any application, and don't know what I should have done, had it not been for the kindness of ———.[11] I came to see you, to "bestow some of my tediousness upon you," [12] but you were gone from home. Everything went on well as to the law-business; and as it approached to a conclusion, I wrote to my good friend P————[13] to go to M———,[14] who had married her sister, and ask him if it would be worth my while to make her a formal offer, as soon as I was free, as, with the least encouragement, I was ready to throw myself at her feet; and to know, in case of refusal, whether I might go back there and be treated as an old friend. Not a word of answer could be got from her on either point, notwithstanding every importunity and intreaty; but it was the opinion of M——— that I might go and try my fortune. I did so with joy, with something like confidence. I thought her giving no positive answer implied a chance, at least, of the reversion of her favour, in case I behaved well. All was false, hollow, insidious. The first night after I got home, I slept on down. In Scotland, the flint had been my pillow. But now I slept under the same roof with her. What softness, what balmy repose in the very thought! I saw her that same day and shook hands with her, and told her how glad I was to see her; and she was kind and comfortable, though still cold and distant. Her manner was altered from what it was the last time. She still absented herself from the room, but was mild and affable when she did come. She was pale, dejected, evidently uneasy about something, and had been ill. I thought it was perhaps her reluctance to yield to my wishes, her pity for what I suffered; and that in the struggle between both, she did not know what to do. How I

---

[10] William Ritchie (1781-1831), editor of *The Scotsman.*
[11] Jeffrey.
[12] *Much Ado About Nothing,* III, v, 25-26.
[13] Patmore.
[14] Roscoe.

worshipped her at these moments! We had a long interview the third day, and I thought all was doing well. I found her sitting at work in the window-seat of the front parlour; and on my asking if I might come in, she made no objection. I sat down by her; she let me take her hand; I talked to her of indifferent things, and of old times. I asked her if she would put some new frills on my shirts?—"With the greatest pleasure." If she could get *the little image* mended? "It was broken in three pieces, and the sword was gone, but she would try." I then asked her to make up a plaid silk which I had given her in the winter, and which she said would make a pretty summer gown. I so longed to see her in it!—"She had little time to spare, but perhaps might!" Think what I felt, talking peaceably, kindly, tenderly with my love,—not passionately, not violently. I tried to take pattern by her patient meekness, as I thought it, and to subdue my desires to her will. I then sued to her, but respectfully, to be admitted to her friendship—she must know I was as true a friend as ever woman had—or if there was a bar to our intimacy from a dearer attachment, to let me know it frankly, as I shewed her all my heart. She drew out her handkerchief and wiped her eyes "of tears which sacred pity had engendered there." [15] Was it so or not? I cannot tell. But so she stood (while I pleaded my cause to her with all the earnestness and fondness in the world) with the tears trickling from her eye-lashes, her head stooping, her attitude fixed, with the finest expression that ever was seen of mixed regret, pity, and stubborn resolution; but without speaking a word, without altering a feature. It was like a petrifaction of a human face in the softest moment of passion. "Ah!" I said, "how you look! I have prayed again and again while I was away from you, in the agony of my spirit, that I might but live to see you look so again, and then breathe my last!" I intreated her to give me some explanation. In vain! At length she said she must go, and disappeared like a spirit. That week she did all the little trifling favours I had asked of her. The frills were put on, and she sent up to know if I wanted any more done. She got the Buonaparte mended. This was like healing old wounds indeed! How? As follows, for thereby hangs the conclusion of my tale. Listen.

I had sent a message one evening to speak to her about some

---

15 *As You Like It,* II, vii, 123. "Of drops that sacred pity hath engender'd."

special affairs of the house, and received no answer. I waited an hour expecting her, and then went out in great vexation at my disappointment. I complained to her mother a day or two after, saying I thought it so unlike Sarah's usual propriety of behaviour, that she must mean it as a mark of disrespect. Mrs. L———[16] said, "La! Sir, you're always fancying things. Why, she was dressing to go out, and she was only going to get the little image you're both so fond of mended; and it's to be done this evening. She has been to two or three places to see about it, before she could get any one to undertake it." My heart, my poor fond heart, almost melted within me at this news. I answered, "Ah! Madam, that's always the way with the dear creature. I am finding fault with her and thinking the hardest things of her; and at that very time she's doing something to shew the most delicate attention, and that she has no greater satisfaction than in gratifying my wishes!" On this we had some farther talk, and I took nearly the whole of the lodgings at a hundred guineas a year, that (as I said) she might have a little leisure to sit at her needle of an evening, or to read if she chose, or to walk out when it was fine. She was not in good health, and it would do her good to be less confined. I would be the drudge and she should no longer be the slave. I asked nothing in return. To see her happy, to make her so, was to be so myself.—This was agreed to. I went over to Blackheath that evening, delighted as I could be after all I had suffered, and lay the whole of the next morning on the heath under the open sky, dreaming of my earthly Goddess. This was Sunday. That evening I returned, for I could hardly bear to be for a moment out of the house where she was, and the next morning she tapped at the door—it was opened—it was she—she hesitated and then came forward: she had got the little image in her hand, I took it, and blest her from my heart. She said "They had been obliged to put some new pieces to it." I said "I didn't care how it was done, so that I had it restored to me safe, and by her." I thanked her and begged to shake hands with her. She did so, and as I held the only hand in the world that I never wished to let go, I looked up in her face, and said "Have pity on me, have pity on me, and save me if you can!" Not a word of answer, but she looked full in my eyes, as much as to say, "Well, I'll think of it; and

---

[16] Mrs. Walker.

if I can, I will save you!" We talked about the expense of repairing the figure. "Was the man waiting?"—"No, she had fetched it on Saturday evening." I said I'd give her the money in the course of the day, and then shook hands with her again in token of reconciliation; and she went waving out of the room, but at the door turned round and looked full at me, as she did the first time she beguiled me of my heart. This was the last.—

All that day I longed to go downstairs to ask her and her mother to set out with me for Scotland on Wednesday, and on Saturday I would make her my wife. Something withheld me. In the evening, however, I could not rest without seeing her, and I said to her younger sister, "Betsey, if Sarah will come up now, I'll pay her what she laid out for me the other day."—"My sister's gone out, Sir," was the answer. What, again! thought I, that's somewhat sudden. I told P———[17] her sitting in the window-seat of the front parlour boded me no good. It was not in her old character. She did not use to know there were doors or windows in the house—and now she goes out three times in a week. It is to meet some one, I'll lay my life on't. "Where is she gone?"—"To my grandmother's, Sir." "Where does your grandmother live now?"—"At Somers' Town." I immediately set out to Somers' Town. I passed one or two streets, and at last turned up King-street, thinking it most likely she would return that way home. I passed a house in King-street where I had once lived, and had not proceeded many paces, ruminating on chance and change and old times, when I saw her coming towards me. I felt a strange pang at the sight, but I thought her alone. Some people before me moved on, and I saw another person with her. *The murder was out.* It was a tall, rather well-looking young man, but I did not at first recollect him. We passed at the crossing of the street without speaking. Will you believe it, after all that had passed between us for two years, after what had passed in the last half-year, after what had passed that very morning, she went by me without even changing countenance, without expressing the slightest emotion, without betraying either shame or pity or remorse or any other feeling that any other human being but herself must have shewn in the same situation. She had no time to prepare for acting a part, to suppress her

---

17 Patmore.

feelings—the truth is, she has not one natural feeling in her bosom to suppress. I turned and looked—they also turned and looked—and as if by mutual consent, we both retrod our steps and passed again, in the same way. I went home. I was stifled. I could not stay in the house, walked into the street, and met them coming towards home. As soon as he had left her at the door (I fancy she had prevailed with him to accompany her, dreading some violence) I returned, went up stairs, and requested an interview. Tell her, I said, I'm in excellent temper and good spirits, but I must see her! She came smiling, and I said, "Come in, my dear girl, and sit down, and tell me all about it, how it is and who it is."—"What," she said, "do you mean Mr. C———?" [18] "Oh," said I, "then it is he! Ah! you rogue, I always suspected there was something between you, but you know you denied it lustily: why did you not tell me all about it at the time, instead of letting me suffer as I have done? But however, no reproaches. I only wish it may all end happily and honourably for you, and I am satisfied. But," I said, "you know you used to tell me, you despised looks."—"She didn't think Mr. C——— was so particularly handsome." "No, but he's very well to pass, and a well-grown youth into the bargain." Pshaw! let me put an end to the fulsome detail. I found he had lived over the way, that he had been lured thence, no doubt, almost a year before, that they had first spoken in the street, and that he had never once hinted at marriage, and had gone away, because (as he said) they were too much together, and that it was better for her to meet him occasionally out of doors. "There could be no harm in them walking together." "No, but you may go some where afterwards."—"One must trust to one's principle for that." Consummate hypocrite! * I told her Mr. M———,[19] who had married her sister, did not wish to leave the house. I, who would have married her, did not wish to leave it. I told her I hoped I should not live to see her come to shame, after all my love of her; but put her on her guard as well as I could, and said, after the lengths she had permitted herself with me, I could not help being alarmed at the influence of one over her, whom she could hardly herself suppose to have a tenth part of

18 Tomkins.
19 Roscoe.

my esteem for her!! She made no answer to this, but thanked me coldly for my good advice, and rose to go. I begged her to sit a few minutes, that I might try to recollect if there was anything else I wished to say to her, perhaps for the last time; and then, not finding anything, I bade her good night, and asked for a farewel kiss. Do you know she refused; so little does she understand what is due to friendship, or love, or honour! We parted friends, however, and I felt deep grief, but no enmity against her. I thought C———[20] had pressed his suit after I went, and had prevailed. There was no harm in that—a little fickleness or so, a little over pretension to unalterable attachment—but that was all. She liked him better than me—it was my hard hap, but I must bear it. I went out to roam the desert streets, when, turning a corner, whom should I meet but her very lover? I went up to him and asked for a few minutes' conversation on a subject that was highly interesting to me and I believed not indifferent to him: and in the course of four hours' talk, it came out that for three months previous to my quitting London for Scotland, she had been playing the same game with him as with me—that he breakfasted first, and enjoyed an hour of her society, and then I took my turn, so that we never jostled; and this explained why, when he came back sometimes and passed my door, as she was sitting in my lap, she coloured violently, thinking if her lover looked in, what a *denouement* there would be. He could not help again and again expressing his astonishment at finding that our intimacy had continued unimpaired up to so late a period after he came, and when they were on the most intimate footing. She used to deny positively to him that there was anything between us, just as she used to assure me with impenetrable effrontery that "Mr. C——— was nothing to her, but merely a lodger." All this while she kept up the farce of her romantic attachment to her old lover, vowed that she never could alter in that respect, let me go to Scotland on the solemn and repeated assurance that there was no new flame, that there was no bar between us but this shadowy love—I leave her on this understanding, she becomes more fond or more intimate with her new lover; he quitting the house (whether tired out or not, I can't say)—in revenge she ceases to write to me, keeps me in wretched

---

[20] Tomkins.

suspense, treats me like something loathsome to her when I return to enquire the cause, denies it with scorn and impudence, destroys me and shews no pity, no desire to soothe or shorten the pangs she has occasioned by her wantonness and hypocrisy, and wishes to linger the affair on to the last moment, going out to keep an appointment with another while she pretends to be obliging me in the tenderest point (which C——— himself said was too much. . . .) What do you think of all this? Shall I tell you my opinion? But I must try to do it in another letter.

No. 126

To James Sheridan Knowles

Liber Amoris

TO THE SAME

(In conclusion.)

I did not sleep a wink all that night; nor did I know till the next day the full meaning of what had happened to me. With the morning's light, conviction glared in upon me that I had not only lost her for ever—but every feeling I had ever had towards her—respect, tenderness, pity—all but my fatal passion, was gone. The whole was a mockery, a frightful illusion. I had embraced the false Florimel instead of the true; or was like the man in the Arabian Nights who had married a *goul*. How different was the idea I once had of her! Was this she,

> —'Who had been beguiled—she who was made
> Within a gentle bosom to be laid—
> To bless and to be blessed—to be heart-bare
> To one who found his bettered likeness there—
> To think for ever with him, like a bride—
> To haunt his eye, like taste personified—
> To double his delight, to share his sorrow,
> And like a morning beam, wake to him every morrow?'[1]

I saw her pale, cold form glide silent by me, dead to shame as to pity. Still I seemed to clasp this piece of witchcraft to my bosom: this lifeless image, which was all that was left of my love, was the only thing to which my sad heart clung. Were she dead, should I not wish to gaze once more upon her pallid features? She is dead to

---

[1] Leigh Hunt, *The Story of Rimini*, III, 205-212.

me; but what she once was to me, can never die! The agony, the conflict of hope and fear, of adoration and jealousy is over; or it would, ere long, have ended with my life. I am no more lifted now to Heaven, and then plunged in the abyss; but I seem to have been thrown from the top of a precipice, and to lie groveling, stunned, and stupefied. I am melancholy, lonesome, and weaker than a child. The worst is, I have no prospect of any alteration for the better: she has cut off all possibility of a reconcilement at any future period. Were she even to return to her former pretended fondness and endearments, I could have no pleasure, no confidence in them. I can scarce make out the contradiction to myself. I strive to think she always was what I now know she is; but I have great difficulty in it, and can hardly believe but she still *is* what she so long *seemed.* Poor thing! I am afraid she is little better off herself; nor do I see what is to become of her, unless she throws off the mask at once, and *runs a-muck* at infamy. She is exposed and laid bare to all those whose opinion she set a value upon. Yet she held her head very high, and must feel (if she feels anything) proportionably mortified.—A more complete experiment on character was never made. If I had not met her lover immediately after I parted with her, it would have been nothing. I might have supposed she had changed her mind in my absence, and had given him the preference as soon as she felt it, and even shown her delicacy in declining any farther intimacy with me. But it comes out that she had gone on in the most forward and familiar way with both at once—(she could not change her mind in passing from one room to another)—told both the same barefaced and unblushing falsehoods, like the commonest creature; received presents from me to the very last, and wished to keep up the game still longer, either to gratify her humour, her avarice, or her vanity in playing with my passion, or to have me as a *dernier resort,* in case of accidents. Again, it would have been nothing, if she had not come up with her demure, well-composed, wheedling looks that morning, and then met me in the evening in a situation, which (she believed) might kill me on the spot, with no more feeling than a common courtesan shews, who *bilks* a customer, and passes him, leering up at her bully, the moment after. If there had been the frailty of passion, it would have been excusable; but it is evident she is a practised, callous jilt, a regular lodging-house decoy, played off by her mother upon the lodgers, one after another, applying them to her different purposes, laughing at them in turns, and herself the probable dupe and victim of some favourite gallant in the end. I know all this; but what do I gain by it, unless I could find some one with her shape and air, to supply the place of the lovely apparition? That a professed wanton should come and sit on a man's knee, and put her arms round his neck, and caress him, and seem fond of him, means nothing, proves nothing, no one concludes anything from it; but that a pretty, reserved, modest, delicate-looking girl should do this, from the first hour to the last of your being in the house, without intending anything by it, is new, and, I think, worth explaining. It was, I confess, out of my calculation, and may be out of that of others. Her unmoved indifference and self-possession all the while, shew that it is her constant practice. Her look even, if closely examined, bears this interpretation. It is that of studied hypocrisy or startled guilt, rather than of refined sensibility or conscious innocence. "She defied any one to read her thoughts!" she once told me. "Do they then require concealing?" I imprudently asked her. The command over herself is surprising. She never once betrays herself by any momentary forgetfulness, by any appearance of triumph or superiority to the person who is her dupe, by any levity of manner in the plenitude of her success; it is one faultless, undeviating, consistent, consummate piece of acting. Were she a saint on earth, she could not seem more like one. Her hypocritical high-flown pretensions, indeed, make her the worse: but still the ascendancy of her will, her determined perseverance in what she undertakes to do, has something admirable in it, approaching to the heroic. She is certainly an extraordinary girl! Her retired manner, and invariable propriety of behaviour made me think it next to impossible she could grant the same favours indiscriminately to every one that she did to me. Yet this now appears to be the fact. She must have done the very same with C——, [2] invited him into the house to carry on a closer intrigue with her, and then commenced the double game with both together. She always "despised looks." This was a favourite phrase with her, and one of the hooks which she baited for me. Nothing could win her but a

---

[2] Tomkins.

man's behaviour and sentiments. Besides, she could never like another—she was a martyr to disappointed affection—and friendship was all she could even extend to any other man. All the time, she was making signals, playing off her pretty person, and having occasional interviews in the street with this very man, whom she could only have taken so sudden and violent a liking to from his looks, his personal appearance, and what she probably conjectured of his circumstances. Her sister had married a counsellor—the Miss F——s, [3] who kept the house before, had done so too—and so would she. "There was precedent for it." Yet if she was so desperately enamoured of this new acquaintance, if he had displaced *the little image* from her breast, if he was become her *second* "unalterable attachment" (which I would have given my life to have been) why continue the same unwarrantable familiarities with me to the last, and promise that they should be renewed on my return (if I had not unfortunately stumbled upon the truth to her aunt)—and yet keep up the same refined cant about her old attachment all the time, as if it was that which stood in the way of my pretensions, and not her faithlessness to it? "If one swerves from one, one shall swerve from another"—was her excuse for not returning my regard. Yet that which I thought a prophecy, was I suspect a history. She had swerved twice from her vowed engagements, first to me, and then from me to another. If she made a fool of me, what did she make of her lover? I fancy he has put that question to himself. I said nothing to him about the amount of the presents; which is another damning circumstance, that might have opened my eyes long before; but they were shut by my fond affection, which "turned all to favour and to prettiness." [4] She cannot be supposed to have kept up an appearance of old regard to me, from a fear of hurting my feelings by her desertion; for she not only shewed herself indifferent to, but evidently triumphed in my sufferings, and heaped every kind of insult and indignity upon them. I must have incurred her contempt and resentment by my mistaken delicacy at different times; and her manner, when I have hinted at becoming a reformed man in this respect, convinces me of it. "She hated it!" She always hated whatever she liked most. She "hated

---

[3] Not identified.
[4] *Hamlet*, IV, v, 189.

Mr. C——'s [5] red slippers," when he first came! One more count finishes the indictment. She not only discovered the most hardened indifference to the feelings of others; she has not shewn the least regard to her own character, or shame when she was detected. When found out, she seemed to say, "Well, what if I am? I have played the game as long as I could; and if I could keep it up no longer, it was not for want of good will!" Her colouring once or twice is the only sign of grace she has exhibited. Such is the creature on whom I had thrown away my heart and soul—one who was incapable of feeling the commonest emotions of human nature, as they regarded herself or any one else. "She had no feelings with respect to herself," she often said. She in fact knows what she is, and recoils from the good opinion or sympathy of others, which she feels to be founded on a deception; so that my overweening opinion of her must have appeared like irony, or direct insult. My seeing her in the street has gone a good way to satisfy me. Her manner there explains her manner in-doors to be conscious and overdone; and besides, she looks but indifferently. She is diminutive in stature, and her measured step and timid air do not suit these public airings. I am afraid she will soon grow common to my imagination, as well as worthless in herself. Her image seems fast "going into the wastes of time," [6] like a weed that the wave bears farther and farther from me. Alas! thou poor hapless weed, when I entirely lose sight of thee, and forever, no flower will ever bloom on earth to glad my heart again!

---

[5] Tomkins.

[6] Shakespeare, Sonnet XII. "That thou amongst the wastes of time must go."

No. 127

To Francis Jeffrey

MS. Yale.
Address: Francis Jeffrey, Esq./Edinburgh.

Oct. 2 [1822] *

Dear Sir,

I understand the Memoirs of Napoleon by Count Montholon are forthcoming. Might I in that case try my hand upon them? [1] I have been thinking, at your suggestion, of doing an article on the Newspaper and Periodical Press, taking in the Times, Chronicle, Magazines, Reviews, etc.[2] The abuses of the Ministerial press might come into this, but I am afraid I know too little of them in detail to make a separate article on that subject. I could make something of the general subject, I know, for it has been some time in my head. I am better than I was, and able to work. If you could lay your hand on the metaphysical article on Bühle,[3] I should take it as a great favour if you would forward it by the Mail to No. 4. Chapel Street West, Curzon Street. You see by this I have moved. I have come away *alive,* which in all the circumstances is a great deal.[4] I believe I did very wrong in not calling on you while in Edinburgh, but the truth is, *I hated the sight of myself* and fancied every body else did the same. Otherwise, I do assure you it would have been the greatest relief my mind was just then capable of. I remain Dear Sir, your much obliged and faithful servant,

W. Hazlitt

---

* Cf. Baker, pp. 417-418.

[1] The review of *Mémoires pour servir à l'histoire de France sous Napoléon* (1823) by Charles Tristan, Marquis de Montholon was not given to Hazlitt.

[2] "The Periodical Press" appeared in May 1823. Cf. *Works,* XVI, 211-239.

[3] An article on Bühle's work on the Rosicrucians and Freemasons which bears many traces of Hazlitt's hand was printed in *The London Magazine,* January 1824. Cf. Letter 65.

[4] In May 1822 Hazlitt had made another trip to Edinburgh for the final proceedings of the divorce. Upon his return to London, he "enacted the final scenes" with Sarah Walker, and removed from Southampton Buildings.

No. 128

To Francis Jeffrey

MS. Yale.
Address: Francis Jeffrey, Esq./Edinburgh.

Dec. 23 [1822] *

Dear Sir,

I sent off a parcel containing an article *On the Periodical Press* a few weeks ago. Might I request the favour of a line from you today whether it came safe to hand, and whether you think of using it? I should be very sorry indeed if you do not think it good enough for the Review, but in that case you would perhaps let me have it again. If you think I am at all in a vein of writing, shall I attempt a sort of critical parallel for the next No. between Lord Byron's Heaven and Earth, and T. Moore's Loves of the Angels? [1] I find my Periodical article was just too late for the last number, which rather disappointed me, for I had fancied myself it was just in time, and just the thing. I am, Dear Sir, your most obliged, and very humble servant,

W. Hazlitt.

4 Chapel Street West,
Curzon Street
May-fair

---

* Cf. Wardle, p. 354.

[1] "Moore and Byron" appeared in February, 1823. The *Wellesley Index* indicates the possibility of Jeffrey's doing this review or having a hand in it. Cf. *Wellesley Index*, I, 1010, "(?) Loves of the Angels," p. 956.

No. 129

To Jane Reynolds[1]

Times Literary Supplement, 21 March, 1936.
Address: Miss Reynolds/Little Britain.

[January 1823]

Dear Madam

On the other side is Mr. Gummow's [2] summons for me to attend him at Cleveland House. I was out of town, and I am afraid it is too late today. If you can manage it, however, I will be there at 3 o'clock. Or will you fix any other time? Or may I call this evening to arrange about it? I thought it possible Mr. Hood [3] might have called in my absence. I am, Dear Madam, your obedient servant,

W. Hazlitt

---

[1] Sister of John Hamilton Reynolds, she married Thomas Hood in 1824. She accompanied Hazlitt to see the paintings collected by the Marquis of Stafford at Cleveland House, later Bridgewater House in St. James's, which Hazlitt described in "The Marquis of Stafford's Gallery," *London Magazine* (February 1823).

[2] The curator, who had published a *Catalogue of the Pictures Belonging to the Marquis of Stafford at Cleveland House* (1814).

[3] Assistant editor of the *London Magazine.* Cf. Letter 133.

No. 130

To Thomas Noon Talfourd

MS. Bodleian Library,
Address: T. N. Talfourd, Esq./26, Henrietta Street/Brunswick Square.

5 Coleman Street Buildings,
Feb. 12. [1823] *

My dear Sir,

I have been arrested this morning and am at a loss what to do.[1] Would you give me a call to talk the matter over, and see if your influence could procure me any terms of accommodation?[2] I am sorry to plague you about my troublesome affairs. Believe me very truly your obliged friend and servant,

W. Hazlitt

---

* Cf. Baker, p. 425.

[1] The result of expenses incurred while obtaining the divorce, but "we do not know at the instance of what creditor he was proceeded against." (Howe, p. 322.)

[2] He was released owing to Talfourd's influence.

No. 131

To Taylor and Hessey

London Mercury, March, 1923.

[February 1823] *

My Dear Sir,

I have been able to do nothing, and have the thing hanging over me. If you could let me have a 30£ at two months for copy-right on ten articles of the Galleries (3 more of which I will deliver in a fortnight), I think I could turn it.[1] I hope you will oblige me in this. Your obliged humble servant,

W. Hazlitt.

P. S. I wish you could send over to Hone's for a copy of my Political Essays, which I want to refer to.[2]

---

* On page 498 of the *London Mercury* for March, 1923, Howe conjectures the date as falling between 12 and 25 February of 1823.

[1] The essays of *Sketches of the Principal Picture Galleries in England* were appearing in *The London Magazine.*

[2] In 1819 William Hone (1780-1842) had published *Political Essays* containing "Mr. Coleridge's Lay-Sermon," a letter which Hazlitt now expanded into his essay, "My First Acquaintance with Poets," *The Liberal* (April, 1823).

No. 132

To Thomas Cadell [1]

Four Generations, I, 142.
Address: Mr. Thomas Cadell/Bookseller/Strand.

4, Chapel Street West,
Curzon Street
April 17, 1823 *

Sir,

Unless you agree to give up the publication of Blackwood's *Magazine,* I shall feel myself compelled to commence an action against you for damages sustained from repeated slanderous and false imputations in that work on me.

W. Hazlitt

---

* Cf. Howe, p. 324.
[1] Bookseller and agent for *Blackwood's* in which Hazlitt was once again attacked in a review of *Table-Talk* and in other articles.

No. 133

To Thomas Hood

MS. Lockwood.

Winterslow Hut, Saturday, July 19 [1823] *
My dear Hood, [1]
I wish you would tell Taylor that something happened which hurt my mind, and prevented my going to Petworth.[2] I had only the heart to come down here, and see my little boy, who is gone from hence.[3] I will do Blenheim [4] for next month. I used to think she saw and perhaps approved these articles: but whatever I can do, implying an idea of taste or elegance, only makes me more odious to myself, and tantalises me with feelings which I can never hope to excite in others—wretch that I am, and am to be, till I am nothing!

Yours truly
W. Hazlitt.

---

* Cf. Howe, p. 326.
[1] Hood (1799-1845) was assistant editor of the *London Magazine*. In December 1822 Hazlitt began a series of articles on paintings in famous English galleries which appeared in the *London Magazine* and the *New Monthly Magazine* before being published anonymously with some additions as *Sketches of the Principal Picture-Galleries in England* (1824).
[2] Petworth House, Sussex, the home of Sir George O'Brien Wyndham, Earl of Egremont (1751-1837), patron of art, whose magnificent collection is discussed in "Pictures at Wilton, Stourhead, Etc.," in the *London Magazine* of October 1823 as well as in other essays *(Works,* X, 61).
[3] The tone of this letter reflects Hazlitt's emotional anguish over Sarah Walker, aggravated by the publication of *Liber Amoris* in May 1823 and the violent attack upon him and his "nasty book—the beastly trash of Billy Hazlitt"—in Theodore Hook's *John Bull* newspaper of 8, 15, and 22 June 1823.
[4] The Duke of Marlborough's collection of paintings.

No. 134

To the Editor of the *London Magazine*

London Magazine.

November 1823

Sir,

Will you have the kindness to insert in the Lion's Head the two following passages from a work of mine published some time since? They exhibit rather a striking coincidence with the reasonings of the "Opium-Eater" in your late number on the discoveries of Mr. Malthus; [1] and as I have been a good deal abused for my scepticism on that subject, I do not feel quite disposed that any one else should run away with the credit of it. I do not wish to bring any charge of plagiarism in this case: I only beg to put in my own claim of priority. The first passage I shall trouble you with relates to the geometrical and arithmetical series, and is as follows:

Both the principle of the necessary increase of the population beyond the means of subsistence, and the application of that principle as a final obstacle to all Utopian perfectibility schemes, are borrowed (whole) by Mr. Malthus from Wallace's work *(Various Prospects of Mankind, Nature, and Providence,* 1761). This is not very stoutly denied by his admireres; but, say they, Mr. Malthus was the first to reduce the inequality between the possible increase of food and population to a mathematical certainty, to the arithematical and geometrical ratios. In answer to which, we say, that those ratios are, in a strict and scientific view of the subject, entirely fallacious—a pure fiction. For a grain of corn or of mustard-seed has the same or a greater power of propagating its species than a man, till it has overspread the whole earth, till there is no longer any room for it to grow or to spread farther. A bushel of wheat will sow a whole field: the produce of that field will sow

---

[1] In the October issue De Quincey had echoed two central passages from Hazlitt's *Reply to Malthus* which had been reprinted in *Political Essays,* 1819.

twenty fields, and produce twenty harvests. Till there are no longer fields to sow, that is, till a country or the earth is exhausted, the means of subsistence will go on increasing in more than Mr. Malthus's geometrical ratio; will more than double itself in every generation or season, and will more than keep pace with the progress of population; for this is supposed only to double itself, where it is unchecked, every twenty years. Therefore it is not true as an abstract proposition, that of itself, or in the nature of the growth of the produce of the earth, food can only increase in the snail-pace progress of an arithmetical ratio, while population goes on at a swinging geometrical rate: for the food keeps pace, or more than keeps pace, with the population, while there is room to grow it in, and after that room is filled up, it does not go on, even in that arithmetical ratio—it does not increase at all, or very little. That is, the ratio, (laid down by Mr. Malthus) instead of being always true, is never true at all: neither before the soil is fully cultivated, nor afterwards. Food does not increase in arithmetical series in China, or even in England: it increases in a geometrical series, or as fast as the population in America. The rates at which one or the other increases naturally, or can be made to increase, have no relation to an arithmetical and geometrical series. They are co-ordinate till the earth or any given portion of it is occupied and cultivated, and after that, they are quite disproportionate: or rather, both stop practically at the same instant—the means of subsistence with the limits of the soil, and the population with the limits of the means of subsistence. All that is true of Mr. Malthus's doctrine, then, is this, that the tendency of population to increase remains after the power of the earth to produce more food is gone; that the one is limited, the other unlimited. This is enough for the morality of the question: his mathematics are altogether spurious.[2]

This passage, allowing for the difference of style, accords pretty nearly with the reasoning in the *Notes from the Pocket-Book of an Opium Eater.* I should really like to know what answer Mr. Malthus has to this objection, if he would design one, or whether he thinks it best to impose upon the public by his silence? So much for his

---

[2] From "Mr. Owen and Mr. Malthus," *The Morning Chronicle* (September 2, 1817). The same article entitled "An Examination of Mr. Malthus's Doctrines" was published in *The Yellow Dwarf,* April 4, 1818 *(Works,* VII, 332-337).

mathematics: now for his logic, which the Opium-Eater has also attacked, and with which I long ago stated my dissatisfaction in manner and form following:

> The most singular thing in this singular performance of our author is, that it should have been originally ushered into the world as the most complete and only satisfactory answer to the speculations of Godwin, Condorcet, and others, or to what has been called the modern philosophy. A more complete piece of wrong-headedness, a more strange perversion of reason, could hardly be devised by the wit of man. Whatever we may think of the doctrine of the progressive improvement of the human mind, or of a state of society in which every thing will be subject to the absolute controul of reason; however absurd, unnatural, or impracticable we may conceive such a system to be, certainly it cannot without the grossest inconsistency be objected to it, that such a system would necessarily be rendered abortive, because if reason should ever get the mastery over all our actions, we shall then be governed entirely by our physical appetites and passions, and plunged into evils far more insupportable than any we at present endure in consequence of the excessive population which would follow, and the impossibility of providing for its support. This is what I do not understand.

It is, in other words, to assert that the doubling the population of a country, for example, after a certain period, will be attended with the most pernicious effects, by want, famine, bloodshed, and a state of general violence and confusion; and yet that at this period those who will be most interested in preventing these consequences and the best acquainted with the circumstances that lead to them, will neither have the understanding to foresee, nor the heart to feel, nor the will to avert the sure evils to which they expose themselves and others; though this advanced state of population, which does not admit of any addition without danger, is supposed to be the immediate result of a more general diffusion of the comforts and conveniences of life, of more enlarged and liberal views, of a more refined and comprehensive regard to our own permanent interests as well as those of others, of correspondent habits and manners, and of a state of things, in which our gross animal appetites will be subjected to the practical controul of reason. If Mr. Malthus chooses to say that men will always be governed by the same gross mechanical motives that they are at present, I have no objection to make to it; but it is shifting the question: it is not arguing against the state of society we are considering from the consequences to which it would give rise, but against the possibility of its ever existing. It is very idle to alarm the imagination by deprecating the evils that must follow from the practical adoption of a particular scheme, yet to allow that we have no reason to dread those consequences but because the scheme itself is impracticable.[3]

This, Mr. Editor, is the writer whom "our full senate call all-in-all sufficient." [4] There must be a tolerably large *bonus* offered to men's interests and prejudices to make them swallow incongruities such as that there alluded to; and I am glad to find that our ingenious and studious friend the *Opium-Eater* [5] agrees with me on this point too, almost in so many words.

I am, Sir, you obliged friend and servant,

W. Hazlitt

---

[3] From "On the Principle of Population, as Affecting the Schemes of Utopian Improvement," *Works*, VII, 343-350.

[4] *Othello*, IV, i, 275.

[5] De Quincey's lengthy reply appeared in December: "I believe that he *has* anticipated me; in the passage relating to the geometric and arithmetic ratios, it is clear that he has."

No. 135

To Taylor and Hessey

London Mercury, May, 1924.
Address: Taylor and Hessey/Fleet St./London.

(PM: Melrose, April 16, 1824)

Dear Sir,

I got the Books and will set about reading them immediately. I return the proof by post.[1] If the new "Picture Galleries" are Colburn's, you must omit that on Burleigh, or he may make some difficulty, as I did not get a formal answer from him.[2] Besides, I think it bad and as well left out. I wish you to get the book out without loss of time, and to send me a copy here. I will let you know if the article is in the Edinburgh. The Preface is on the other side.

Yours very truly,
W. H.

The Principal Picture Galleries in England	or	Sketches of the Principal Picture Galleries in England

By the author of T.T. (or not.)
With a Criticism on the Marriage-a-la-Mode.
Advertisement.

It is the object of the following little work to give an account of the principal Picture-Galleries in this country, and to describe the

---

[1] *Sketches of the Principal Picture-Galleries in England,* which Taylor and Hessey published.

[2] P. G. Patmore's anonymous collection, *British Galleries of Art,* which had appeared in Colburn's *New Monthly Magazine,* was an imitation of Hazlitt's essays on art in *The London Magazine.* Since Colburn was not the publisher of Patmore's volume, the "Pictures at Burleigh House" was included in Hazlitt's book.

feelings which they naturally excite in the mind of a lover of art. Almost all those of any importance have been regularly gone through. One or two, that still remain unnoticed, may be added to our *Catalogue Raisonnée* at a future opportunity. It may not be improper to mention here that Mr. Angerstein's pictures have been lately purchased for the commencement of a National Gallery, and are still to be seen in their old places on the walls of his house.[3]

---

[3] This advertisement was included at the beginning of the book.

No. 136

To Francis Jeffrey

MS. Keynes. *Bibliography,* 83.

Melrose, [1824]
Sunday evening, 25th April.

Dear Sir,

I fear this will hardly do.[1] The two passages I am apprehensive of *most* are p. 10-12, "This was the reason" to "farthing about," and p. 64-66, "If these pragmatical personages" to "Liberty and Humanity." They are easily left out. In case of the worst, may I request you to let me have it again, as I can make use of the first dozen pages for an Essay. I hope to make something better of Salvator [2] which I will send you the end of the week, and remain Dear Sir your most obliged humble servant

W. Hazlitt.

---

[1] The essay on "Landor's Imaginary Conversations" which appeared in the *Edinburgh Review* in March 1824.Cf. *Works,* XVI, 240-264.

[2] The review of "Lady Morgan's Life of Salvator" was published in July, 1824.

No. 137

To Walter Savage Landor [1]

MS. The Historical Society of Pennsylvania.

Rome, 28 March [1825]

Dear Sir,

I beseech you send me word (by return of post) if the copy of Table-Talk you have received is perfect, with Regal Character and Advice to a Schoolboy at the end; [2] also if the Spirit of the Age is a bookseller's copy, or the one I left at Paris, and forwarded to you

---

[1] In April 1824 Hazlitt had married a Mrs. Isabella Bridgwater whose maiden name is unknown and whose identity therefore remains something of a mystery. Howe assumed that they were married at Edinburgh, but no record of the marriage has been found in parish registers. However, some information about the second Mrs. Hazlitt is contained in a letter from one of her early acquaintances, G. Huntly Gordon, who wrote to W. C. Hazlitt on 15 February 1866: "I knew her slightly in Scotland when she was a most beautiful girl of 20, on her way to one of the West India Islands, where she was soon married to a planter who died in a year or two" (Ms. BM.). Writing to Leigh Hunt on 31 August 1824, John Hunt mentions that "Hazlitt and his new bride have departed for France: he proposes to pass Florence on his way to Rome. This Mrs. H——— seems a very pleasant and ladylike person. She was the widow of a Barrister, and possesses an independence of nearly £300 a year." This first tour of the continent lasted until October 1825. Temporarily relieved from the strain and anxiety of financial worries caused by his divorce, Hazlitt contributed a delightful narrative of the journey to the *Morning Chronicle* in a series of articles that were later published as *Notes of a Journey through France and Italy* (1826). Arriving in Florence in January 1825, Hazlitt called upon Landor (1775-1864), who had made his home there since 1821 and whose *Imaginary Conversations* Hazlitt had reviewed "with great pleasure" in the *Edinburgh Review* for March 1824. Landor found the pleasure mutual, according to John Forster: "Many were the points of agreement, indeed, between Hazlitt and his host; and so heartily did each enjoy the other's wilfulness and caprice, that a strong personal liking characterized their brief acquaintance" (*Howe*, p. 343).

[2] The last edition of *Table-Talk* published in Hazlitt's lifetime by A. and W. Galignani in Paris included a selection from the two volumes of 1821-1822.

for me? ³ Yesterday the first fine day. Remember me to all friends, and believe me yours truly.

W. Hazlitt

33 via Gregoriana ⁴
Tuesday
Severn is well.⁵

---

³ The Galignani Edition of *The Spirit of the Age* also differs from the two editions published in London. Hazlitt arranged the text, omitting the essays on Moore and Irving and adding those on Canning and Knowles.

⁴ The former home of Salvator Rosa. "I have now lived twice in houses occupied by celebrated men, once in a house that had belonged to Milton, [No. 19, York St.] and now in this, and find to my mortification that imagination is entirely a *thing imaginary,* and has nothing to do with matter of fact, history, or the senses" *(Notes of a Journey Through France and Italy, Works,* X, 231-232).

⁵ Joseph Severn (1793-1879) the painter and friend who had accompanied Keats to Italy in 1820. After Keats' death in February 1821, Severn remained in Rome where he and Hazlitt now met for the first time. It was probably Severn who praised the galleries in Rome as "equal to the Louvre," but which disappointed Hazlitt *(Notes of a Journey Through France and Italy, Works,* X, 237).

No. 138

To Walter Savage Landor

MS. Victoria and Albert Museum.
Address: Walter Savage Landor, Esq./Poste Restante/
Florence.

Rome, April 9 [1825]*

Dear Sir,

I did not receive your obliging letter till a day or two ago. Mrs. H. and myself crossed the mountains pretty well, but had rather a tedious journey. Rome hardly answers my expectations; the ruins do not prevail enough over the modern buildings, which are commonplace things. One or two things are prodigious fine. I have got a pleasant lodging but find everything very bad and dear. I have thoughts of going to spend a month at Albano, but am not quite sure.[1] If I do not, I shall return to Florence next week and proceed to Venice. I should be glad, if I settle at Albano, if you could manage to come over and stop a little. I have done what I was obliged to write for the Papers [2] and am now a leisure man, I hope, for the rest of the summer. I am much gratified that you are pleased with the Spirit of the Age. Somebody ought to like it, for I am sure there will be plenty to cry out against it. I hope you did not find any sad blunders in the second volume; but you can hardly suppose the depression of body and mind under which I wrote some of these articles. I bought a little Florentine edition of Petrarch and Dante the other day, and have made out one page.

---

* Cf. Howe, p. 343-344.

[1] He did not spend a month at Albano but returned to Florence.

[2] *Notes of a Journey Through France and Italy* had appeared in *The Morning Chronicle* throughout 1824-1825 before it was published as a book in 1826. In addition, many of the essays which compose *The Plain Speaker* were written abroad.

Pray remember me to Mrs. Landor, and believe me to be, Dear Sir,
Your much obliged friend and servant,
W. Hazlitt.

33 via Gregoriana.

Jacobo III.
Jacobi II. Magnae Brit. Regis Filio,
Karolo Edwardo
Et Henrico Decano Patruum Cardinalium
Jacobi III. Filiis,
Regiae Stirpis Stuardiae Postremis,
Anno M.V.CCC.XIX.
Beati Mortui qui in Domino moriuntur.

What do you think of this inscription on Canova's monument to the Stuarts in St. Peter's . . . ordered by the R. Revd. Superior? . . . Ask Southey for his opinion.

No. 139

To William Hazlitt, Jr.

Four Generations, I: 185-186.
Address: Master Hazlitt, at Mrs. Hazlitt's/Crediton/Near Exeter/England.

Vevey, near Geneva
[June or July 1825] *

Dear Baby,

We are got as far as Vevey in Switzerland on our way back. I propose returning by Holland in the end of August, and I shall see you, I hope, the beginning of September.

The journey has answered tolerably well. I was sorry to hear of poor Miss Emmet's death, [1] and I hope Grandmother and Peggy are both well. I got your letter at Florence, where I saw Mr. Leigh Hunt [2] and Mr. Landor. I have a very bad pen.

The *Table-Talk* and the *Spirit of the Age* have been reprinted at Paris; but I do not know how they have succeeded. The *Advice to a School-boy* [3] is in the first. If you should be in London, remember me to all friends, or give my love to my Mother and Peggy. I am, dear Baby,

Your ever affectionate father,
W. Hazlitt.

We are stopping here. Write to me, and tell me all the news.

---

* Cf. Howe (pp. 344, 347) who implies the dates of mid-June or shortly thereafter.

[1] A sister of Robert Emmet (1778-1803), the Irish patriot, whom the Rev. Mr. Hazlitt had probably known. Miss Emmet had lived with the elder Hazlitts since 1816.

[2] After Shelley's death, Hunt quarrelled with Byron and moved to Florence with his family where they remained until September 1825. The meeting there with Hazlitt is described in the *Autobiography of Leigh Hunt,* II, 149, edited by Roger Ingpen (Westminster, Archibald Constable & Co., Ltd. 1903).

[3] This essay was written for his son, now nearly fourteen years old. William, Jr. was now in school in Devonshire, having left Mr. Dawson's of Hunter Street, London, his location when the letter of advice on the conduct of life was originally addressed to him in 1822. Cf. Letter 99.

No. 140

To John Black

Hazlitts, 479.

August 31, 1825

Dear Black,

Will you insert this, [1] or hand it over to J. Hunt?

Yours ever,
W. H.

I shall be at home in about a month. I have been to Chamouny. [2]
Vevey.

---

[1] *The Damned Author's Address to His Reviewers,* Hazlitt's reply to the *Edinburgh Review*'s notice of *The Spirit of the Age,* and his "only known verse-attempt" was not printed either by John Black in *The Morning Chronicle* (in which *Notes of a Journey Through France* and Italy were appearing) nor by John Hunt in *The Examiner.* It first appeared in W. C. Hazlitt's *Lamb and Hazlitt* (1900), pp. 128-129. Cf. *Works,* XX, 392-393.

[2] For an account of his excursion to Chamouni and Mont Blanc see Chapter XXVI of *Notes of a Journey Through France and Italy, Works,* X, 288.

No. 141

To Henry Colburn [1]

Four Generations, I, 193.

[January 1826]

Dear Sir,

Did you receive the extracts from Donne in good time for the Essay, as I feel uneasy about it? Could I see the proof?

Your obliged humble servant,
W. Hazlitt.

---

[1] This note refers to the essay "Of Persons One Would Wish to Have Seen" *(Works,* XVII, 122-134) which contains passages from Donne's *Epithalamion on the Lady Elizabeth and Count Palatine* and *Lines to His Mistress.* It does not refer to the *Lectures on the English Poets,* as W. C. Hazlitt thought, which does not include Donne. The essay was first published in Colburn's *New Monthly Magazine* (January 1826).

No. 142

To Henry Colburn

MS. Princeton Univ. Library, John Wild Autograph Collection.
Address: Henry Colbourn, Esq./New Burlington St.

[January 1826]

Dear Sir,

I have corrected the copy, [1] and am much obliged by the error being pointed out.

Yours very truly
W. Hazlitt

---

[1] The proof "Of Persons One Would Wish to Have Seen."

No. 143

To P. G. Patmore

Works, XIII, 354.

Early in August [1826] *
My dear Patmore,
   I am damnably off here ¹ for money, as I have taken a house and garden (No. 58, Rue Mont-Blanc) and have been disappointed in two remittances which I ought to have received. If you could by any possibility raise 20£, I will send you back Manuscript ² to that amount by return of post, written on the spot since I have been here. My best remembrances at home, and believe me ever truly yours,

W. Hazlitt.
I have made a rough copy of the Titian, and get into nothing but rows and squabbles. I shall be glad to hear from you *tandem-wise.*

G. P. Patmore, Esq. [sic]
3 North-Terrace
Fulham, near London.

---

* Cf. Baker, p. 456.
¹ From July 1826 to October 1827, Hazlitt lived in Paris for the purpose of writing *The Life of Napoleon.*
² Patmore must have been successful, for "On the Want of Money," appeared in the *Monthly* in January 1827, followed by "On the Feeling of Immortality in Youth," "On Reading New Books," "On Means and Ends," and "On Disagreeable People," Cf. *Works,* XVII, Nos. 17, 18, 19, 20, and 21 respectively. The essay," On Means and Ends," contains the following: "I lately tried to make a copy of a portrait [of a Man in Black] by Titian (after several years' want of practice) with a view to give a friend in England some notion of the picture, which is really remarkable and fine" *(Works,* XVII, 219).

No. 144

To Isabella Jane Towers [1]

MS. Stanford.

Nov. 21st. 1827

My dear Madam,

Your brother has not dropped the slightest hint whether you are maid, wife, or widow; whether you are black, brown, or fair, tall or short, plump or slender; whether you are gay or grave, whether you laugh or weep oftenest; I am lost in conjectures whether your complexion rivals the rose or is of a lovely pale; whether you are a heroine of romance or a pattern in common life; whether you are fond of Rousseau or of Mrs Inchbald's Simple Story; whether you are reserved, timid, distant, or frank, heedless, playful; whether wit, sense, or good nature prevails most in you: how then should I be able to write a single line that can be agreeable to you or not ridiculous in itself? [2]

"Come, draw the curtain, show the picture." [3]

And then—I fear I shall be more at a loss than ever how to express my admiration. Of one thing I am sure, that you are very good; and if you are ugly, old, or disagreeable, I'll be hanged! I find dreams very troublesome things; and wish you would put me out of doubt, though I might run into greater danger.

Believe me, Dear Madam,
your most obliged humble servant,
W. Hazlitt.

Since I am got into quotation, do not think it impertinent if I quote something of my own. My sending it to you shews too well the good opinion I have of it. [4]—"Could I have had my way, I

---

[1] Sister of Charles Cowden Clarke and contributor of occasional verses to Hunt's journals.

[2] Mrs Towers had asked Hazlitt to write something for her Memory Book.

[3] Cf. *Twelfth Night,* I, v, 252.

[4] The passage, with some minor revisions, is taken from "On Personal Identity," which Hazlitt had just written at Winterslow *(Works,* XVII, 268-269).

would have been born a lord: but one would not be a booby lord neither. I am haunted with an odd fancy of driving down the Great North Road in a chaise and four and coming to the inn at Ferry Bridge, about fifty years ago, with out-riders, white favours, and a coronet on the pannels—and then I chuse my companion in the coach—really there is a witchcraft in the thought that makes it necessary to divert my attention from it lest in the conflict between imagination and impossibility I should grow feverish and light-headed! On the other hand, if one had been born a lord, should one have the same idea (that every one else has) of a *peeress in her own right?* Is not distance, elevation, romantic mystery, an impassable gulph necessary to form this idea in the mind, that fine ligament of "ethereal braid, sky-woven, [5] that lets down Heaven upon earth, soft as enchantment, fair as Berenice's hair, bright and garlanded like Ariadne's crown;—and is it not better to have had this idea all one's life, to have caught but glimpses of it in passing, to have known it but in a dream, than to have been born a lord ten times over with twenty pampered menials at one's back and twenty descents to boast of? If I had been a lord, I would have married Miss ———, and then my life would not have been one long sigh, made up of sweet and bitter regrets! If I had been a lord, I would have been a Popish one, and then I might have been an honest man; poor, and then I might have been proud and not vulgar!"———

Pray, ask Miss Lamb (not Mr Southern) [6] if she does not think this in my very best manner? But why send it to you? Nay, if you tell me with a saucy air to throw it in the fire and have a little common sense, I shall be more out of my wits than ever. W.H.

Wm Hazlitt

Winterslow,
Nov. 21st. 1827.

Dear C. [7]

"I am ill at these numbers." [8] Pray, tear out the above, if you think proper.

---

5 Collins, "Ode to Evening," 7, echoing *Paradise Lost,* VII, 356 and V, 285.
6 Editor of the *Retrospective Review* and last owner of the *London Magazine.*
7 Charles Cowden Clarke. Cf. Letter 145.
8 *Hamlet,* II, ii, 120.

P.S. Hang those fellows the poets, say I. They are always getting the start of us poor prosers on the most precious occasions. Now would I give my fingers to be able to indite a Sonnet *To the fair unknown.* As it is, I must beg, borrow, or steal. It is has [sic] been my fate all my life to admire genius and beauty without expecting a return; but I as yet see no reason to repent. I will tell you, my dear Madam, what I think the prettiest love-verses in the world. Now does M.ʳ Moore get out his guitar, prepared to accompany some of his own melodies; Lord Byron from the other world seriously inclines his ear; M.ʳ Leigh Hunt (my most excellent friend—I like his foibles (if he has any) better than the best virtues of many others) turns over the pages of Rimini with a gay anxiety. These gentlemen will excuse me. Poor Burns is my favourite in such matters.

> "Here's a health to one I love dear,
> Here's a health to one I love dear;
> Thou art sweet as the smile when fond lovers meet,
> And soft as their parting tear,
>   Jessy.
> Altho' thou canst never be mine,
> Altho' even hope is denied;
> Tis better for thee despairing
> Than aught in the world beside,
>   Jessy!" [9]

---

[9] An English version of the chorus and first stanza of Burns's *A Health to Ane I Loe Dear.*

No. 145

To Charles Cowden Clarke

MS. Lockwood.

December 7 [1827] *

Dear Sir,

I thought all the world agreed with me at present that
Buonaparte was better than the Bourbons or that a tyrant was
better than tyranny.[1] In my opinion, no one of an understanding
above the rank of a lady's waiting-maid could ever have doubted
this, though I alone said it ten years ago. It might be impolicy then
and now for what I know, for the world stick to an opinion in
appearance long after they have given it up in reality. I should like
to know whether the preface is thought impolitic by some one who
agrees with me in the main point or by some one who differs with
me and makes this excuse not to have his opinion contradicted? In
Paris (Jubes regina renovare dolorem)[2] the preface was thought a
masterpiece, the best and only possible defence of Buonaparte, and
quite new *there!* It would be an impertinence in me to write a Life
of Buonaparte after Sir W.[3] without some such object as that
expressed in the Preface.[4] After all, I do not care a *damn* about the

---

* Cf. *Memoirs,* II, 218; Howe, p. 358; Baker, p. 459.

[1] Clarke and Henry Hunt (Leigh Hunt's nephew) published the first two
volumes of the *Life of Napoleon* in 1828, but after their bankruptcy in 1829 the
book was taken over by Effingham Wilson and Chapman and Hall, who brought
out the four volumes as a uniform set in 1830.

[2] Virgil, *Aeneid,* ii, 3:

infandum, regina, iubes renovare dolorem.
Queen, you bid me renew an unspeakable grief.

[3] Sir Walter Scott's *Life of Napoleon* in nine volumes was published this year.

[4] The original preface was incorporated in Chapter XXXI of Volume Three
but was reprinted in its proper place in the *Works,* XIII, lx-x *(Bibliography,* p. 97).
The "object" of the *Life* is a vindication of "the child and champion of the
Revolution . . . the one reputation in modern times equal to the ancients."

Preface. It will get me on four pages somewhere else. Shall I retract my opinion altogether, and forswear my own book? Rayner [5] is right to cry out: I think I have tipped him fair and foul copy, a lean rabbit and a fat one. The remainder of vol. ii. will be ready to go on with, but not the beginning of the third. The Appendixes had better be at the end of second vol. Pray get them if you can: you have my Siéyes [6], have you not? One of them is there. I have been nearly in the other world.[7] My regret was "to die and leave the world 'rough' copy." Otherwise I had thought of an epitaph and a good end. *Hic jacent reliquiae mortales Gulielmi Hazlitt, auctoris non intelligibilis: natus Maidstoniae in com[it]atu Cantiae, Apr, 10, 1778. Obiit Winterslowe, Dec. 1827.* I think of writing an epistle to C. Lamb Esq. to say that I have passed near the shadowy world, and have had new impressions of the vanity of this with hopes of a better. Don't you think this would be good policy? Don't mention it to the severe author of the Press, a Poem, [8] but methinks the idea *arridet* Hone. He would give six-pence to see me floating upon a pair of borrowed wings, half way between Heaven and Earth and edifying the good people at my departure, whom I shall only scandalise by remaining. At present, my study and contemplation is the leg of a stewed fowl. I have behaved like a saint and been obedient to orders. *Non fit pugil,* [9] etc., I got a violent spasm by walking fifteen miles in the mud, and getting into a coach with an old lady who would have the window open. Delicacy, moderation,

---

[5] The printer.

[6] L'Abbé Sieyès' *Qu'est ce que le Tiers Etat?* was one of the works used in writing the *Life.*

[7] He was at Winterslow recovering from one of the increasingly frequent attacks which developed into cancer of the stomach.

[8] J. McCreery, the printer of *Political Essays,* which William Hone had published.

[9] He is not turning boxer. Horace, *Satires,* II, iii, 30 runs

ut lethargicus hic cum fit pugil et medicum urget.

for example, this fellow with the lethargy turns boxer and kicks out the doctor.

complaisance, the *suaviter in modo,* [10] whisper it about, my dear Clarke, these are my faults and have been my ruin.

Yours ever,
W. H.

Dec. 7.

I can't go to work before Sunday or Monday. By then the Doctor says he shall have made a new man of me. Pray, how's your sister? [11]

---

[10] "Gentle in manner."
[11] Isabella Jane Towers.

No. 146

To Charles Cowden Clarke

MS. Edinburgh.

[January 1828]

Dear C.

Tell Henry I am much obliged to him.[1] Pray has the London Review had the Essays or did Baylis get them? [2]

Yours truly

W. H.

My pet Reviewer.—I formerly took my little book of Characteristics [3] to Baldwyn [4] in Newgate Street (now with God) who gave me for answer the next day that he did not think "this Editor (*viz.* of the Retrospective) would like them to put their name in the title-page of a work by one of the *Cockney School.*" And yet you doubt my being of a patient and sweet temper.

---

[1] Probably a partial payment for *The Life of Napoleon,* the first two volumes of which were published in this month.

[2] "On Public Opinion" appeared in *The London Weekly Review* on 19 January 1828 followed by "On the Causes of Popular Opinion" (16 February) and "A Farewell to Essay-Writing" (29 March). Baylis was associated with Henry Southern's review, *The Retrospective.*

[5] *Characteristics in the Manner of Rochefoucault's Maxims* was published by Simpkin and Marshall in 1823.

[4] One of the publishers of the *London Magazine.* Cf. Letters 89, 90, and 91.

No. 147

To David Constable [1]

MS. Edinburgh.

Winterslow, near Salisbury
Jany. 10th, 1828

Dear Sir,

I have to thank you for your obliging letter, which I received in due course. It has come into my head that I could make a little volume of outlines or elements of the following subjects. 1. Of Law. 2. Of Morals. 3. Of the Human Mind. 4. Of Taste. 5. Of Political Economy. 6. Of English Grammar. On all of these but the fifth, I have something new to offer. Do you think you could print such a work (I would leave the price to you) or that it might possibly do for the Miscellany? [2] You will perhaps see that the papers have taken to praise me: [3] I suppose they are tired of abusing me. As to Titian, I have no theory: [4] but one of our wiseacres at Rome (seeing a sketch of it in the room of a young artist there) asked if it was not intended for Christ and the woman of Samaria? [5] If you want to see how dry I can be in the way of elementary analysis, Ritchie [6] has a book of mine *On Human Action* which no one can

---

[1] Succeeded his father as head of the firm in 1827.

[2] "Outlines of Morals," "The Human Mind," and "Political Economy," were not published until long after Hazlitt's death. "On Law" ("Project for a New Theory of Civil and Criminal Legislation"), based on the essay written at Hackney, was published in the *Literary Remains.* "English Grammar" appeared in *The Atlas* (March 15, 1829).

[3] Favorable notices of *The Life of Napoleon,* from advance copies, had recently appeared in the *Athenaeum* and *London Weekly Review.*

[4] An art enthusiast, Constable may have been interested in acquiring one of Hazlitt's copies of Titian.

[5] St. John, IV. The painting may have been "The Woman Taken in Adultery" (*Works,* X, 54).

[6] Leitch Ritchie, editor of *The London Weekly Review* and William Ritchie, the editor of *The Scotsman* were both acquainted with Hazlitt.

charge with being florid or *ad captandum vulgus.*[7] I remain, dear Sir, your truly obliged, humble servant,

W. Hazlitt

How the years slide on! If I should go to Paris in the spring, could you find any use for a series of papers on French plays and players. [8] I am a great admirer of their theatre—as much so as I abominate their style of art.

[7] To catch the masses.

[8] He returned to Paris in June to gather more material for the biography of Napoleon and contributed an article to *The Examiner* on Edmund Kean as Richard III at the Théâtre Français.

No. 148

To Henry Hunt

MS. Lockwood.

Jany. 16, 1828

Dear Sir,

I am obliged by the 2£. and am glad the account is no more against me. The Appendix, Nos. 4 and 5, must be given at the end of vol. 4 (To be said so in a note).[1] No. 6, Character of Marat by Brissot, will be found infallibly at the end of one of Miss Williams's volumes from France, year 1794, which can be had at any library, Saunders and Ottley's, certainly.[2] Also, I sent it up to Clarke some time ago. Tell him, I received the letter and am much gratified by it, vanity apart. I am not surprised at what you tell me, but drowning men catch at Buckinghams.[3] Still so far so good. What follows is important, not a drowning but a shooting matter. You *must* give me one cancel, p. 209, vol. II and alter the word Buccaneer to cruiser. An Erratum won't do. Second, do learn the width of the valley of the Nile from some authentic person *(forsan* Travels in Mesopotamia) and if it is more than five leagues (which I suspect it must be) cancel and change to fifteen, fifty, or whatever is the actual number. It is five in Napoleon's Memoirs, followed by Thibaudeau *in vita.*[4] Is the preface to go? You'll see I can bear it out, and perhaps play the devil with some people. Don't you think an extract in the Examiner would tell in just now, after the

---

[1] In *The Life of Napoleon.*

[2] Appendix No. IV, "Character of Marat," is taken from *State of Manners and Opinions in the French Republic* by Helen Maria Williams.

[3] James Silk Buckingham (1786-1855), editor of the *Athenaeum,* published an extract from Chapter III of the *Life* which Hazlitt had sent without Clarke's and Hunt's approval.

[4] Antoine Thibaudeau's *Histoire Générale de Napoléon Buonaparte* and *Mémoires sur le Consulat de 1799 à 1804* were sources for the *Life.* The number given is "five in breadth" *(Works,* XIV, 26).

London Review [5]and Athenaeum and give us a kind of pre-possession of the ground? Tell St. John I wrote to thank him last week, but find I directed the letter wrong to 150 instead of 159. Have the kindness (if you have room) to insert the inclosed paragraph. I see your leader of Sunday confirms my theory of good-natured statesmen.[6]

Yours ever very truly,
W. H.

P.S. I won't send Clarke any more of my Georgics—Buckingham *had* an article the day before, which I daresay he has yet, unless he has given it to Colburn to keep.[7] Pray send me down the second vol. corrected, in a day or two. I won't send any more to B[uckingham] unless he *remits,* which he does not seem inclined to do. I think this book will put your uncle's head above water, and I hope he will keep it there—*to vex the rogues.* I wish he had not spoken so of Hook,[8] but Colburn *has a way with him!*

Jany 16, 1828

---

[5] A notice of the *Life* as forthcoming had appeared in the *London Weekly Review,* edited by J. A. St. John.

[6] Hunt and Clarke were now the publishers of *The London Magazine.*

[7] The article—"Illustrations of Toryism from the Writings of Sir Walter Scott"—had appeared in Buckingham's weekly newspaper, *The Sphynx,* on 5 January.

[8] Theodore Hook (1788-1841), dramatist, novelist, and editor of the *New Monthly Magazine* who figures in "The Dandy School" as having "a fellow-feeling with low life" *(Works,* XX, 147). His *John Bull,* a weekly newspaper, on June 22, 1823, violently attacked Hazlitt as the author of the *Liber Amoris.* Cf. Letter 103.

No. 149

To Charles Cowden Clarke

Four Generations, I, 191.

[January 1828]

Dear Clarke,

Do you think it would be amiss to give Buckingham the first vol.
for next week's Athenaeum, though Hunt, etc. do not write in it? [1]
The public are to be won like a widow,—
> "with brisk attacks and urging,
> not slow approaches, like a virgin." [2]

unsigned.

---

[1] A Notice of the first two volumes of *The Life of Napoleon* with a long extract
from it appeared in *The Athenaeum* on 12 February 1828.

[2] Loosely quoted from *Hudibras,* First Part, Canto I, 905-908, which reads
> Honour is, like a Widow, won
> With brisk Attempt and putting on;
> With entring manfully, and urging;
> Not slow approaches, like a Virgin.

No. 150

To Charles Cowden Clarke

Four Generations, I, 189-190.

[1 February 1828]

Dear Clarke,

"To you Duke Humphrey must unfold his grief" [1] in the following queries.

1. Is it unworthy of our dignity and injurious to our interest to have the Life noticed favourably in a journal that is not the pink of classical elegance? [2]

2. Are we to do nothing to secure (beforehand) a favourable hearing to it, lest we should be suspected or charged with being accomplices in the success of our own work by the Charing Cross Gang who would ruin you and me out of their sheer dogmatism and malignity? [3]

3. Must we wait for Mr. Southern [4] to give his opinion, before we dare come before the public even in an extract? Or be first hung up by our enemies, in order to be cut down by our zealous Whig and Reform friends?

4. When the house is beset by robbers, are we to leave the doors open, to show our innocence and immaculateness of intention?

5. Were you not pleased to see the extracts from Hunt's book in the *Athenaeum?* and do you not think they were of service? Why then judge differently of mine? [5]

6. There is a puff of Haydon in the *Examiner,* like blue ruin, *out of*

---

[1] *2 Henry VI,* I, i, 71.

[2] A notice of *The Life of Napoleon* had appeared in *The London Weekly Review.*

[3] Scott's *Life of Napoleon* was published by Longman, Rees in 1827. Two volumes of Lockhart's *History of Napoleon* (Murray) came out before Hazlitt's.

[4] Editor of the *Retrospective Review.*

[5] Extracts from Hunt's *Lord Byron and Some of his Contemporaries* were published in the January 1828 *Athenaeum* along with a long extract from Chapter III of the *Life,* which Hazlitt had sent without Clarke's approval.

pure generosity. But with respect to ourselves we shut our mouths up like a maidenhood, lest it should look like partiality. So Hunt said he could not notice my lectures, or give me a good word, because I had praised him in the *Edinburgh,* and it would be thought a collusion.

7. You sent me L. H.'s [6] letter in the *Chronicle,* which I was glad to see, particularly that part relating to a literary cut-throat; but why, my dear Clarke, did you not send me the puff of myself in the *London Review,* which I was perhaps—perhaps not—more pleased to see? [7]

If you continue to use me so ill, I shall complain to your sister. Think of that, Master Brook.[8] I like the *Companion* very well.[9] Do not suppose I am vexed; I am only frightened.

Yours ever very truly,
W. H.

---

[6] Leigh Hunt.
[7] The favourable notice of *The Life of Napoleon.*
[8] The name assumed by Ford to trick Falstaff in *The Merry Wives of Windsor.*
[9] Hunt's new journal, which Clarke and Hunt published.

No. 151

To Charles Cowden Clarke

Lamb and Hazlitt, 144.

[Winterslow February 1828]

Dear Clarke,

Convey (the wise it call) [1] the enclosed hare and Wiltshire bacon to the most agreeable of biographers at Highgate;[2] and the other thumper and the article [3] to the Editor of editors, J. S. Buckingham, Esq.

W. H.

Tell Henry [Hunt] if he has a sweet tooth that way to detain the hogs-flesh.

---

[1] *The Merry Wives of Windsor,* I, iii, 32.

[2] Leigh Hunt. His *Lord Byron and Some of his Contemporaries,* containing a character of Hazlitt, was published in February 1828 by Hunt and Clarke. Hazlitt's "agreeable" is not entirely complimentary, for in "A Farewell to Essay-Writing," completed on 20 February, he took occasion to disagree with Hunt's picture of himself: "I am neither a buffoon, a fop, nor a Frenchman, which Mr. Hunt would have me to be. He finds it odd that I am a close reasoner and a loose dresser. I have been (among other follies) a hard liver as well as a hard thinker; and the consequences of that will not allow me to dress as I please. People in real life are not like players on a stage, who put on a certain look or *costume,* merely for effect. I am aware, indeed, that the gay and airy pen of the author does not seriously probe the errors or misfortunes of his friends—he only glances at their seeming peculiarities, so as to make them odd and ridiculous; for which forbearance few of them will thank him" *(Works,* XVII, 317-318).

[3] The article was probably "A Farewell to Essay-Writing," but Buckingham did not publish it in the *Athenaeum.* It appeared in the *London Weekly Review* (March 29, 1828).

No. 152

To the Postmaster, Salisbury

MS. The Historical Society of Pennsylvania.

Winterslow, near Salisbury,
Oct. 6, 1828.

Sir,

I live at this place, the distance of which from Winterslow Hut is a mile and a half, and from Winterslow Hut to Salisbury six miles and a half. Each letter or newspaper I receive (brought out from Salisbury) is charged 4d. additional, which I understand is too much. This imposition is accompanied with impertinence and collusion, which make it worse. I sent a man down last night for a newspaper which I was particularly anxious to see, and it was refused to be given up because the messenger had not brought 2d. though the landlady had in her possession 2d. of mine that had been left as change out of a letter paid for yesterday. This happens whenever the landlady at the Hut (Mrs. Hine) is in the humour, and the object is to keep the 2d. for the letter-carrier the next day. Nor is this all. The letters received in so unpleasant manner do not reach Winterslow till the morning or middle of the next day after they arrive in Salisbury. They are brought out by the Guard at night, and sent up to the village at their leisure the next morning. For the additional 4d. many persons would be glad to fetch them out from Salisbury the same day, so that they would be received here two hours after they reach Salisbury, which would be a great convenience, and in some cases an object of importance.

I am, Sir,
Your very obedient, humble servant,
W. Hazlitt.

No. 153

To Leigh Hunt

MS. Lockwood.
Address: H. L. Hunt, Esq.

March 2, 1829.

Please to deliver the hamper left out by Mr. Hunt's direction to the bearer.

W. Hazlitt.

To—
4 York Street,
Covent-Garden

No. 154

To the Editor of *The Atlas*

The Atlas.

19 April 1829.

Sir

In a criticism in your last Sunday's paper on a *Life of Napoleon*, just published by Mr. Murray, you take occasion to observe that a popular work on this subject was much wanted, as Sir Walter Scott's was entirely taken up with unwieldy documents and long descriptions, and Mr. Hazlitt's was a mere tissue of dissertations, or a series of essays, the facts and points of character being either obscured or wholly omitted in both, and now, for the first time, introduced into the two small volumes of the *Family Library*.[1] Will you allow me to dissent from the justness of this criticism? Of Mr. Murray's publication I know nothing but from the extracts you have given; but all the three anecdotes you have quoted as characteristic of its peculiarly popular style, I had read before in both the works you condemn as too much filled with irrelevant matter to leave room for such trifles. For instance, the anecdote of Junot is thus given in Mr. Hazlitt's account of the siege of Toulon.

> On one occasion, while constructing a battery, he wanted some one to write a letter for him. A young man stepped forward to offer his services. The letter was hardly finished, when a cannon-ball striking near him, covered him all over with earth. 'Good,' said the writer, 'we shall not want sand this time.' This sally, together with the coolness he displayed, was the making of the young soldier's fortune. It was Junot.[2]

---

[1] John Lockhart's anonymous *History of Napoleon Buonaparte* was published in Murray's *Family Library*, 1829.

[2] *The Life of Napoleon Buonaparte, Works*, XIII, 178-79.

The story of Bonaparte's crossing the Great St. Bernard and "spoiling his hat," is taken nearly *verbatim* from Sir Walter.[3] Three pages are devoted to the details of the same subject in Mr. Hazlitt's work. As to the poisoning the soldiers at Jaffa, the statement in the new Life is incorrect. It is said that Napoleon had repeatedly acknowledged at St. Helena that he had suggested the idea, though it was not carried into execution. The real account which he gave was this.

"Previous to leaving Jaffa," continued Napoleon, "and after the greatest number of the sick and wounded had been embarked, it was reported to me that there were some men in the hospital so dangerously ill as not to allow of their being removed. I immediately ordered the chiefs of the medical staff to consult together on what was best to be done, and to deliver their opinion on the subject. Accordingly they met, and found that there were seven or eight men so dangerously ill, that they conceived it impossible for them to recover; and also that they could not exist twenty-four or thirty-six hours longer; that moreover, being afflicted with the plague, they would spread that disease amongst all those who approached them. Some of them, who were sensible, perceiving that they were about to be abandoned, demanded with earnest intreaties to be put to death. Larrey was of opinion that recovery was impossible, and that these poor fellows could not exist many hours; but as they might linger long enough to be alive when the Turks entered, and be subjected to the dreadful tortures which they were accustomed to inflict upon their prisoners, he thought it would be an act of charity to comply with their desires and accelerate their end by a few hours. Desgenettes did not approve of this, and replied that his profession was to cure the sick and not to dispatch them. Larrey came to me immediately afterwards, informed me of the circumstances and of what Desgenettes had said, adding that perhaps Desgenettes was right. But, proceeded Larrey, those men cannot live for more than a few hours, twenty-four or thirty-

---

[3] Scott's *Life*, in nine volumes, was published in 1827.

six at most, and if you will leave a rearguard of cavalry to stay and protect them from advanced parties, that will be sufficient. Accordingly I ordered four or five hundred cavalry to remain behind, and not to quit the place until all were dead. They did remain, and informed me that all had expired before they left the town; but I have heard since, that Sidney Smith found one or two alive when he entered it. This is the truth of the business." [4]

But the truth of the business would not have served as a peg for the author of the *Family Library* to hang a reflection upon of Bonaparte's "readiness to sport with the laws of God and man:" it is, therefore, altered into a repeated avowal on his part, of "having suggested the idea of the poisoning." He is, however, acquitted even in this, of "cruelty to his soldiers;" and this has a savour of candour and impartiality. Thus a gross and gratuitous falsehood is at one time invented and industriously propagated; and the giving up one half of the lie to save the other half is thought to be a notable compromise between truth and courtesy, and constitutes modern and *popular* history. It is, however, a great step gained by Mr. Murray, and I congratulate him on the change. Even Sir Walter still *lumps* this poisoning business among Bonaparte's "other atrocities." With respect to Mr. Hazlitt's frequent and lengthened "reflections," it is to be remembered that he had to contend with a strong prejudice on the other side, on which he could hope to make no impression without giving his reasons at length. If he had been disposed to be "dogmatic," he might have been shorter.

I am, Sir, your obedient servant and constant reader,

Philalethes.[5]

---

[4] *Life of Napoleon, Works,* XIV, 38. Hazlitt quotes from Barry E. O'Meara, *Memoirs of Napoleon,* 1822.
[5] "Lover of Truth." Cf. Wardle, p. 464.

No. 155

To Macvey Napier [1]

MS. British Library.
Address: Macvey Napier, Esq./Edinburgh.

No. 3, Bouverie Street, Fleet Street.
July 13, 1829.

Dear Sir,

I was pleased to hear that you had been so good as to make some inquiries after me through Messrs. Longman. I need not say that I shall be happy if you will lay your commands upon me to do anything that lies in my power. There are two works lately published that I think I might make something of, *viz.*, the Life of Mr. Locke by Lord King and Southey's Dialogues of Sir Thomas More.[2] But I only suggest these for your better consideration. I hope that Mr. Jeffrey is well, and I remain, Dear Sir, very respectfully, your obliged humble servant,

W. Hazlitt.

---

[1] Succeeded Jeffrey as editor of the *Edinburgh Review* in 1829. Hazlitt now enters upon his last association with the *Review*.

[2] Neither of these works was given to Hazlitt to review.

No. 156

To Macvey Napier

MS. British Library.

July 21st, 1829
3, Bouverie Street, Fleet
Street.

Dear Sir,

I was favoured with your obliging communication this morning, and I shall be glad to attempt some account of Dr. Channing's character as a writer, though I am afraid from what I know of it at present I cannot estimate it very high.[1] I will however do my best and let you know in time. He appears to me an ambitious common-place writer who makes his impressions bend to certain preconceived pulpit notions, a scholastic rhetorician, but able and an American. In case this and the others should fail, let me suggest another subject, the forthcoming *Life & Writings of Defoe,* in which I should be somewhat *au fait* and could treat *con amore.*[2] I should be sorry to do an indifferent article for a commencement. Tell Mr. Jeffrey I am much pleased by his kind recollection of me and believe me to be, Dear Sir, your obliged and faithful servant,

W. Hazlitt.

P.S. I do not know whether I have much natural piety in my constitution, but Dr. Channing preaches at an Unitarian Meeting in Boston the Liturgy (formerly Trinitarian) was drawn up by my father forty years ago and upwards, who went to America to plant Unitarianism there.

---

[1] "American Literature—Dr. Channing," a review article based on W. E. Channing's *Sermons and Tracts,* appeared in the *Edinburgh Review* for October 1829. Cf. *Works,* XVI, 318-338.

[2] The article on Walter Wilson's *Life and Times of Defoe* was published in the *Edinburgh Review* for January 1830.

No. 157

To Macvey Napier

MS. British Library.

3, Bouverie Street
26th August, 1829

Dear Sir,

I send the article on Channing that you may have time to see if it will do. I hope to do better with some other subject. I will get the account of Defoe as soon as I can, and look into Flaxman.[1] What do you think of the *Fashionable Novels* as a subject? [2] That would be safe and light ground. Do not let the Southey go undone. I am afraid you will think I am presuming too far. I have only to add that if you think the article I have sent will do, I would beg for a small advance upon it. I would not thus early appear in *forma pauperis,* but the loss of £200 on my Life of Napoleon through the failure of Messrs. Hunt and Clarke has driven me to great straits at the present moment.[3] I remain, Dear Sir, your very respectful and obedient servant,

W. Hazlitt.

---

[1] *Flaxman's Lectures on Sculpture* was in the *Edinburgh Review* for October, 1829. Cf. *Contributions to the Edinburgh Review, Works,* XVI, 338-363.

[2] If written, it has not been found.

[3] Cf. Letter 145.

No. 158

To Basil Montagu

MS. Lockwood.
Address: Basil Montagu, Esq./to the care of B. W. Procter,
Esq.

August, 1829

Dear Sir,
Will you let Mr. Procter have 8£ out of the bill for 100£?

Wm. Hazlitt

No. 159

To Macvey Napier

MS. British Library.

3, Bouverie Street,
October 5, 1829.

My Dear Sir,

I received your very obliging communication in due course and availed myself of your kindness. If you would send me the introductory lines of the part where you wish to begin the article on Channing, I would see if I could improve it. I hope to send you something on Flaxman in about a week's time. I am promised a copy of the Life of Defoe shortly. I see a new edition of Horne Tooke advertised. Would you dislike my trying my hand upon that? [1] I remain, Dear Sir, your truly obliged humble servant,

W. Hazlitt.

---

[1] No article on Horne Tooke's *Diversions of Purley* (Pt. I, 1786) appeared in the *Edinburgh Review.* For Hazlitt's discussion of Tooke's "genuine anatomy of our native tongue" as well as his political career, cf. "The Late Mr. Horne Tooke," *The Spirit of the Age* (1825).

No. 160

To Macvey Napier

MS. British Library.

Nov. 7, 1829
3 Bouverie Street.

Dear Sir,

I was glad to find you think the *Flaxman* will do. I am about the Defoe, and shall attend to your advice. The only reason why I presume to think that my articles may *do* for the *Edinburgh* (not in the sense in which some people would pretend) is that they make perhaps a variety. If not so good, they are different from others, and so far, are the better for being worse. There are licenses in criticism, as well as in poetry. I am glad to find that the Life of Locke is in the present number. Perhaps whether the review of Flaxman is included or not, you might be able to let me have the amount of the two articles on account, and this would, I hope, be the last irregularity of the kind I shall be guilty of. But as I said before, I have been sadly thrown out in my finances. I shall take care to let you have the account of Defoe in good time. You say nothing of Horne Tooke. Perhaps you are afraid to trust me with it; but I think if you would turn to my account of him in a certain work [1] that shall be nameless, you would perceive that I know something of the matter. If you suggest a subject to me, I will make the best I can of it; but I will promise never to suggest one myself that I do not feel master of. I remain, Dear Sir, ever your obliged, humble servant,

W. Hazlitt.

P.S. May I add that if you could favour me with a copy of the number, I could get it spoken of early in one or two quarters? What is more to the purpose, I should be glad to receive one. This postscript, I am afraid, is a blundering one. Pray, overlook it, if it is wrong.

---

[1] The chapter on Horne Tooke in *The Spirit of the Age.*

No. 161

To Macvey Napier

MS. British Library.

15 January 1830

Dear Sir,

I have done as well as I could.[1] I hope it will do. I hope you will let me know soon. If it is inserted, I shall be glad of a remittance for it as soon as convenient: but though I have put some strength and truth into it, I fear there is very little discretion. Your ever obliged servant,

W. Hazlitt.

---

[1] The review of the *Life and Times of Defoe* by Walter Wilson, which appeared in the *Edinburgh Review* of January 1830.

No. 162

To Macvey Napier

MS. British Library.

March 19, 1830
6 Frith Street, Soho

Dear Sir,

I have looked at Cloudesley [1] and think I may make an article of it whether as a failure or successful, if you will give a certain latitude, I do not mean of space but style. I have a design upon Jefferson's Memoirs, if you please, and promise to do it well. [2] I am not sorry I had not *Southey* as it is so ably done. [3] I received your remittance and am thankful for that, and still more for your approbation of my last. Pray tell me if there is any hurry: I hope to send you in a fortnight, if I am not prevented by accidents. I remain, Dear Sir, ever your truly obliged, humble servant,

W. Hazlitt.

---

[1] An article on Godwin and his *Cloudesley; A Tale* appeared in the *Edinburgh Review* for April 1830. Cf. *Works,* XVI, 398-408.

[2] Articles on "Fashionable Novels" and Jefferson's *Memoirs* were published, but they are not by Hazlitt.

[3] The essay on Southey's *Sir Thomas More; or Colloquies on the Progress and Prospects of Society* was by Macaulay.

No. 163

To George Bartley [1]

Four Generations, I, 196.

Monday 14th June 1830
6 Frith Street, Soho

Dear Sir,

I should feel most extremely obliged if you could possibly favour me with a couple of orders for to-morrow night (Tuesday).

I remain, Dear Sir, very respectfully yours,
W. Hazlitt.

---

[1] Actor and stage-manager at Covent Garden, 1829-1830, whom Hazlitt had known since his days as drama critic on *The Examiner,* 1816. He was requesting tickets for "Cinderella, or the Fairy and the Little Glass Slipper," an English adaptation of Rossini's *La Cenerentola.*

No. 164

To James Northcote

MS. Cornell.
Address: James Northcote, Esq. R.A./8 Argyll Place/Great
Marlborough Street

6 Frith St.
July 29, 1830

My dear Sir,

I heard of the letter you sent me yesterday a week ago.[1] The subject of complaint in it is one that occurred four years ago, and is entirely and sedulously removed in the forth-coming work.[2] What cause of alarm there is from the evil of passages that are struck out, I cannot well comprehend. If there is to be the same outcry about these obnoxious expressions after they have been cancelled as before, they might as well have remained to afford some rational ground for your fears and reproaches. At present, the first appear to me as entirely gratuitous as the others are (in what concerns the papers in their corrected state) unmerited on my part. I cannot pretend to say what the character you have drawn of me is in your letter to Mr. Campbell,[3] but I almost regret that the present subdued tone of the *Conversations* may be the means of depriving the world of another master-piece.

I remain Dear Sir, with much respect
and some little disappointment, your
obliged very humble servant,
W. Hazlitt

---

[1] Northcote had sent via Colburn a letter from one Richard Rosdew threatening a libel action against Northcote for remarks about the Mudge family of Plymouth included in the *Conversations* of Northcote that Hazlitt had contributed to Colburn's *New Monthly Magazine, London Weekly Review,* and *Court Journal.*

[2] The remarks about Northcote's friends were either cancelled or disguised through the use of initials before the *Conversations of James Northcote* was published in 1830.

[3] Thomas Campbell was at this time editor of *The New Monthly Magazine.*

No. 165

To Martin Archer Shee,
President of the Royal Academy

Four Generations, I, 197.

6 Frith Street, Soho,
[August] 1830

Mr. Hazlitt takes the liberty to leave this little work [1] with Mr. Shee, but would feel obliged to have it returned to him at No. 6, Frith Street. When the vol. is published, Mr. H. will have the honour of leaving a perfect copy of it with Mr. Shee.

---

[1] The *Conversations of James Northcote.* For the February 7 *Atlas,* Hazlitt wrote two short articles: One of them on the "New President of the Royal Academy," was a tribute to Martin Archer Shee . . . (Wardle, p. 477).

No. 166

To Basil Montagu

MS. Keynes.

[Early September 1830] *

Dear Sir,

I am confined to my bed with illness, or I would have come out. The second vol. of the Titian is at p. 304, and I will be done this week.[1] Could you in the course of today let me have 15£ on account to prevent law expences,[2] which I dread? *Ceci devient trop longue.*

I remain, Dear Sir, your truly obliged humble servt.,

W. Hazlitt

Monday morning

In another hand: I believe the Mackintosh has been of service to me.

---

* Cf. Baker, p. 468n.

[1] The *Life of Titian,* supposedly by Northcote, but most of which Hazlitt wrote. (Howe, p. 372).

[2] Probably connected with the loss of £200 through the bankruptcy of Hunt and Clarke. Cf. Letter 157.

No. 167

To Messrs. Longman and Co.[1]

Works, XVII, 429.

6 Frith St.,Scho,
Sept. 6th, 1830

Mr. Hazlitt is very sorry that he has been obliged to keep the Pelham, &c.,[2] but he was not quite sure as to whether he had to write an article respecting them. He has been some time confined to his bed, dangerously, and is consequently unable to take them himself or to see about sending another with them. If Messrs. Longman would direct any of their persons passing in this neighbourhood to call for them, Mr. Hazlitt would feel much obliged: he is already so for the loan of them.

---

[1] Publishers of the *Edinburgh Review.* Too ill to write himself, Hazlitt dictated this note to his son in connection with an article on Bulwer-Lytton's novels which he had planned to write for the *Edinburgh Review.* In one of his last essays, "The Sick Chamber" (*New Monthly Magazine,* August 1830), Hazlitt mentions *Paul Clifford* (published May 1830), which he had just read.

[2] The novels sent to him were: *Falkland* (1827), *Pelham* (1828), *The Disowned* and *Devereux* (1829), and *Paul Clifford* (1830).

No. 168

To the Editor of the *Edinburgh Review*

Thomas Carlyle, *Reminiscences,* ed. Froude, II, 38.

[September 1830]

Dear Sir,[1]
I am dying; can you send me 10£, and so consummate your many kindnesses to me?

W. Hazlitt

---

[1] Hazlitt was on his deathbed when he dictated this note to Martin Burney. It was intended for Francis Jeffrey, whom Macvey Napier had succeeded as Editor in 1829. According to Carlyle, "Jeffrey, with true sympathy, at once wrote a cheque for 50£."

A passage from Hazlitt's last essay, "The Letter-Bell," reflecting on the part played by letters in his life, seems appropriate:

As I write this, the Letter-Bell passes: it has a lively, pleasant sound . . . and . . . rings clear through the length of many half- forgotten years . . . it wakes me from the dream of time, it flings me back upon . . . the period of my first coming up to town, when all around was strange, uncertain, adverse . . . and when this sound alone, startling me with the recollection of a letter I had to send to the friends I had lately left . . . made me feel that I had links still connecting me with the universe, and gave me hope and patience to persevere.

In the *Memoirs* (II, 238), W. Carew Hazlitt, the editor, says: "His last words were: 'Well, I've had a happy life.' " The editor does not give any authority for this last paradoxical utterance. He adds that his grandmother left a memorandum stating that Charles Lamb, J.A. Hessey, Mr. Edward White, and William Hazlitt, Jr., were present at the time of his death: Saturday, 18 September 1830 at about half past four in the afternoon, aged 52 years, five months, and eight days.

Appendix A

Hazlitt's diary-notes of the testing of Sarah Walker's virtue were last published in *The Journals of Sarah and William Hazlitt: 1822-1831* in February 1959 (University of Buffalo Studies, v. 24, no. 3), edited by Professor Willard Hallam Bonner. They are here published with some revisions.

HAZLITT'S JOURNAL OF
MARCH 4-16, 1823

[Page 1]

March 4. Mr. F.[1] goes to No. 9 S.B.[2] at my request to see the lodgings. Sees Mrs. W.[3] who is very communicative—says there is no one but herself and *her daughter*—her eldest daughter [4] married one of the Mr. Roscoes of Liverpool—gentlemen generally staid

---

[1] A close friend of Hazlitt's.
[2] Southampton Buildings.
[3] Mrs. Walker, Sarah's mother.
[4] Martha.

there 2 or 3 years—the gentleman that last occupied the front room staid there three years—a Mr. Crombie (no, the last person that occupied it was a Mr. Tomkins [name inked out], who did not stay there quite so long) She concluded Mr. F. from the country and let the front-room, second floor, to him at 15 s. a week. The back-room (my poor room) was empty at 14 s. a week.

March 5. Goes. Is introduced into the back-parlour—meets Miss shawled and bonnetted going out to meet Tompkins. Mrs. W. has my name up as having lodged there and says that except when I am at Salisbury, I lodge there still—speaks of the quantity of money I got by my writings, and [of several presents] 5 I had [given] her daughter—She returns, and takes

2

off her bonnet and shawl, throws them down on Mr. F.'s great-coat which he had put in a chair. This is her first move, thus putting these little matters together and mingling persons by proxy. She then went out and gave one of her set looks at the door.

March 6. The next morning she comes up to light his fire, and he wanting his pantaloons brushed, she comes to take them out of his hands, as he gives them to her naked at the door. She is not dressed to wait at breakfast, but is very gracious and smiling, and repulses a kiss very gently. She afterwards expressly forgives this freedom, and is backwards and forwards all day. On his asking for a newspaper or a book, she brings him up the *Round Table,* 6 with my name and sincere regards written in the title-page.

March 7. This morning she is dressed to wait on the gentleman. The day before it was too early. Nothing occurs, but she regularly answers the bell, yet does not bring up the things that are wanted, smirks and backs out of the room in her marked manner. A circumstance happened decisive of her lying character. Mr. F. going into the parlour for his umbrella met her going out to meet T. her mother repeating the old cant that it was too late to go to Mr. Roscoe's. She however went, and her father after her, probably to watch and entrap T. But F. going upstairs again found Betsey 7

---

5 Phrase illegible. Present reading supplied by W. C. Hazlitt, *Lamb and Hazlitt,*, N.Y., 1899, p. 120.

6 The bound volume of Hazlitt's essays reprinted in 1817 from the *Examiner.*

7 Sarah's younger sister.

in the room and on telling her the bed was not made, she said "her sister told her it was, but not turned down." This no doubt was a lie to keep the job to close up and be there on his return.

3

March 7. At night Miss was gone to bed, and on being asked next morning whether she did not return sooner than usual, said, "She sometimes went to bed earlier and sometimes later." This was just like one of her common place answers on all occasions. Mr. F. went down for a glass of water, and the brother (Cajah [8] as they call him) was there. He observed Mr. H. always drank water and they didn't like it at the Southampton Arms. He continued, "I was rather an odd man, a little flighty," he believed, and added smiling, "I was in love." F. did not ask with whom, but said the manner and tone convinced him more than anything that the whole was a regularly understood thing, and that there was nothing singular in gentlemen's being *in love* in that house.

March 8, Saturday. Mr. F. got a paper and lent it to the Father to read. Saw Miss several times. In the evening pressed her to stay tea which she declined, but he followed her to the door, and kissed her several times on the stair case, at which she laughed. While this passed he had hold of one hand, and the other was at liberty, but she did not once attempt to raise it so as to make even a show of resistance. This is what she calls "being determined to keep every lodger at a proper distance." Her aunt must know that she has not stuck to her advice.

March 9. Miss was seen in close conference with T.[omkins] at a landing [just?] opposite her own door. I wondered what divine music he poured into her ear, to which my words were harsh discord. What, I thought, would I not give to hear words of that honeyed breath that sinks into her heart, that I might despair and feel how just has been her preference! The next moments were enough. I had a specimen of that

4

sort of conversation to which "her ear she sweetly inclined." Not T[omkin]'s [name inked out] but any man's. F. insisted on her drinking tea with him, declaring he would not sit alone, that he

---

[8] Sarah's younger brother.

was not used to that sort of thing, and that if she did not stay, he would not have any tea at all, and would take his hat and walk out. By that terrible threat she was awed, she did not "show an independent spirit," and let the gentleman go, but said if she *must* stop, she would sit on the chair next the door instead of the one next to him. Wonderful delicacy! F. then got up and shut the door that she might not be exposed to the draught, and Emma [9] who was waiting on the stairs went down to announce this new arrangement. "Sarah, they all knew you never staid five minutes with anybody but me." She then poured out F.'s tea and the talk commenced. F. asked her which of the Essays in the *Round-Table* was a favourite with her, to which she seemed at a loss for an answer. He said he thought that on Methodism was a good one and asked what she thought of the remark that "David was the first Methodist?" [10] She laughed and said "Mr. H. was full of his remarks." F. answered "To the men or the ladies?" "No—Mr. H. thought very little about the ladies—indeed she believed he cared very little about them." F. "In a prose writer this was not so necessary, but a poet could hardly do without them. What did she think of Mr. Moore's Loves of the Angels?" [11] "She thought it impious to make angels fall in love with women." "Had she any of Lord Byron's works." She had read Cain, which she thought very fine (I think I know which part). Had she read Don Juan? "No, for her sister said it was impious." F. repeated the word "Impious" and laughed, at which she laughed. "Had Mr. F. read any of Mr. Procter's poetry?" He could not say. On which she explained Mr. Barry Cornwall's." Oh yes. Had she. Yes: she had Marcian Colonna and Mirandola[12] and had seen Mirandola. Mr. Proc-

5

ter was a particular friend of Mr. Hazlitt's, and had very gentle and pleasing manners. Miss Foote [13] played Isidora when she saw

---

[9] Emma Roscoe, Sarah's niece.

[10] "The first Methodist on record was David." This is the first sentence in *On the Causes of Methodism* No. 22 in the *Round Table.*

[11] The last long poem by Thomas Moore, very recently published and in great vogue.

[12] *Marcian Colonna,* a poem, 1820; *Mirandola,* a tragedy produced at Covent Garden, 1821.

[13] Maria Foote, later Countess of Herrington (1797?-1867). She was the original Isadora in *Mirandola.*

it: she was a pretty girl but no actress. She liked Miss Stephens [14] as a singer, her voice was very clear and good but her acting was deficient. "Did she like going to the play?" "She was fond of tragedy, but did not think comedy worth going to see."—She had not been to Drury-Lane: this was a hint that she should like to go. We shall see. And so she cackled on with her new gallant; T [inked out] being in the street with her every night and I in hell for this grinning, chattering ideot. F. said he is sure she is quite incapable of understanding any real remark, and shut up her lips with him for fear of being found out for what she is, a little mawkish simpleton. Sd that it was more stupidity than unkindness She rose to go in about ten minutes and then being pressed sat down again for another quarter of an hour, and then said she must go to her sister's to take home the child. F. kissed her and let her go. I thought no $\begin{cases} \text{lodger} \\ \text{body} \end{cases}$ [15] was ever to kiss her again but T. The next morning she came up to answer the early call but being in her bed gown would not come in, but ran up with the breakfast things in ten minutes, drest all in her best [ruff]. Decoy! Damned, treble damned ideot! [several words inked out] When shall I drive her out of my thoughts?—Yet I like to hear about her—that she had her bed-gown or her ruff on, that she stood or sat, or made some insipid remark, is to me to be in Heaven—to know that she is a whore [16] or an idiot is better than nothing. Were I in Hell, my only consolation would be to learn of her. In Heaven to see her would be my only reward.

6

March 10. In the evening Betsey waited at tea, her sister, she said, being busy. Mr. F. went down afterwards and sat with the family in the back parlour just opposite to her and then next to her. She said little, but laughed and smiled and seemed quite at her ease

familiar. Oh low life! God deliver me from thee! This was with a person, a perfect stranger to her, and whose only introduction was

---

14 Catherine Stephens, later Countess of Essex (1794-1882), "sweetest soprano voice of her time." She was at Covent Garden from 1813 to 1822.

15 Where words are placed above similar ones in the line, both appear in the manuscript and are in the same hand.

16 W. C. Hazlitt prints "nane."

that he obtruded himself upon her and her friends without
ceremony and without respect, under the pretext that he was too
dull to sit alone. T[ompkins] [name inked out], a lover of different
stamp, will not even be seen with her or come near the house. So
that she reasons by the familiar and the distant—all but true regard
which requires a return which she cannot feel. Me, poor, tortured
worm, she rejected on this account. I asked F. how she looked. He
said, "She had more flesh on her bones than her mother." On
rising to go upstairs, he saw three books piled on the drawing
[-room table], and on going toward them, Mrs. W. said they were
three books he had asked Sarah to lend him. One of mine and two
of Procter's. He was going to take them, but said he thought he
had better not, as he wanted a good night's rest, and they might
prevent him. Mrs. W. accorded this, intending her daughter to
bring them up in the morning. *N.B.* Mrs. W. among other things
said that Mr. H. had been in the neighborhood the other evng at a
literary party in Castle Hunt.[17]

March 11. She came up with the books, drest. F. asked her to
point out a passage in Marcian Colonna which she liked. She
declined this, and said she admired the whole. She in fact I daresay
had not read a word of it. He then read some of it, and on her
coming up again pretended it was so savory it had made him
sentimental and melancholy so that he should be obliged to turn to
Mr. Moore. He then said he wanted to look at Mirandola but he
was afraid of venturing on a tragedy—so hoped Miss would point
out a passage. So she took the book and turning to the place where
was the description [18] of herself, said—"This was Mr. H.'s favorite
passage." F. said he could hardly believe his eyes when he saw it,
for she seemed perfectly unmoved. He then read [it] off and [19] said
"he thought

---

[17] Coldbath Fields Prison (?) where John Hunt was confined in 1822. Patmore
records that Hazlitt and he visited Hunt on May 21. (*My Friends and Acquaintance,*
London, 1854, III, 20.) Leigh Hunt was in Italy in 1823.

[18] The passage in *Mirandola* goes:
> See with what a waving air she goes
> Along the corridor. How like a fawn!
> Yet statelier. No sound (however soft)
> Nor gentlest echo telleth where she treads.
> But every motion of her shape doth seem
> Hallowed by silence.

[19] The passage from "for she" to "off and" omitted by W. C. Hazlitt.

it very pretty; but could not reconcile what she said of its [being] my favourite passage with her declaring the day before that I cared very little about the ladies, as it was all about love." She hesitated a bit and he repeated, but she didn't think I did, adding "I don't think Mr. H.'s love lasts very long." Incomparable piece of clock work! To suppose that any one could count upon her even to be a friend is ridiculous. She is not good or bad; she is defective in [certain] faculties that belong to human nature, and acts upon others, because you can make no impression on her. I was only wrong in not pulling up her petticoats yet F. says he thinks it would be impossible to offer her rudeness, if he did not know beforehand which she was. "Being a thing majestical, it were a violence," &c. He kissed her heartily and put his arms round her neck [20] going away, at which she seemed as pleased as punch. In the evening she brought up the tea-things but said significantly she couldn't stop then, as there was nobody in the house but her father. He had done [just this] for he came to me and found she was gone out as far as Fleet Street to get Mr.— some coffee. That is, to meet Tomkins. If she has two, why not three? One of them thought her a punk! [21] Her sister was sitting with the child in the afternoon when Mr. F. bolted into the room for his umbrella and as she had her back to him, he mistook her for Mrs. W. and said How do you do Mam." She seemed a little dissatisfied at such familiarity, but the other said, It's only my sister [22] and handed him the umbrella, quite swiftly. Who could suppose that under such a name there was a heart of marble or that a mask could smile? Mrs. Roscoe was rather ashamed and hurt after the blow-up with me on account of her attachment to Tomkins to see the new affair in sweet friendship. She perhaps did not wish her little girl Emma to see her aunt a whore in the street a few years hence.

8

March 12. The little ideot came up with the breakfast, drest as usual, or rather varied, that is, she had a cap on and a shawl,

---

[20] Following "neck" there are 4½ finely written interlinear lines that are illegible.

[21] Sentence omitted by W. C. Hazlitt.

[22] W. C. Hazlitt omits everything between "sister" and "smile?"; also the rest of MS p. 7 following "attachment to Tomkins."

which I gave her on. F. had got his Marcian Colonna lying on the chair beside him and when she came in, read her some lines, and asked if she remembered them No: but she had the whole. He then asked her to look at them, and for that purpose she came round the table to his side, and on his asking her, she sat down. After looking them over, the book was laid aside,[23] and he laid his hand upon her thigh, to which she made not the slightest objection. He then put his arm round her neck, and began to play with her necklace and paddle in her neck, all which she took smilingly, being determined to keep every lodger at a proper distance, having been guilty of improprieties enough with me. He told her she would make a pretty nun. That, she said, she was sure she never should be. She was not to be shut up. F. asked her if she ever went out, and she said very seldom and only in the neighborhood, to her sister. In the afternoon the conversation was resumed in the parlour downstairs while her sister was in bed in the inner room and she was mending a stocking; and she then declared she did not like to be confined to the conversation of his on nuns, although she believed the nuns had leave to talk with their Confessors. F. observed that one Confessor was hardly enough for fifty or sixty nuns. "No!" "If," he said, "there was a Confessor for every Nun?" "That indeed!" said the lady of individual attachments. Half a dozen would be better. F. then asked her to go to the play. She said, she was afraid her mother might object to her going with a stranger. "Phoo! nonsense that was nothing: she really *must* go. She should have her choice of any part of the house, except the one shilling gallery. She supposed her ambition was not so high as that." "No, her ambition was not so high and laughed at this as an excellent jest. "But any part of the boxes: [24] In the pit they would be equally exposed." It was left indetermined and tonight we are lovers. I thought

9

I am exculpated by all this. I asked F. if he wanted to take a girl into keeping would he allow her half a guinea a week to be his

---

[23] Five lines between "laid aside" and "He told her she would make a pretty nun" are omitted by W. C. Hazlitt. For "He then put his arm," which the sense requires, Hazlitt wrote "She then put his arm. . . ."

[24] The last line of MS p. 8 and the first 12 lines of p. 9 (excepting only the short sentence, "He thought at first . . . she could not") are omitted by W.C.H.

whore? and he said, No, for one might get girls that would have some conversation in them for that, and she had not. He thought at first she would not talk, but now he was convinced she could not. He asked what was to be done if she consented to come to bed to him. I said Why you had better proceed. He did not seem to like the idea of getting her with child, and I said I supposed he didn't like to have a child by a monster," which he said was really his feeling. In this child-getting business we are however reckoning without our host, for she has evidently some evasion for that. It remains to be seen what her theory and practice on this subject are.—F. speaking of Mr. T[omkins] [25] said, he seemed out of sorts the other evening. She said, Mr. T. knew his ill-humour had no effect upon her And added, "We have not had the pleasure of seeing you in an ill-humour yet." F. answered, Suppose I was to give you a specimen? She said, I hope not till *I* give you cause." Mr. T. hearing F. above-stairs called out Who's that? F. said Sir? on which the other replied gruffly,[26] Oh, it was not you I wanted to see, but somebody else." So that she is not [through?] breaking this poor man's heart and probably his wife's, and she feels very happy that his ill-humours have no effect upon her.

March 14. F. got her between his legs so that she came right into contact with him. She made no resistance nor complaint. She retired a step or two and he followed and then she retreated a little further like the Tygers and the Dove in Nevys.[27] He said M[iss] I will kill you with kissing, if I catch you." "But you must catch me first," she said, and bounded down stairs and stood looking up and laughing at the ⎰bottom ⎱first landing place. By God, there isnt such another scheming punishing [?] devil in the world. F. is I think already in love [28] with her and thinks she likes him and I shant be able to get him to move. She didn't go to the play the other night

[25] In this passage Hazlitt writes "F" for both "F" and "Mr. T." As he always speaks of Tomkins elsewhere as "Mr. T," his intention is clear. I have accordingly regularized these initials.

[26] W.C.H. ends MS p. 9 here and does not begin again on p. 10 till "F. is I think . . .",—an excision of 11 lines.

[27] Not identified.

[28] For "love" W.C.H. prints "force"; and by misreading "world" prints "mild F," which has been repeated by P. P. Howe *(Life of William Hazlitt,* new ed., 1947, p. 323).

but was backwards and forwards with her sist[er] all the evening as an excuse. Yesterday he says he could make nothing of her. They had a parley in the evening. She didnt come up with the tea-things, but on ringing afterwards, she answered the bell. She would not come in: she could hear where she was—her old word. F. got up and sat near her. He began to say he was sorry he staid out at night and was afraid she thought him wild. She said she was not his keeper. He then said he could bear to live by himself [if] he could [have] something to kiss and fondle and muss. They should make good company.[29] She asked if [he thought it would be] proper. Oh! he said, hang propriety. What, she said, you would not hang propriety! [She half hangs it and cuts it down again.] [30] Would it be seemly? Oh, he said, as to seemly, there was nobody to see them but themselves. While this delicate negotiation was going on, she kept sobbing and crying [31] all the time and at last said she must go now. But she could come and sit with him when they were gone to bed. She made no promises [32] and so it stands. F. swears he'll

11

put it home to her today: but I doubt she has already denied him.

Saturday, March 15. She did not come up in the morning and nothing was done but that as she put down the curtains at night, he kissed her and saying he was determined to give a good tickling for her tricks in running away from him the day before, put his hand between her legs on that evening. She only said "Let me go Sir.", and retiring to the door, asked if he would have the fire lighted. She did not come up again. She was altered in her manner, and probably begins to make something. In lighting F. upstairs she waits for him to go first, and on his insisting on her leading the way, they had a regular scamper for it, he all the way tickling her legs behind. Yet she expressed no resentment nor shame. This is she who murdered me that she might keep every lodger at a proper

---

[29] These two sentences are paraphrased and euphemized by W.C.H.

[30] The square brackets are Hazlitt's.

[31] For "she kept sobbing and crying," W.C.H. has, "she kept on his lap."

[32] After "promises" at the bottom of MS p. 10, W.C.H. omits almost everything until the entry for March 16, which is three-fourths through p. 11. It is doubtless because of this abridgment particularly that some biographers of Hazlitt find it possible to picture Sarah Walker as a gentle, fawnlike girl always evading F.'s advances firmly but resolutely, offended even at the thought of violence.

distance.—I met Tomkins in the street who looks bad. I fancy we are all in for it; and poor F. will be over[head] and very [?] with her in another week.

March 16. Saw nothing of her in the morning, but asked her to tea—answered "she never drank tea with gentlemen," and was high. F. was in despair when returning home at dusk, he met my lady with her muff on going along Lincolns Inn Fields by herself. He saw [her] turn at the corner of Queen Street to go down towards the New Inn. Followed her—asked to accompany—she refused—and on his offering to take her arm, stood stock still, immoveable, inflexible—like herself and on his saying he could not then press her and offering his hand, she gave it him, and then went on to her lover. I also am her lover and will live and die for her only, since she can be true to any one. F. met her brother at the door and said, "I just met your sister." "Why she is gone to her grandmother's." Let her [and then cross hatched up the right side of the page is:] be to hell with her tongue—. She is as true as heaven wished her heart and lips [to] be. My [own?] fair hell.

Appendix B

The "Liber Amoris" letters fall together because of their common theme (Sarah Walker) and their concentration within the year 1822. No original manuscript letters to Sarah Walker have survived, but Hazlitt himself chose to print matter from three in his little book of love, *Liber Amoris, or the New Pygmalion* (1823). The entire letter from which a part of one of these was taken, however, was acquired (presumably purloined) and printed in *John Bull*, a weekly paper, on June 22, 1823, as a part of a scurrilous Tory attack on the liberal Hazlitt. Ironically, this letter, as may be seen, is probably the most relaxed and socially agreeable in the whole "Liber Amoris" group. And its source in *John Bull* remains our only source today.[1]

Besides talking to anyone who would listen, Hazlitt sought relief in four other ways: 1) letters to his friends, 2) the book called *Liber Amoris,* 3) testing Sarah Walker's virtue by an emissary (a "Mr. F.") whose daily adventures Hazlitt graphically recorded, and 4)

---

[1] Stanley Jones, who republished this letter, discusses it at length in *Rev. of Eng. Studies,* NS 17 (1966), pp. 163-170. Hazlitt's letter "TO THE SAME" near the end of Part I, *Liber Amoris* is taken from it.

philosophizing on women and love in many essays.[2] Few people comprehend how entangled are these acts of literary composition. "I write what I think; I think what I feel," he once wrote.[3] And he lost no time in composing the first part of *Liber Amoris,* beginning it almost at once upon removing to Scotland to establish legal residence required in his divorce proceedings. Thus the book developed under the hand that was at the same time recording his feelings in long personal letters.

Liber Amoris was in three parts. Part I was a series of seven short separately entitled conversations between "H" and "S" plus the two letters or fragments of letters Hazlitt had sent to the real S(arah). This may be all that he at first planned inasmuch as he wrote at the end (or planned to), "The End," suggesting rather clearly the kind of work of art he then was attempting.[4] Part II was a *mélange* of increasingly obvious personal matter, grounded on his long letters to Peter George Patmore, his friend and confidant since their excursion together to see the great prize fight now immortalized in the zestful essay, "The Fight." For Part III Hazlitt composed three long letters to his friend James Sheridan Knowles, the Scottish dramatist. *Liber Amoris,* therefore, began as a series of conversations whose form (such as captions and plot device) brings to mind Sterne's *Sentimental Journey* and Mackenzie's *Man of Feeling,* but whose spirit is quite otherwise. He intended to work within a recognized genre, but as the work evolved, it appeared with two-thirds of it a heavily autobiographical display of anguish. Thus *Liber Amoris* became in part both a product and a source of Hazlitt's letters, for where originals no longer exist we follow the judgment of P.P. Howe and accept such isolated epistolary matter as substantially what Hazlitt wrote.

The largest group within the extant "Liber Amoris" letters are eleven to Patmore, which Hazlitt asked Patmore to keep. The

---

[2] Cf. "On Great and Little Things," *Works,* VIII, 226-242, and Stewart C. Wilcox, *The Manuscript of the Fight* (Baltimore, 1943), p. 9.

[3] Preface to *A View of the English Stage* (1818), Works, V, 175.

[4] MS. Book, Lockwood Library. Howe and a few others have pointed out our need to understand this. In 1916 Howe crisply remarked that *Liber Amoris* has suffered by not being considered a deliberate and highly characteristic work of art, a picture of what the havoc of love will do to a man. "Hazlitt and Liber Amoris," *Fortnightly Rev.* NS 99 (February 1916), pp. 300-310.

manuscripts of these letters are still preserved in the Goodyear Collection at the Lockwood Library. Previous printings have been scattered and fragmentary, the first being an exhibition of literary curiosities unaided by any editing in the modern sense.[6] In 1894 Richard Le Gallienne brought out a privately printed edition of *Liber Amoris* which presented two versions of the text: Hazlitt's of 1823 and an emendation based on handwritten revisions which still may be seen in the "manuscript book" of Part I of *Liber Amoris.*[7] In addition he printed the eleven letters to Patmore, as he put it, "now first literally transcribed from the original MSS." Adjoined at the end he printed Mrs. Hazlitt's Journal of her "Trip to Scotland" along with her letters to the Hazlitts' son. In doing all this Le Gallienne managed to cloud his own understanding (and ours) of just what Hazlitt had attempted to do with them. Le Gallienne's intention was to present the Patmore letters as part of a hypothetical original manuscript of *Liber Amoris* instead of original personal letters which had served as source materials which Hazlitt manipulated for his own purposes.

Until recently Le Gallienne's private printing, falling just short of completeness, has been the standard printed source of the bulk of Hazlitt's letters to P.G. Patmore, and it has been generally depended on. It contains, however, about sixty-five errors of omission, misreading, or sophistication of the text. Hazlitt's practice in these letters was to crowd in extra matter or after-thoughts, either between original lines, up and down the margins, at the tops and bottoms of pages, or in bold and sometimes quite legible over-writing at right angles to the already written lines. Some of this "writing both ways" Le Gallienne omitted. A postscript to the letter dated April 21 was carelessly attached to the previous letter of April 7. "Receipt of the sonnet" appeared for "receipt of the same." Hazlitt's obvious phallic "prick of a fellow" was rendered "brick of a fellow." The word "some" served to euphemize "seven" (also in a phallic connection). Among the

---

[6] P.G. Patmore, *My Friends and Acquaintance* (1854), I, vi; III, 171-178. W.C. Hazlitt, *Memoirs of William Hazlitt* (1867), v.II, 30-68.

[7] Now in the Lockwood Memorial Library, State University of New York at Buffalo.

deviations from the autograph originals, the most serious was the omission of matter, such as the full page of over-writing on page one of the letter of June 10.

The Patmore letters have thus been handled often, though no biographer of Hazlitt except Professor Ralph M. Wardle has made any extensive use of them. Hazlitt himself became in a way their first editor when he decided to use them in *Liber Amoris,* marking scattered passages for omission and making minor revisions of words and phrases. He himself split up letters at will, using only the postscript of the letter of June 25 for "Letter XII to C.P___," for example, and employing only the first two or three sentences from the long letter of June 10. Also he added new matter, as his muse dictated. By such cutting and patching Hazlitt constructed fourteen literary letters out of eleven real ones.

However, whole letters for which we now have the originals, do appear in *Liber Amoris,* leaving us the right to conjecture that the four such letters for which no manuscripts are now at hand ("I," "II," "VI," and "Letter the Last") consist substantially of Hazlitt's original sentences as sent. Two of them can be validated in part by the lucky fact that two of Patmore's "Extracts" in *My Friends and Acquaintance* (1854) are word for word from them.

There are no known originals for the three open letters to "J.S.K—" (James Sheridan Knowles). They are included for the following reasons: 1) they are a premeditated series addressed to a single well known, specified person, 2) their rich autobiographical data can be substantiated (such as the abortive day's outing in the Highlands), 3) they help to extend our knowledge of the stormy events of 1822 (especially Hazlitt's futile return from Scotland to London in May to see Sarah Walker), 4) reputable biographers have already with confidence used the letters as letters. Hazlitt's friendship with the young Scottish dramatist is well known, and there is no reason to doubt that Knowles acted as the confidant and friend he is pictured as being in the letters. Knowles was in Scotland in 1822. He arranged for Hazlitt to lecture in Glasgow. And he met and talked and walked with Hazlitt. It would be straining a point to question the epistolary character of these intimate writings simply because we do not know for sure whether they were ever sent by public or private carrier. They round out for us Hazlitt's amorous adventure, completing the tale of William Hazlitt and his "Infelice," Sarah Walker, so far as it appears in his correspondence.

Willard Hallam Bonner,
Professor Emeritus, English Department,
State University of New York at Buffalo.

Index